Norway's Pharmaceutical Revolution

Norway's Pharmaceutical Revolution

Pursuing and Accomplishing Innovation in Nyegaard & Co., 1945–1997

Knut Sogner

OXFORD
UNIVERSITY PRESS

Great Clarendon Street, Oxford, OX2 6DP,
United Kingdom

Oxford University Press is a department of the University of Oxford.
It furthers the University's objective of excellence in research, scholarship,
and education by publishing worldwide. Oxford is a registered trade mark of
Oxford University Press in the UK and in certain other countries

Published in the United States of America by Oxford University Press
198 Madison Avenue, New York, NY 10016, United States of America

British Library Cataloguing in Publication Data
Data available

Library of Congress Control Number: 2022934654

ISBN 978–0–19–286900–5

DOI: 10.1093/oso/9780192869005.001.0001

Printed and bound by
CPI Group (UK) Ltd, Croydon, CR0 4YY

Preface

This book is the culmination of a long journey. In May 1990, as a young historian, I entered the premises of Nycomed, a company known until 1986 as Nyegaard & Co. My task was to prepare a possible history project for the company. The project became a reality, and a book by Rolv Petter Amdam and me was published in 1994 in coffee-table format.

The story included an innovative success of international significance, something developed and sharpened into a doctoral thesis I defended in the summer of 1996. This won the European Business History Association prize for the best doctoral thesis in 1998. Senior UK and US colleagues then promoted it to major international publishing houses, only to be told that the manuscript was not sufficiently international in focus. Other professional commitments meant that publication was pushed into the future, and that future is now.

I have many people to thank. The manuscript revision and extension in 2019 was done in communication with the excellent US editor Madeleine Adams. Afterward, my old opponent at the doctoral defense, Professor Louis Galambos of Johns Hopkins University, pointed to areas that needed strengthening and parts that were redundant. Armed with his and Madeleine's insight into publishing procedures, and a renewed confidence in the merit of what I brought to market, I approached Oxford University Press. I am grateful for the constructive reception Adam Swallow gave me.

Many more people deserve credit, and you will find them in the references to the interviews in the project. In the revision process my several conversations with Åse Aulie Michelet, a long-term employee of the company, were important in shaping the new chapter. I also got crucial help and moral support from Aksel Reksten, at the time head of GE Healthcare in Norway, the successor company to Nycomed.

Two people who contributed in the early stage of this work also need to be mentioned. I learned much from my co-author Rolv Petter Amdam while working with him on the first book. My supervisor, Professor Even Lange, was also very helpful, urging me to make the most of my findings in the final stages of my doctoral thesis.

Eamonn Noonan has improved the language — in the 1990s and now.

Two people at Nyegaard & Co. must be mentioned. The retired, humorous and very friendly pharmacist Fridtjov Rakli was organizing the company archive when I first visited. He proved to be a very serious man who gave highly illuminating insights into company culture and company affairs. He personified professional commitment to the history he had experienced, and he wanted this history to be told and understood. Hugo Holtermann, the chemist with a doctorate from the University of Oxford who more than anyone organized the innovative breakthrough, did not originally want to speak to me for reasons that had to do with difficult internal affairs. When he did, he opened up many doors to insights, some of which I found difficult to pursue fully. But I believe and hope that, this time around, I present an interpretation of events that does justice to what actually happened.

Contents

List of Figures, Tables, and Boxes

Figures

Tables

Boxes

1

Introduction

The rise of the modern pharmaceutical industry shaped many aspects of
life in nineteenth- and twentieth-century Europe, including the relationships between the large industrial powers and Scandinavian economies.
At first, Denmark, Sweden, and Norway only provided markets for the
advanced products from Germany and Switzerland—the smaller-country
exception. But as this science-based industry evolved in the twentieth century, all three of these Scandinavian nations developed their own pharmaceutical firms and innovations. They thus provide an excellent opportunity
to describe and analyze the factors shaping the spread of the global industry and its impact on smaller nations with medium-sized economies.
The focus will be primarily upon Norway, which lagged behind Denmark
and Sweden, and particular attention will be paid to one innovative firm
and the institutional and economic context that shaped its success. We will
consider whether these developments mimicked, on a smaller scale, those
in the successful US pharmaceutical industry; as J. Rogers Hollingsworth
has said with reference to the US industry: "Without obligational networks
embedded in promotional networks involving multilateral relations with
universities, various agencies and departments of the federal government,
and numerous business firms, these technologies and products could not
have occurred in the United States at the time they did" (Campbell et al.,
1991). This is the context we will be examining in Scandinavia (Galambos
and Sewell, 1995).

The rise of pharmaceutical innovation was tightly connected with the
scientific effort in universities in each of the major nations (Galambos,
1991). This was clearly the case in nineteenth-century Germany and in
twentieth-century America. The huge US federal research effort in medical sciences through the National Institutes of Health brought forward
new understandings of disease that the industry could utilize. In a recent
book about the emergence of the biotechnology industry in the 1970s and
1980s, it is argued convincingly that the biotech industry commenced in
the university sector (Rasmussen, 2014). Yet, the question of why these innovations actually emerged in such numbers from the 1930s into the 1960s

Norway's Pharmaceutical Revolution. Knut Sogner, Oxford University Press.
© Knut Sogner (2022). DOI: 10.1093/oso/9780192869005.003.0001

and how this second phase of the pharmaceutical revolution impacted the smaller nations is more difficult to answer. If the model of academic–business relationship that functioned so well from the 1930s is important to the success with innovation, why were the subsequent results from this model in the 1990s and later disappointing (Henderson and Cockburn, 1996)?

It would be tempting from a purely scientific standpoint to assume that somehow the scientific foundation for new innovations had been eroded. The low-hanging fruit had been picked, and in the 1970s there was a need for scientific reorientation. In this perspective, the time of organic chemistry and biochemistry—practices that were behind the successes of the past—needed to be supplemented and replaced with the new understanding of gene modification and the rise of biotechnology. To some extent, this has been true, and biotechnology has provided new and important pharmaceuticals. Yet the pharmaceutical industry has not been able to recapture the dynamics of the era of the pharmaceutical revolution. Rather, the industry has gone through an age of consolidation, a huge merger movement that has created much larger and more transnational corporations.

Current theories of innovation would not accept that basic science has had such a fundamental role that it could explain the fortune of the entire pharmaceutical industry. Innovation is rather seen as a phenomenon that occurs within complex networks of actors of many sorts—scientists indeed, but also companies, regulatory agencies, users, experts, and the whole mix of what constitutes a modern market economy constitutes "systems of innovation" (Edquist, 2005). Innovation is thus an interactive phenomenon that may indeed more often than not be rooted in national institutional contexts like those that clearly have contributed to the rise of the innovative pharmaceutical industry. But this concept of the institutional context includes a lot more than just the scientific undertakings in academic institutions. A pertinent example is the German dye industry, which not only pioneered industrial research and development as such but whose efforts to use its knowledge base constructively also made important pharmaceutical innovations and contributed to the direction of activity within German academic institutions (activity that would again support such activities at a later date) (Achilladelis, 1999). The actual companies and their choices and aspirations were not neutral to scientific efforts within the academic institutions but were influential participants in an ongoing process of knowledge creation. Thus, a better understanding of what has gone on within pharmaceutical companies provides a fruitful path to a better understanding of the development of this innovative industry.

Surprisingly, Norway provides an interesting case of global innovation: the development of non-ionic X-ray contrast media (Sogner, 1993; de Haën, 2019). Contrast media are liquids that are inserted into the blood veins, the spinal canal, and the liquid-filled parts of the brain to make X-ray pictures of soft body parts. Contrast agents, because of their iodine content, stop X-rays. Contrast agents are regarded as pharmaceuticals because of their intrusive use in all of the body; they serve very important diagnostic functions that are tightly connected with the use of therapeutic medicine. X-ray contrast media started to emerge in the 1920s. They were vastly improved in the early 1950s, making for more detailed pictures, and the concept that was synthesized in the small Norwegian company Nyegaard & Co. in 1969 made them safer, with fewer side-effects, and opened them up for use in really sensitive areas of the body.

Non-ionic contrast media is still the dominant contrast agent globally in 2020. Figure 1.1 shows the development of patient doses that has been provided by the Norwegian company from 1984 to 2016.

One of the questions this book sets out to answer concerns this innovation process and thus the mechanisms that contributed to innovation in the pharmaceutical industry for a century and a half. How did that

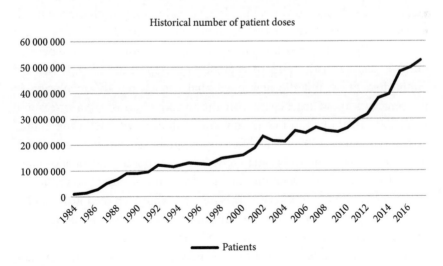

Fig. 1.1 Historical number of non-ionic patient doses.
Source: GE Healthcare AS

small Norwegian company, Nyegaard & Co, invent and innovate? How did it achieve scientific as well as commercial success? How could a company from Norway, a small nation not known for its pharmaceutical excellence, break through internationally with a major research-based innovation? What factors fed into the success of this company's deliberate, single-minded pursuit of innovation despite its location outside the major national ecosystems that have produced the great majority of pharmaceutical innovations in the past? And, once successful in the 1980s, why did the company's success in research-based innovation peter out? This is a story that mirrors the general trend of the international industry, except to say that this company—along with its Scandinavian brethren—was located outside the nations dominating pharmaceutical innovation.

Neither Norway nor its Scandinavian cousins in Denmark and Sweden are populous enough to provide those all-encompassing medical ecosystems that the large nations have prioritized. Yet the experience of these three rather similar nations—all with modern and well-financed health services—contain insights into other developmental avenues for successful pharmaceutical companies. Sweden and Denmark have been rather more successful than Norway even though they did not have the type of large enterprises that were the leading innovators in pharmaceuticals during the decades immediately following the Second World War.

Alfred Chandler, the historian who more than anyone else singled out the importance of big business in twentieth-century economic development, emphasized the role of large corporations in pharmaceuticals (Chandler, 2005). Those firms, he said, which started early in a sector subsequently built organizational knowledge and competence and became durable, lasting institutions of capitalist development. "Thus it was the established firms, not the new ones, that carried out the revolution in pharmaceuticals which began with the introduction of sulfa drugs and penicillin. They did so in Germany and Britain as well as in the United States" (Chandler, 1990: 603f). But as subsequent scholars have repeatedly pointed out, the great firms had to renew their corporate knowledge—their "established base"—by hooking up with emerging scientific communities (Galambos and Sturchio, 1996). This network approach obviously catches something crucial about pharmaceutical innovation. It has illuminated the larger story of the development of pharmaceuticals from the 1930s to the present as one of collaboration between university scientists and corporations (Achilladelis, 1999).

While we have thus learned a great deal about this industry, we still need to delve deeper into processes of innovation to catch their essential dynamics. We know that these processes were performed by individual scientists, but we do not really know what drove them and what in their context mattered the most (Sciabine, 1999). How did the corporate contexts matter? An individual like James Black, who twice (in two different companies) made important contributions to drug discovery, underlines the importance of going deeper into the processes of innovation and working out what mattered from an inside position to the actual discovery process. How much did he matter, or the corporation, or the networks? When we know more about such specificities, we should also know more about what mattered to achieve the actual accomplishments. This book seeks to provide answers to these questions about the process of innovation.

Any study of a pharmaceutical company and its innovations must place it within its scientific context. For this book, that scientific context must be in part Norwegian but must also bring into focus international scientific settings. It was not just university sciences that were international in scope and content but so were twentieth-century medical practices. To innovate with an internationally relevant pharmaceutical was an international undertaking. Yet, Nyegaard & Co. was also a Norwegian company with Norwegian owners, employees, and connections, working under Norwegian laws, regulations, and industrial policies that also influenced its fate.

Norway: A Scandinavian laggard

Among the three Scandinavian countries, Norway proved to be the laggard. While Nyegaard & Co. was one of many pharmaceutical companies to invent and innovate after the end of the Second World War, it was the only Norwegian firm to do so until about 2000. The five other Norwegian pharmaceutical companies of some significance existing in the 1940s all followed generic strategies—that is, they sold pharmaceuticals not invented by themselves. Until one of them, Apotekernes Laboratorium (AL Pharma), internationalized as a generic company in the 1980s, they were all small (Amdam et al., 2003). On the international stage, Nyegaard & Co. is one example of many, on the domestic front it is an exceptional case.

Historically, the three Scandinavian countries had very similar preconditions for meeting the challenges and opportunities of the new, science-based pharmaceutical industry. Although often being at war with one another since the Middle Ages and up to the Napoleonic wars, the three countries shared a common approach to the pharmaceuticals of the day. Being influenced by the German and continental approach, sales and production of drugs were highly regulated by the state (Amdam and Sogner, 1994; Johannessen et al., 1995). Norway got its first pharmacy in Bergen in 1595, while in union with Denmark. The three nations imported drugs, raw materials, and knowledge from Europe in general and Germany in particular, and although the products imported—and made in Scandinavia—were modernized at an increasingly rapid pace in the twentieth century, all three countries gave little heed to originality. All three countries developed a national industry at the beginning of the twentieth century; it was small-scale and based on imported medicinal knowledge; it competed by being more productive than the local pharmacies.

Consisting of fairly wealthy countries coming into the twentieth century, Scandinavia was a growing market for both imported and domestically made pharmaceuticals. All three countries developed their university and "hochschule" sectors; as the pharmaceutical revolution commenced in the 1930s, an increasing number of Scandinavian research projects and finished candidates were relevant to the emergence of a national pharmaceutical industry.

Two of these projects were particularly significant. The Danish insulin industry was founded on the work of Nobel laureate August Krogh at the Animal Physiological Laboratory in Copenhagen (Richter-Friis, 1991; Sindbæk, 2019). Two important companies, Novo and Nordisk (which merged at a much later date), had their origins in this environment. The Danish pharmaceutical industry achieved export ratios of 30–40 percent in the 1930s because of its insulin capacity based on pancreases sourced from the large and modern Danish agricultural sector. Danish exports were as much as one-and-a-half times larger than imports, and the sectoral trade surplus continued to grow after the Second World War.

Meanwhile, Norwegian researchers—led by Axel Holst of the University of Oslo—did deep studies of nutritional ingredients and came very close to isolating vitamin C (Carpenter, 1986). This research was motivated by Norway's strong fisheries sector and the possibilities attached to cod liver oil and other raw materials from the sea. There was also a need to address the dietary conditions of the many Norwegian sailors who suffered defi-ciency diseases from their long time spent onboard the ships of the large Norwegian merchant marine. Vitamin research was a Norwegian priority, and it was by forging links with this state-financed research that Nyegaard & Co. can be said to have started its own research activity in 1924 (Amdam and Sogner, 1994).

These two academic projects were historically important for what they produced, but they were also significant because they emphasize two points about the Scandinavian preconditions for entering the age of innovative pharmaceuticals. Even though Denmark and Norway were small nations, they were well positioned to contribute to the pharmaceutical revolu-tion. Yes, they were latecomers compared with the large countries, but even in the1920s they had already created research of international signif-icance. These examples also make clear that the Scandinavian route was to follow narrower and more specialized pathways than the big nations did. Not for the Scandinavian countries was a full-blown, broad research agenda that could compete with the more populous nations in all relevant scientific niches. The Scandinavians would have to depend on individ-uals and groups—of which August Krogh and his team were significant examples—to explore and exploit their particular niches.

The various avenues created by their specializations help explain the sub-stantial differences in the development of these three countries from the 1930s to the 1990s, shown in Table 1.1. Even in the 1930s, Denmark's ex-port of pharmaceuticals was higher than its import, as we noted earlier. Denmark was able to hold on to its Scandinavian leadership afterward, primarily because of the growth of its insulin business. Sweden was also developing a very successful pharmaceutical industry during these years. Astra and Pharmacia became world renowned companies, although the value of exports did not reach the value of imports until the 1980s. In these same years, however, Norway was unable to build effectively on its vitamin starting point; it was still a huge consumer of imported pharmaceuticals. Its national industry continued to concentrate on producing generic drugs for the national market. It was only with the innovation of non-ionic contrast media in the 1970s and beyond that Norway was able to achieve substantial exports of pharmaceuticals.

While concentrating on the Norwegian case, this book will use the other two countries to compare the Norwegian development. How could three such similar countries with more or less the same living standards, the same ideals behind their scientific endeavors, and similar political systems,

Table 1.1 Production, imports, and exports of pharmaceuticals in Norway, Sweden, and Denmark in selected years, 1931–1980

Norway						
	Production	Import	Exports	Export/ production	Export/ import	Import/ production
	100 NOK				Percent	
1931	1,723	2,698	118	6.9	4.4	156.6
1939	6,218	7,079	2,546	41.0	36.0	113.9
1950	21,016	16,381	8,767	41.7	53.5	78.0
1955	34,200	28,200	9,500	27.8	33.7	82.5
1960	50,100	48,600	9,300	18.6	19.1	97.0
1970	125,000	189,200	37,000	29.6	19.6	151.4
1980	581,300	679,400	179,900	31.0	26.5	116.9

Sweden						
	Production	Import	Export	Export/ production	Export/ import	Import/ production
	100 NOK				Percent	
1931	3,985	5,307	343	8.6	6.5	133.2
1939	13,574	11,865	1,160	8.6	9.8	87.4
1950	67,361	22,182	7,870	11.7	35.5	32.9
1955	107,660	52,871	18,770	17.4	35.5	49.1
1960	211,500	110,102	32,334	15.3	29.4	52.1
1970	556,300	372,800	180,900	32.5	48.5	67.0
1980	2,521,900	1,377,700	1,291,800	51.2	93.8	54.6

Denmark						
	Production	Import	Export	Export/ production	Export/ Import	Import/ production
	100 NOK				Percent	
1931	7,000	5,063	2,378	34.0	47.0	72.3
1939	20,400	6,383	9,490	46.5	148.7	31.3
1950	79,500	18,343	47,283	59.5	257.8	23.1
1955	117,900	40,425	74,515	63.2	184.3	34.3
1960	254,400	97,421	156,347	61.5	160.5	38.3
1970	485,300	335,100	452,600	93.3	135.1	69.1
1980	2,432,200	1,177,000	2,096,000	86.2	178.1	48.4

Sources: These figures are taken from the official Norwegian, Swedish, and Danish statistics, SITC after 1953. The figures for Norway have been compiled by Jon Skeie, who has also compiled the Swedish and Danish numbers from 1960 to 1989. I have taken the earlier figures from Sweden and Denmark from the historical archives of Nycomed: NFR. 17. B. 2. drawer. Industri. Farmasøytisk II: "Farmasøytisk Industri."

develop so differently? And how could the Norwegian firm Nyegaard & Co.—an enterprise bitten by the research bug in 1924—emerge successfully almost half a century later? Unfortunately, very little has been written on the development of research-based Norwegian industrial companies. Generally, the interplay between government and business in Norway in the post-Second World War period is little studied. No serious analysis exists of Nyegaard & Co. prior to the 1994 book that is partly the basis for *this* book (Amdam and Sogner, 1994).[1] A former employee wrote a history of Nyegaard & Co. in 1974, but this took the form of a loose, publicity-oriented narrative. This is nevertheless of interest for its emphasis on the company's long-term research effort (Bjørnson, 1974). Another former employee of Nyegaard studied the different developments of the pharmaceutical industries of the three Scandinavian countries and related the lagging development of Norway to the pharmaceutical industry's fear of being nationalized (Holtermann, 1965).

That the Norwegian pharmaceutical industry feared nationalization is also not a topic that has been developed outside the above-mentioned analyses. What has been rather extensively covered is the strong and professionally led Health Directorate that emerged after the Second World War. Trond Nordby's book about the Norwegian Director General of Health, Karl Evang, is important in this regard. Evang dominated the Norwegian health authorities in the post-war period, and Nordby emphasizes that Evang's regime created rule by professionals—doctors held sway over the whole area of health. Nordby did not, however, address the impact of the regulatory practices on the pharmaceutical sector (Nordby, 1989).

On a more general level, historian Francis Sejersted has argued that Norway and Sweden are rather more different politically and institutionally than commonly perceived. He has summed up the Norwegian economy under the term "democratic capitalism" (Sejersted, 1993, 2011). According to Sejersted, Norwegian capitalism has been characterized by "the strong petite bourgeoisie—with its special democratic-anarchistic norms and its localistic orientation" (Sejersted, 1993: 11). This parliamentary system, developed after 1814, placed great importance on the political control of business's relations to broader societal needs and demands. The construction of local savings banks, dairies, and eventually local power companies has been at the heart of many political considerations about business's role

---

[1] I deliberately omit my part of the book but include the part where Amdam gives a contextual account of Nyegaard & Co.'s history until 1940.

in society (Sejersted, 1993: 163–208). Especially important compared to Sweden and the general Western European pattern, Norwegian companies were smaller and did not have support of national investment banks, quite possibly reflecting—not least compared with Sweden—the lack of strong military and aristocratic traditions.

According to Sejersted, there were important differences between Norway and Sweden after 1945 too. Building on Swedish historian Rolf Torstendahl's approach to the shifting role of the state in the development of north-western European capitalism, Sejersted argues for a particular Norwegian development path (Torstendahl, 1989). Torstendahl focuses specifically on phases in the development of the state. He labels the period from the coming of state economic interventionism in the 1930s to around 1973 as participatory capitalism: the state and (big) business were allies seeking to increase national wealth. While progressive industry-friendly social democratic parties dominated parliaments and governments for the good part of the first twenty years after the war, Sejersted argues that the Swedish development was characterized by much smoother collaborative environment between the state and private business. Norway had a gap to close left by the "democratic-capitalist created" absence of big business; closing the gap led to the use of an activist industrial policy (for structural transformation, for research, for exports) aiming to correct the lack of influence from big banks, and this activism did not fit well into the efforts of the existing small businesses. Important strands of the Norwegian society also represented in the Parliament wanted less state activism and more attention to local needs.

These are important perspectives to bring into a discussion about the relative stagnation of the Norwegian pharmaceutical industry. What kind of world did the state–business relationship in the pharmaceutical sector of Norway constitute? Who were the industry leaders and owners and how did they perceive the state regulatory system? And vice versa: How did the "rule by professionals" that seemed to characterize the General Director of Health impact the pharmaceutical industry? Being a small pharmaceutical company in 1945 was no hindrance to innovation internationally but was it in Norway?

Basically, there are two approaches to innovation. Some scholars see innovations as the results of entrepreneurial activities by individuals and firms that launch new products. Innovations may also be seen as the outcome of structures in the economy, fairly stable configurations of networks, institutions, and organizations that mutually reinforce each other. They provide for the kind of interaction that may be conducive for innovation. Such structures are often called systems of innovation, and they may be analyzed on many levels: nation state, region, sector, and company (Nelson, 1993). Indeed, those science-based communities in the United States and the large European nations mentioned previously are where one would expect innovative products to emerge from networking and interactions between government financed researchers and the private pharmaceutical industry.

Throughout the book, there is an emphasis on national innovation systems. In the post-war period, all the Scandinavian nations combined state planning efforts of mixed economies with a US-led creation of an orderly international trade system meant to facilitate economic growth around the world. The nation state took on a new purpose, that of creating economic growth by having export-ambitious and open economies; this purpose was not only recognized by other nations but also encouraged by international organizations like the Organisation for Economic Co-operation and Development (OECD), the General Agreement on Tariffs and Trade (GATT) 1947 and eventually what is now known as the European Union. Thus, the national systems of innovations very clearly became politicized, with state apparatuses and their policies taking part in all of the interactions of the actors and organizations within the economy.

The other important approach to innovation is the entrepreneurial one. In his 1911 book *The Theory of Economic Development*, Joseph Schumpeter launched a forceful approach to change within the economy by ascribing the innovative drive to entrepreneurs (Schumpeter, 1934). Later, with the broad concept of "creative response," Schumpeter pointed to the possibility for firms to take opportunities and to play active, constructive roles in the economy (Schumpeter, 1947: 149–159). He highlighted something fundamentally different from the assumptions of standard economic theory that firms develop within a competitive framework where they respond to more or less given circumstances.

While Schumpeter's entrepreneurs were part of a macro theory, one particularly important continuation of his emphasis on supply-side action is the resource-based theory originally developed by Edith Penrose (Penrose, 1995). Penrose ascribes a firm's growth to the use of available (human) resources. Firms are collections of resources put together by different individuals; they perform according to how these individuals combine as a collective. For these reasons, firms differ from one another even though they may look very much alike from the outside. Through their resource base, firms are both enabled to develop productively and constrained. They cannot do more than their resource base is able to achieve. Small companies are, of course, constrained by their narrower resource base and the shortcomings of their managerial capacity. Their outcomes will depend largely on their ability to extend and develop their resources. Penrose's approach is further developed by others to be operative as a lens with which to understand corporate action. Authors like David Teece emphasize that entrepreneurial actions within enterprises may utilize its resources in powerful ways (Teece, 2014). Penrose also made an important distinction between knowledge that can be "objectified" and knowledge that is based on "experience" (Penrose, 1995). The first kind of knowledge is formal and can be taught, the other one—which may also be referred to as tacit—may also be scientific, but it is the kind of knowledge that follows experience.

This book approaches the act of innovation as simultaneously a corporate and a contextual effort. Given that the context in the phase of the pharmaceutical revolution is primarily national in kind, particular emphasis is placed on the Norwegian experience in a comparative Scandinavian perspective. Norway's experience was important for what it tells us about those smaller nations outside of the core that created the revolution. It is also important that Nyegaard & Co. and Norway innovated with one of the most important pharmaceuticals in the twentieth century.

The structure of the book

This book includes an introduction (Chapter 1), a conclusion (Chapter 10), and eight chapters that dig into the details and personalities involved in an innovative process. The 2nd chapter deals with the new era of pharmaceutical revolution and how it was experienced in Norway and the rest of Scandinavia after the Second World War. This was a time of optimism and great ambitions, with new ideas of building novel, innovative pharmaceutical companies. In the 3rd chapter, optimism meets reality in the form not only of strict and inhibiting price regulation from the Norwegian state but also of a leadership culture that is firmly rooted in the pre-war pharmaceutical culture. Moreover, this leadership culture sees the state more as an enemy than a partner. In chapter 4, there is a generational change within what is a family company. The new generation represents a more optimistic attitude about developing original products in the Norwegian ecosystem; now, the role of the state was also interpreted differently. Chapter 5 explains the research breakthrough with a product of global importance. Chapter 6 examines the daunting tasks of testing and marketing an entirely new product; here, there is an experience with a shift in regulatory demands from a price to a safety focus that draws the whole organization into an intense collective effort. Chapter 7 analyzes the marketing of the new product and the preparation for the next follow-up innovations during the 1970s, while Chapter 8 discuss the challenging consequences of success and how that led to the integration of the company into larger Norwegian conglomerates. In this big business framework of chapter 9, a Norwegian enterprise with a distinctly collective culture gives way to a framework shaped by maximizing shareholder value logic. Chapter 10 reflects on the long path from launching a research agenda in the 1940s, to the success in 1969, to the new developments in a global context. The conclusion in Chapter 10 reflects on what was gained and what was lost in the transition from a Scandinavian to a global enterprise.

References

Achilladelis, B. 1999. "Innovation in the Pharmaceutical Industry." *In*: Landau, R., Achilladelis, B., and Scriabine, A. (eds) *Pharmaceutical Innovation: Revolutionizing Human Health*. Philadelphia, PA: Chemical Heritage Press, pp. 1–147.

Amdam, R. P. and Sogner, K. 1994. *Wealth of Contrasts: Nyegaard & Co.—a Norwegian Pharmaceutical Company 1874–1985*. Oslo: Ad notam Gyldendal.

Amdam, R. P., Hagberg, A. E., and Sissener, E. W. 2003. *A.L. 1903–2003: Internasjonalisering med lånte penger*. Oslo: A.L. industrier.

Bjørnson, O. 1974. "Nyegaard & Co 100 år." Oslo, private publishing.

Campbell, J. L., Hollingsworth, J. R., and Lindberg, L. N. 1991. *Governance of the American Economy*. Cambridge: Cambridge University Press.

Carpenter, K. C. 1986. *The History of Scurvy and Vitamin C*. New York: Cambridge University Press.

Chandler, A. D. 1990. *Scale and Scope: The Dynamics of Industrial Capitalism*. Cambridge, MA: Belknap Press.

Chandler, A. D. 2005. *Shaping the Industrial Century: The Remarkable Story of the Evolution of the Modern Chemical and Pharmaceutical Industries*. Cambridge, MA: Harvard University Press.

Edquist, C. 2005. "Systems of Innovation: Perspectives and Challenges." *In*: Fagerberg, J., Mowery, D. C., and Nelson, R. R. (eds) *The Oxford Handbook of Innovation*, 1st edn. Oxford: Oxford University Press, pp. 181–208.

Galambos, L. 1991. Values. *In*: Sturchio, J. L. (ed.) *Values & Visions: A Merck Century*. Rahway, NJ: Merck, Sharp and Dohme, pp. 5–156.

Galambos, L. and Sewell, J. E. 1995. *Networks of Innovation: Vaccine Development at Merck, Sharp & Dohme, and Mulford, 1895–1995*. Cambridge: Cambridge University Press.

Galambos, L. and Sturchio, J. L. 1996. "The Pharmaceutical Industry in the Twentieth Century: A Reappraisal of the Sources of Innovation." *History and Technology*, 13, 83–100.

de Haën, C. D. 2019. *X-Ray Contrast Agent Technology. A Revolutionary History*. Boca Raton, FL: CRC Press.

Henderson, R. M. and Cockburn, I. 1996. "The Determinants of Research Productivity in Ethical Drug Discovery." *In*: Helms, R. B. (ed.) *Competitive Strategies in the Pharmaceutical Industry*. Washington, DC: AEI Press, pp. 167–193.

Holtermann, H. 1965. "Farmasøytisk industri." Tidsskrift for kjemi, bergvesen og metallurgi, 25, 25.

Johannessen, F. E., Skeie, J., and Norsk Farmasihistorisk, M. 1995. *Bitre piller og sterke dråper: norske apotek gjennom 400 år, 1595–1995*. Oslo: Norsk Farmasihistorisk Museum.

Nelson, R. R. 1993. *National Innovation Systems: A Comparative Analysis*. New York: Oxford University Press.

Nordby, T. 1989. *Karl Evang: en biografi*. Oslo: Aschehoug.

Penrose, E. T. 1995. *The Theory of the Growth of the Firm*. Oxford: Oxford University Press.

Rasmussen, N. 2014. *Gene Jockeys: Life Science and the Rise of Biotech Enterprise*. Baltimore, MD: Johns Hopkins University Press.

Richter-Friis, H. 1991. *Livet på Novo*. Copenhagen: Gyldendal.

Schumpeter, J. A. 1934. *The Theory of Economic Development: An Inquiry into Profits, Capital, Credit, Interest, and the Business Cycle*. Cambridge, MA: Harvard University Press.

Schumpeter, J. A. 1947. "The Creative Response in Economic History." *Journal of Economic History*, 7, 149–159.

Sciabine, A. 1999. "Discovery and Development of Major Drugs Currently in Use." *In*: Landau, R., Achilladelis, B., and Scriabine, A. (eds) *Pharmaceutical Innovation. Revolutionizing Human Health*. Philadelphia, PA: Chemical Heritage Press, pp. 148–270.

Sejersted, F. 1993. *Den norske "Sonderweg." Demokratisk kapitalisme*. Oslo: Universitetsforlaget.

Sejersted, F. 2011. *The Age of Social Democracy: Norway and Sweden in the Twentieth Century*. Princeton, NJ: Princeton University Press.

Sindbæk, H. 2019. *De renfærdige. Fortellingen om Novo-Nordisk.* Copenhagen: Politikens forlag.

Sogner, K. 1993. "Nations, Clusters and Culture: Nycomed and World Leadership in the Field of X-Ray Contrast Media." *Scandinavian Economic History Review,* 41, 209–220.

Teece, D. J. 2014. "A Dynamic Capabilities-Based Entrepreneurial Theory of the Multinational Enterprise." *Journal of International Business Studies,* 45, 8–37.

Torstendahl, R. 1989. "Teknologi och samhällsutveckling 1850–1980. Fyra faser i västeuropeisk industrikapitalism." *In*: Nybom, T. and Torstendahl, R. (eds) *Byråkratisering och maktfördelning.* Lund: Studentlitteratur, pp. 85–102.

2

Scandinavia and the Pharmaceutical Revolution

The pharmaceutical revolution was both a challenge and an opportunity for the Scandinavian societies, their medical systems, and their pharmaceutical companies. Sulfa preparations had introduced a new era. In the first place, the 1932 discovery of sulfa's inhibitory effect on the growth of bacteria was a tremendous breakthrough for therapeutic medicine; it was the first pharmaceutical product that actively destroyed disease-causing bacteria. Formerly, scientifically researched pharmaceutical products had been based primarily on principles of replacement or immunity. Vitamins and hormones (like insulin) were isolated from plants or animal organs and were used to compensate for nutritional deficiencies or failures in bodily functions. In the constant fight against contagious disease, vaccines had been the main weapon. But now, the opportunities for further advances were seen to be immense. The development of penicillin as another potent antibiotic during the Second World War emphasized the huge possibilities in pharmaceutical research.

The possibilities for research progress were readily apparent to scientists and business leaders in Scandinavia. Denmark surged ahead, led by the two insulin companies Novo and Nordisk with their early start based on August Krogh's pioneering work (Sindbæk, 2019). Especially, Novo broadened its product base, taking in penicillin. In Sweden, the war and the immediate post-war years were used to forge research networks between universities and firms (Norgren, 1989). For the management of Norway's Nyegaard & Co., the new horizon was inspiring in a different way. As early as 1948, its fledgling research effort prior to the war was confirmed as a contributing pathway to the isolation of vitamin B_{12}, something US Merck and British Glaxo managed to do independently of each other that year (Jones, 2001; Galambos, 1991). Lester Smith, the man behind Glaxo's breakthrough, had been in Oslo in 1936 and studied Nyegaard's methods of isolation of an active substance in ox liver.

Norway's Pharmaceutical Revolution. Knut Sogner, Oxford University Press.
© Knut Sogner (2022). DOI: 10.1093/oso/9780192869005.003.0002

The business implications of the renewed importance of research were, however, still difficult to interpret from a Norwegian perspective. At this time, there really did not exist any clear architecture for doing research in the pharmaceutical industry. Even for Glaxo, Smith's breakthrough was not an automatic signal for its top management to go wholeheartedly into the uncertainties of explorative research. For the management of a Norwegian firm, there were even more uncertainties. It recognized that something had profoundly changed in the Scandinavian context luring Danish and Swedish companies to innovate. And Nyegaard & Co. had been gaining experience with original research since the 1920s. But as a small national provider in a highly regulated industry, its management found it difficult to maneuver in a clear and consistent way when it came to research. The government's policies were restrictive and it was not at all clear that the nation's political leaders could be trusted. As a result, a strong and unambiguous belief in the importance of pharmaceutical research did not materialize.

War and chemical renewal

Despite these concerns, praise was plentiful on Nyegaard & Co.'s seventy-fifth anniversary in 1949. The little agency that pharmacist Morten Nyegaard started in 1874 had grown into one of the biggest Norwegian pharmaceutical companies. In 1912, Nyegaard had started production, and in 1924 it had started its own in-house research activities (Amdam and Sogner, 1994: chs 1–5). The Director General of Health, Karl Evang, head of the Directorate of Health, was among those who spoke in recognition of the company's achievements, noting that he found that particular task both easy and pleasant.[1] There were many reasons to celebrate in 1949. The company had passed through three-quarters of a century of development and had survived both the wartime crisis and those difficult years that followed. The company had been abruptly and brutally confronted by the war in 1940, but it had managed to accomplish more than simply maintaining its 1940 position. It had expanded and progressed beyond its old product portfolio, adding new categories of more modern and revolutionary pharmaceuticals, including sulfa preparations. Expectations were high. "We feel that our future is secure," company personnel affirmed in their anniversary

---

[1] "Nyco—75 år [. . .]," *Nationen*, November 25, 1949.

message.[2] Nyegaard & Co. was financially sound and had a broad range of products and product development activities.

To some degree, the war effort had prepared Nyegaard & Co. for a leap forward. The war period had been characterized by a dual development. On the one hand, the war had been strenuous and had led to efforts that did not have any long-term benefits. On the other hand, the war had brought opportunities to upgrade the company's chemical capabilities. Nyegaard & Co. entered the war years as a pharmaceutical company, but by the time the war was over, it had become a *pharmaceutical-chemical* company.

Traditionally, Nyegaard's product development had its roots in the nation's pharmacies. Pharmacists used age-old recipes to produce specific drugs. Industrial production had brought significant changes to both the process of making drugs and the task of product development. As early as the 1930s, the firm was using considerable chemical expertise in its product development. But it was still just reminiscent of a large pharmacy, extracting substances from plant and animal material (Amdam and Sogner, 1994: ch. 5).

The family of sulfa drugs changed that situation. The company started to concentrate on organic-synthetic chemistry in 1937 by initiating work on a copy of the important sulfa discovery. Nyegaard launched its product in 1938 and quickly followed up with copies of other new sulfa preparations.[3] This effort was not research in the strict sense of the word; it involved developing methods for the production of copies of the new preparations. To oversee this work, Nyegaard employed its first chemical engineer in 1937.[4] Reidar Gording's work paralleled the traditional role of Norwegian pharmacists, searching for new methods of manufacturing products already on the market. The crucial difference was that work on sulfa preparations required knowledge of the organic chemistry needed for synthesis rather than just extraction.

There clearly was more to the effort than mere copying. That is why, in 1939, the firm hired Trygve Holmsen, an industrial chemist who had worked in the United States, to replace Gording. The experienced Holmsen set about developing products in the newly established synthesis department.[5] He ran this department until 1944, and by 1947 the company

---

[2] "Anniversary Message," *VG*, November 25, 1949.
[3] NFR, 11, Streptan: Laland to Per Hanssen, August 10, 1938; NFR, 11, "Utgåtte prep. III": "Ad Pneumotan-Thiotanfremstilling," unsigned, August 29, 1941.
[4] Interview with Reidar Gording, February 13, 1991.
[5] Board meeting, December 5, 1938.

Table 2.1 Operating revenues in million
kroner, 1937–1950; fixed prices: 1985 = 100
(SSB consumer price index)

Year	Million kroner
1937	26
1938	27
1939	30
1940	25
1941	29
1942	27
1943	29
1944	27
1945	24
1946	37
1947	48
1948	52
1949	54
1950	61

Source: NADM, Øk.20: yearly accounts, 1918–1958.

had added seven other chemists to the staff. These were important additions. Technical Director (and pharmacist) Per Laland maintained close
ties with Professor Nils A. Sørensen at the Norwegian Institute of Technology (NTH), who helped Laland hire its best students.[6] The new (1946)
Royal Norwegian Council for Scientific and Industrial Research (NTNF)
provided support by awarding scholarships to young chemists taking
doctorates in fields relevant to pharmaceutical innovation.

Developments within the company during the war laid the foundation
for this cooperation. The war promoted an upgrading of the company's
chemical capabilities, and it had also been able to reap new turnover in the
home market. As is shown in Table 2.1, Nyegaard's turnover was high immediately after the war, as was turnover for Norwegian industry as a whole.
The company had also done reasonably well during the war years. Yet, in
Nyegaard's case, there were some significant reverses. Virtually no investment had been made in production equipment between 1942 and 1945. In
addition, the company's sales of its two most important products, Globoid
and Nyco Fruktsalt, almost disappeared because of lack of raw material

---

[6] Interview with Hugo Holtermann, August 5 and 10, 1991.

Table 2.2 Net operating profit pharmaceuticals (NOP) and income before taxes (IBT) in percent of operating revenue; solidity (SOL) in percent, 1939–1945a

	1939	1940	1941	1942	1943	1944	1945
NOP	12	14	15	13	12	13	12
IBT	13	13	10	7	7	8	8
SOL	34	33	33	32	30	34	31

Source: NADM, Øk.20: yearly accounts, 1918–1958.

for their production.[7] Globoid was a copy of Bayer's Aspirin, while Nyco Fruktsalt was a copy of Eno Fruitsalt. Nyegaard had started production of both of them in the 1910s. These two products were, however, impossible to make with Norwegian raw materials during the latter part of the war.

Instead, Nyegaard & Co. placed more than 30 new pharmaceutical products on the market, most of which were chemically synthesized. Among the most important were the barbiturates, Prodorm and Citopan (sedatives). In addition, Hydrokon, a cough-relieving substance later known as Nyodid, was synthesized during the war. The war years thus brought about a general renewal of the company's product line (Bjørnson, 1974).

The company exploited a number of new opportunities (Amdam and Sogner, 1994: ch. 6). At the start of the war, most of the pharmaceuticals that had been imported from Great Britain and the United States disappeared from the Norwegian market and were replaced by Norwegian, Swedish, and German products.[8] In retrospect, the war made it possible to enter into areas in which the allied countries were already established, and the ensuing peace made it possible to maintain this foothold. Now, markets that had been dominated by Germany offered further opportunities that depended on the production of synthetic pharmaceuticals. In this setting, Nyegaard & Co. was able to become a significant producer of *primary products*. It was able to produce the basic substances used in medications. Previously, these substances had been purchased and then used in *pharmaceutical production*, the final stage of the production process. By expanding its range of primary products, the company developed a strong foundation in chemical synthesis.[9]

[7] Board meetings, August 26 and December 2, 1941; September 15, 1942; and October 28, 1943.
[8] "Importation of Pharmaceuticals, 1925–52 from Denmark, Sweden, Great Britain, Germany, and Switzerland." Unpublished memo, c.1992, Jon Skeie.
[9] "Syntetisk laboratorium" by Sigurd F. Jermstad, *Nyco-Mix*, 3, 1948; "Syntetisk fabrikk" by Knut Paul Brekke, *Nyco-Mix*, 4, 1948.

Table 2.2 shows that operations were profitable. The net operating profit was stable at a high level throughout the war. In general, shareholders' equity in relation to the balance sheet was relatively constant, indicating that assets had neither been depleted nor increased greatly.[10] Clearly, Nyegaard came through the war years quite successfully.

Nevertheless, the company's research activities had yet to develop original, patentable products for the international market. Management had instead followed the very conservative course of developing synthesizing capabilities for the production of existing pharmaceuticals. Many new products were launched on the domestic market but all were Norwegian versions of already established pharmaceuticals. Working under challenging conditions, the company's executives did not focus any of its new research capabilities in chemical synthesis on breakthrough products. That was somehow related to the war conditions. All through the war, the German occupation was a source of tension and uneasiness. The majority owners—Chief Executive Officer (CEO) Sverre Blix and sons—were, to differing degrees, involved in the Norwegian resistance, as would be other employees. These activities happened in secrecy as informers and members of the Norwegian Nazi party could be anywhere. Members of the resistance working in the same company did not necessarily know about each other. What was not secret was the company's effort to help employees and their families with food and other items that were difficult to obtain.

New opportunities in a new chemical setting

The end of the war created euphoria and general optimism and, indeed, very satisfying recognition of the company's pre-war research. The general idea that science could provide opportunities for companies swept the world, and in Norway the government created several new research institutions. The pharmaceutical revolution offered particularly important opportunities to small companies from small countries with a high level of relevant technology. Denmark did well, which is not so surprising given its firm footing before the war. During the course of the war and the first post-war years, four small Swedish companies managed to develop proprietary

---

[10] Income from its shipping activities (see later) had come to a halt during the war as contact with D/S Nyco was lost. This would add to the profits, while lack of investments, on the other hand, make the profits seem too high.

Table 2.3 Pharmaceutical exports from Norway, selected years, 1946–1959

	Total	Various	Vitamins	Antibiotics
1946	1,663	270	1,393	–
1950	8,767	493	8,274	–
1955	9,535	931	7,173	1,431
1959	10,258	1,607	4,985	3,663

Note: Current prices in 1,000 kroner.
Sources: National archives; Statistics Norway's Archive for Industrial Statistics.

products with the help of research performed in Swedish universities (Norgren, 1989).

That there were no similar breakthroughs in Norway can be largely attributed to the German occupation of the country from 1940 to 1945. Sweden managed to remain neutral throughout the war, which obviously was an advantage. Norwegian industry had to concentrate on ersatz production of simpler non-medical products and raw material for its own medical output. Meanwhile, many of Norway's leading scientists had either emigrated or become involved in the resistance. The industry as a whole also had problems with changing conditions in vitamin production. There were six significant Norwegian pharmaceutical companies. Two (Collett & Co. and A/S Inta) specialized in vitamins, while four (A/S Farmaceutisk Industri, Apotekernes Laboratorium, Weider, and Nyegaard & Co.) were old-style, domestically oriented firms with broad assortments of generic products as well as vitamins (Amdam and Sogner, 1994: ch. 5). During the Second World War, several other countries began producing vitamins, and later many of the competitors turned to synthetic vitamin products. This reduced the advantage of Norway's readily available raw material from fisheries and the whaling industry (Benterud, 1958).

This process was gradual, as is shown in Table 2.3. The ten years after 1945 saw a boom in Norwegian vitamin exports. Yet, this was of no long-term benefit to the Norwegian pharmaceutical industry as a whole. This would seem to reflect the way the boom was handled as much as the above-mentioned technological matters. Three of the companies involved in vitamins before the war, Nyegaard, AL, and AFI, did not take part in the boom. The firms which expanded were those which specialized in vitamins, such as Collett & Co. in Oslo and Inta at Nøtterøy.[11]

---

[11] "About Inta": interview with one of the company's four partners, Karsten Berner, November 22, 1994.

The Norwegian pharmaceutical industry comprised a group of small companies, but it had a dual character. On one side stood a group of "large pharmacies," almost without exports. On the other side stood some companies which specialized in vitamin production and which had neither the will nor the capability to develop a lasting pharmaceutical or research-based chemical industry. Table 2.3 shows Norwegian pharmaceutical exports and reflects this dualism. Exports of pharmaceuticals were almost nil; this is the sum total of the efforts of the "large pharmacies." The figure for antibiotics is accounted for by exports of AL's Bacitracin, a generic product, which serves as evidence of AL's desire to expand (Amdam et al., 2003).

Vitamins, moreover, were not medically important in the same way as insulin, the Danish specialty. Insulin was critical for some patients and had to be produced in a meticulous and antiseptic fashion, as it was administered by injection. The industrialization of insulin depended on a large medical-industrial complex in or around an industrial company. Vitamins were entirely different. People could take vitamins in a number of ways. They did not have to be produced in an antiseptic environment. Much of the output went into foodstuffs and pills and in the 1940s and 1950s did not depend on a medical-industrial complex. While the small Norwegian pharmaceutical industry did not have the resources to take full advantage of the vitamin boom, it had a subtle but important impact on several of the nation's firms. For instance, the Norwegian industry began to collaborate with some of the world's foremost researchers in the field—such pioneers as Axel Holst and Theodor Frølich, ocean researcher Johan Hjort, and the leading interwar vitamin researcher Edvard Poulsson (Carpenter, 1986: 173–178). Nyegaard's technical director, Per Laland, had been trained partly in this way. He and fellow pharmacist Aage Klem developed the products Pernami and Examen, which contained vitamins and became export articles. They both contained what was later known as Vitamin B_{12} and remedied pernicious anemia. This proved to be a stage in the process to isolate Vitamin B_{12}, which Glaxo and Merck did after the war (Amdam and Sogner, 1994: ch. 5).

Per Laland, pharmacist by education, biochemist and industrialist by practice, was the main source of inspiration for Nyegaard's scientific endeavors. According to one of his colleagues, he conversed with the medical profession about chemistry and with chemists about medicine, building up good relationships with both groups.[12] Laland was the organizer

---

[12] Interview with Bjørn Sinding-Larsen, December 10, 1991.

who created a scientific climate within the company and who developed external contacts. In the 1940s, the business recruited young chemists Torleif Utne, Bjarte Løken, and Sigurd Jermstad. Laland had strong scientific ambitions, and he ensured that his son, Søren Gustav, and CEO Sverre Blix's son, Ulf, followed the best possible academic programs in England. Laland wrote to his good friend at Glaxo, Hector Walker, in June 1946 about various possibilities for Søren Gustav, and Walker was more than willing to help: "Please let me know at any time exactly what you would wish him to do, and I will make any contacts necessary."[13]

Laland and Walker both had in mind Sir Norman Haworth in Birmingham. Haworth received the Nobel Prize in Chemistry in 1937 for his work on Vitamin C, an area in which Per Laland had been active. Norway could also boast of its traditions in this field through Axel Holst's work at the beginning of the century. Haworth, who was deeply involved in vitamin research, had received an honorary doctorate at the University of Oslo in 1946, on which occasion he met Laland (Carpenter, 1986: 194–197).[14] Nyegaard & Co. established contact with one of the world's foremost research environments when Søren Gustav Laland and Ulf Blix were sent to Professors Haworth and Stacey in Birmingham. Søren Laland studied for one year in Birmingham before the death of Haworth in 1950.[15] The afore-mentioned Torleif Utne was also supported when he was accepted for doctoral studies at Harvard University under the guidance of Professor Louis Fieser.

Per Laland also brought a recently graduated chemical engineer, Hugo Holtermann, to Nyegaard. Holtermann quickly established a reputation as a particularly bright scientist and a future leader, something that was noticed and not too popular among the other young chemists.[16] Shortly after being hired, he received a government scholarship to study with Sir Robert Robinson at Oxford. Laland was enthusiastic and saw to it that Nyegaard made a financial contribution to this project.[17] Robinson, who was one of this century's greatest chemists, received a Nobel Prize in 1947 while Holtermann was at Oxford (Todd and Cornforth, 1976: 414–527). Holtermann wrote his doctoral thesis in steroid chemistry and defended

---

[13] NFR, 14, Glaxo 1945–1949: Walker to Laland, June 21, 1946.
[14] NFR, 14, Glaxo 1945–1949: Walker to Laland, March 18 and June 21, 1946, February 9, 13, and 18, 1948 and February 2, 1949 and Laland to Walker, June 6, 1946, February 4, 1948, and February 16, 1949; Glaxo 1949–1951: Macrae to Laland, September 22, 1949.
[15] Interview with Søren Gustav Laland, August 11, 1992.
[16] Interview with Torleif Utne, June 30, 1992.
[17] Interview with Hugo Holtermann, August 5, 1991.

his thesis in 1952. With this, the comprehensive steroid project that Robinson had started in 1932 was concluded; Holtermann, Robinson, and three other researchers who made important contributions published "Completion on the Synthesis of Androgenic Hormones and of Cholesterol Group of Sterols" in the *Journal of the Chemical Society*, in 1953 (Todd and Cornforth, 1976: 414–527; Holtermann, 1951).

It is fair to assume that Laland was interested in, and perhaps inspired by, the breakthrough research in the United States during the war. Merck—a company he would be well aware of because its vitamin research paralleled his own—had, in the 1930s, created a very successful research group that isolated and synthesized vitamins (Galambos, 1991). During the war, the research effort was enormously expanded to complete the mastering of full-blown production of penicillin, and at the end of the war Merck's research and development team counted around 500 people. Merck's Karl Folkers, who led the 1948 breakthrough in B_{12} isolation, came to acknowledge the work of Laland and Klem (Amdam and Sogner, 1994: 67). That and Merck's advances in medical science seem to have opened up new possibilities in Laland's mind. With the vitamin field closing off and new opportunities opening up in organic chemistry and biochemistry, Per Laland recognized that the business needed to turn in this new direction. Nyegaard & Co. thus began to recruit and nurture young chemists—a new profession within the company—for the longer-term future.

The contours of new national networks

Nyegaard was particularly well placed to interpret the new developments in pharmaceuticals and shift toward prioritizing science and organizing scientific efforts on grander scales than before. Possibilities for cooperation between the Norwegian pharmaceutical industry and medical doctors were increasing. Breakthroughs in clinical chemistry were an important part of the pharmaceutical revolution. This brought a new understanding of the chemical properties of diseases. The 1940s saw the institutional breakthrough of clinical chemistry in Norway in that several hospital laboratories were set up. Before the war, only the National Hospital and Ullevål Hospital, both in Oslo, had their own laboratories. After the war, both these hospitals—and especially the National Hospital—expanded their central laboratories (Palmer, 1992: 120–127). Each of the new or the expanded labs provided an opportunity for constructive collaboration between the pharmaceutical industry and the hospitals. Sweden provided a good example of successful institutionalized collaboration at the national level (Norgren, 1989).

During the war, Norwegian big business had developed an interest in the pharmaceutical industry,[18] awakened by the advances in industrial synthesis based on organic chemistry. The new sulfa drugs originally developed at the German chemical company Bayer (part of IG Farben) aroused interest. The first sulfa drug originated as a by-product of the manufacture of a chemically synthesized red dye. This event turned out to have major implications for the future structure of the industry. The Norwegian chemical industry, led by Norsk Hydro and Borregaard, would in theory be able to provide a totally different foundation for a Norwegian pharmaceutical industry than the one previously furnished by the isolated efforts of small Norwegian pharmaceutical companies.

With this in mind, Nyegaard and Norsk Hydro established contacts, though only on the basis of individual products. Hydro had a similar experience to Bayer. During the war, in connection with a process for separating potassium from salt water, an engineer at Norsk Hydro came upon a process for manufacturing "polyaminostyrene," a substance that could be used as a remedy for excess stomach acid. Polyaminostyrene was later launched under the brand names Macrin and Macrostyrin, with Nyegaard & Co. marketing the product on behalf of Norsk Hydro (Olsen, 1955: 461 and 556). Macrin never became more than a minor product, but it provided export opportunities for Nyegaard & Co. and was a pharmaceutical "spin-off" for Norsk Hydro, just as sulfa had been for Bayer.

These developments may partly explain the inclusion of the pharmaceutical industry in a post-war plan for industrial development that had been prepared in 1944 by a group of industrialists who wanted to communicate with the Norwegian government in exile in London and New York. The plan foresaw a need for a more systematic effort to promote industrial development in post-war Norway (Sevje, 1977). A major portion of this plan dealt with the organic chemistry industry and, by extension, with the pharmaceutical industry. Norwegian representatives abroad were urged to investigate the possibility of establishing primary pharmaceutical production in Norway.[19] Nothing came of this, but Reidar Gording, who had been

---

[18] RA,IKNY, box 9, A-243: Ik i London professor F. Vogt saker tilsendt. Appendix of August 24, 1944 to letter of August 1944.

[19] RA,IKNY, box 9.A-243: Ik i London prof. F. Vogt saker tilsendt. Appendix of August 24, 1944 to letter of August; box 12.A-325: Med.dir. i Washington. Jebsen to Evang, January 31, 1944.

Nyegaard's first chemical engineer in 1937 and was well acquainted with the Norwegian government in New York, took it upon himself to promote a Norwegian effort to produce penicillin. He was familiar with the new deep-tank method for producing this potent antibiotic.[20] Penicillin had been originally discovered by the Scotsman Alexander Fleming in 1928. During the war, English and American researchers had developed penicillin into a highly effective antibiotic, and much public and private effort had been devoted to the development of large-scale production methods. The recently discovered deep-culture method from the United States made mass production possible on a far larger scale than the English surface method.[21] This opened up possibilities in Gording's mind for Norwegian production.

Gording's plan for Norwegian production of penicillin was well received by Sven Oftedal, Minister of Health and Social Affairs, and the government granted Gording the necessary licenses. Penicillin was the most important pharmaceutical discovery up to that time, and the Norwegian Medicines Council in New York had in effect paved the way for Gording with a lengthy report on the development of penicillin during the war. The report included projections for producing penicillin in Norway. In July 1946, it became evident that large-scale Norwegian production of penicillin would entail a joint project between Nyegaard, the entire pharmaceutical industry in Norway, and Thor Dahl A/S, where Gording had previous contacts.[22]

For the Norwegian government, an important consideration was the strengthening of the country's pharmaceutical industry as a whole. In 1946, both Prime Minister Einar Gerhardsen and Minister Sven Oftedal were eager to develop this industry as quickly as possible. The issue had been raised previously in connection with the possible establishment of a state-owned wholesale monopoly for pharmaceuticals, but the industry itself apparently knew nothing of this. Gerhardsen had asked Oftedal to investigate whether such a medicinal wholesale depot could help to build up the industry in Norway, and the director of Health Karl Evang had confirmed to Oftedal that this might be feasible.[23] In strengthening the Norwegian pharmaceutical industry, the government was also acting on national security and foreign exchange considerations.

---

[20] Interview with Reidar Gording, February 13, 1991.

[21] NKT, 637: "Penicillin. Hovedtrekk fra industriell framstilling i USA" by T. Guthe, April 1, 1945.

[22] RA, IKNY, eske 12.A-325: Med.dir. i Washington: Guthe to dr. Jebsen February 14, 1945; NFR, 1, 100: "PM ad penicillin" and "Referat fra møte 26.7.46 på vårt kontor" by Bjørn Sinding-Larsen, 1946.

[23] RA, Sd, Hd, Ak, box 794: Oftedal to Evang, February 25, 1946; box 788: Evang to Oftedal, December 30, 1946.

Nyegaard occupied a strategic position in this effort. Its pharmaceutical expertise and strong connections within the industry had won Nyegaard the rights to sell Hydro's product, Macrin. Attempts had also been made to market Macrin through Glaxo's international network. Nyegaard worked toward the acquisition of production rights for Glaxo products in *Scandinavia*. These rights would enable the firm to export Glaxo products from Norway to Sweden, Denmark, and Finland.[24] Of primary importance was the right to use Glaxo's production method for penicillin, which Nyegaard obtained in 1945.[25]

After considering the governmental penicillin plan, however, Nyegaard withdrew from the project, bowing to strong opposition from Glaxo.[26] As the company reported to Glaxo: "We have constantly been in close contact with the Government, and we were largely instrumental in preventing the proposed deep-culture plant being built in Norway, a matter in which the Government was interested."[27] When Nyegaard withdrew, Gording also gave up on the plan.[28] Nyegaard thus forfeited an opportunity for securing a foothold in a major product area. Penicillin was made in both Sweden and Denmark. Nyegaard did not exactly play along with the new and progressive government either.

Nyegaard prioritized its desire to maintain a good relationship with Glaxo, hoping its pre-war contribution to the development of vitamin B_{12} would be a ticket to further collaboration. There were no binding agreements for the rights to penicillin production based on Glaxo's surface method. As early as 1945, it was obvious to most of those directly involved that penicillin would have to be produced by the American deep-culture method to have a high yield. Shortly before Gording announced his plan, Glaxo declared that it was discontinuing all of its surface production of penicillin and converting to the deep-culture method.[29] Glaxo was forced to admit to Nyegaard in December 1945 that they "had sold something of no value" when Nyegaard obtained rights for the surface method (Tweedale, 1990).[30] Glaxo's conduct would have justified discontinuing all

---

[24] NFR, 14, Glaxo (1949–1951): Glaxo to Nyco, February 22, 1950 and ". . . forhandlinger i Glaxo 1.–7. mars 1950" by Olav Bjørnson, 1950.

[25] NFR, 1, 100: Prop. Heads of Agreement between Nyco and Glaxo; board meeting, June 9, 1947.

[26] NFR, 1, 100: "PM ad penicillin" and "Referat fra møte 26.7.46 på vårt kontor" by Bjørn Sinding-Larsen, 1946.

[27] NFR, 14, Glaxo (1945–1949): Nyco to Glaxo, May 8, 1947.

[28] NFR, 1, 100: "Referat fra møte 26.7.46 på vårt kontor" by Bjørn Sinding-Larsen, 1946.

[29] NKT, 637: "Penicillin. Hovedtrekk fra industriell framstilling i USA" by T. Guthe, 1946, p. 10.

[30] NFR, 1, 100: "Referat fra møte 26.7.46 på vårt kontor" by Bjørn Sinding-Larsen, 1946.

association with this company, but Nyegaard had its sights on other products for the Norwegian and Scandinavian markets as well as continued scientific collaboration.

When the question of research collaboration with Glaxo was raised in May 1948, however, the British firm turned Nyegaard down, despite the fact that it had managed to bring in the Danish pharmaceutical company, Løven, to start a "Scandinavian Research Department."[31] Glaxo maintained that its own clearly stated research strategy, limiting research to a few selected areas, was not consistent with the plans of the two Scandinavian companies. In 1950, it became clear that Glaxo did not regard Nyegaard & Co. as its extended arm in Scandinavia, but merely as its representative in Norway and its partial representative in Sweden. Glaxo was not satisfied with Nyegaard's poor export results in Denmark and Finland.[32]

This was a major defeat for Nyegaard & Co. The fact that a company of Glaxo's size was not interested in closer cooperation with a small Norwegian company is easy to understand. In March 1950, Glaxo had 3,800 employees. Its research department alone had about 160 personnel, more or less the number of employees in all of Nyegaard & Co. On the other hand, Glaxo and Løven in Denmark managed to work out an agreement for penicillin.[33] This must have been a bitter pill for Nyegaard to swallow since the company had rejected the idea of a Norwegian penicillin plant in order to maintain its relationship with Glaxo.

Nor was this the only problem Nyegaard confronted in these years. The objectives of the new Labour Party government were seen as a threat to the existence of private pharmaceutical companies. While cabinet Minister Oftedal favored a private penicillin plant and a progressive wholesale monopoly working for the benefit of the national industry, the industry as a whole was under the de facto authority of the Director General of Health, Karl Evang. Industry was at the mercy of Karl Evang's policies in general, and they included far more than the production of penicillin.

To a considerable extent, business wariness reflected a general fear of nationalization. Evang, although a civil servant, was a prominent member of

[31] NFR, 14, Glaxo (1949–1951): "Forhandl. i London 11.–16. mai 1948 . . ."; AIDE-MEMOIRE, May 12, 1948; Walker to Laland, May 13, 1948 and "Rapport . . . mars 1950" by Olav Bjørnson, March 9, 1950; board meeting, June 9, 1947.
[32] NFR, 14, Glaxo (1949–1951): Glaxo to Nyegaard & Co., February 22, 1950 and "Rapport . . . mars 1950" by Olav Bjørnson, March 9, 1950.
[33] NFR, 14, Glaxo (1949–1951): Walker to Laland, June 21, 1948; Glaxo to Nyegaard & Co., April 24, 1951.

the Labour Party. The leaders of Norway's two other major pharmaceutical companies, AFI and AL, believed that, together with Fredrik Steen of
Nyegaard & Co., the Labour Party planned to nationalize both the industry and the pharmacies.[34] In Steen's words: "personally I am convinced that
The Labour Party [. . .] will gradually nationalize the whole pharmaceutical industry in this country [. . .] ."[35] And nationalization was only part of
the picture. The immediate problems were Evang's price and product policies since his position as Director General of Health gave him the final say
in the Proprietary Medicines Board. This board was responsible for autho-
rizing all pharmaceutical products and prices, and Evang's strong position
created uncertainty in the industry.

The pharmacies and Norwegian industry had both converging and di-
verging interests. They competed against one another in the Norwegian
market, while they were united in their efforts to limit foreign competition. During the First World War, conflict had existed between pharmacies
and industry, but wartime production requirements had helped the pharmacy owners accept the necessity of a separate pharmaceutical industry
in Norway. This understanding was strongly emphasized through the Acts
of 1928 and 1938, which established collective opportunities for pharmacies and Norwegian industry to provide pharmaceuticals to the Norwegian
populace. The intention of the 1928 Act was to stem the flow of pharmaceutical imports. In 1938, a Need Clause was introduced, a clause which
legally established that medicines could be kept from the Norwegian market if, as implied, there was no need for them. This gave explicit protection
to pharmacies and the national industry (Johannessen et al., 1995).

Evang was now obliged to take a position on Norwegian production of
drugs in the new era of the pharmaceutical revolution. Many new medicinal preparations originally developed outside of Norway had appeared
on the market, and the question was whether they in addition to the foreign companies who had launched them, were to be produced by the
pharmacies or by Norwegian industry. The pharmacies were on the offensive. Throughout the 1930s and 1940s, modern production technology
had undermined the advantageous position industry had held relative to
the pharmacies. For instance, the pharmacies had developed techniques for

---

[34] NFR. 14, No-Fa-Ki (1944–1948): Sissener (AL) to No-Fa-Ki, May 19, 1947, "Dir. Brantsæters
forslag til parallell-preparater," October 4, 1949 and Med.fabr.for. (Denmark) to AFI, October 11, 1946
(copy).
[35] NAFI, 739: PM by F. Steen, May 26, 1950.

producing tablets in large quantities. The Norwegian Association of Proprietor Pharmacists (NAF) had initiated a large-scale project with Kongsberg
Våpenfabrikk, and shortly after 1935, 170 tablet machines were distributed
to Norwegian pharmacies (Ødegaard, 1981: 97–103). With this advance,
pharmacies suddenly became competitive in a sector that had formerly
been industry's special area of competence, that is, tablet production.

Government legislation was little impediment to the pharmacies; they
worked under one set of laws and industry worked under another. Industry's products were approved by the Proprietary Medicines Board, and
approval applied only for a period of five years at a time. By contrast, pharmacies were free to produce any product which was registered in their
formulary. They could add new products to these lists of medicinal substances and formulas if they had not been patented; for example, they
could copy industrial preparations that sold well. In practice, this could
lead to industry being refused registration renewal for products which they
had developed and produced on the grounds that there was no need for
them.[36] These loopholes were primarily caused by the fact that the legislation had been adopted before the arrival of the Kongsberg machines. In
1944, when Sverre Blix called for a meeting with the other sizable Norwegian pharmaceutical companies, Apothekernes Laboratorium (AL) and
A/S Farmaceutisk Industri (AFI), their relationship to Norwegian pharmacies was the first item on the agenda. The problem was that, "if NAF
[the Association of Proprietor Pharmacists], freely and without control can
take our products and duplicate them, the future of our factories will be
threatened."[37]

Industry reacted in a variety of ways. No-Fa-Ki, Norway's
Pharmaceutical-Chemical Industry Association, was founded unof-
ficially in April 1944, to look after the interests of the Norwegian
pharmaceutical industry. On behalf of No-Fa-Ki, Supreme Court Attorney Henning Bødtker wrote to the Ministry of Health and Social Affairs
in October 1946 describing the industry's situation relative to that of the
pharmacies. He noted that legislation "was clearly characterized by the fact
that until a short time ago, all medicines were made at pharmacies."[38] In
the future, industry alone would be able to withstand *foreign* production
and maintain standardization requirements. Only industry would be able

---

[36] NFR, 14, No-Fa-Ki (1944–1948): Bødtker to the Ministry for Social Affairs, October 26, 1946.
[37] NFR, 14, No-Fa-Ki (1944–1948): meeting, April 19, 1944 between Sissener (AL); Brantsæther
(AFI); and Blix, Steen, and Laland (Nyco).
[38] NFR, 14, No-Fa-Ki (1944–1948): Bødtker to the Ministry for Social Affairs, October 26, 1946.

Table 2.4 Net operating profit pharmaceuticals (NOP) and income before taxes (IBT) in percent of operating revenue; solidity (SOL) in percent, 1945b–1951

	1945b	1946	1947	1948	1949	1950	1951
NOP	13	5	6	–	–	–	3
IBT	13	12	3	6	5	6	6
SOL	16	15	23	25	25	26	23

Source: NADM, Øk.20: årsregnskaper, 1918–1958.

to carry out the necessary research for further development. Bødtker drew a parallel between the revolt against the new machinery in the textile industry in Nottinghamshire during the First Industrial Revolution and the pharmacists' struggle against industrialization in the 1930s and 1940s.

Bødtker's argument was in line with the Labour Party's industrial policies, but at first, little was done to address the issue. Not until 1949 was a committee formed to study the question, and this is the subject of Chapter 3. In the years after 1946, Nyegaard had been struggling against low price levels. Despite large price increases for the industry's raw materials, prices for pharmaceuticals had not been adjusted. The company was desperate. Steen declared that "with the pricing policy of the government it is virtually impossible to raise prices, as the authorities maintain that profit on certain products shall cover the loss on others."[39]

In 1948, the company explained its poor results: "The reason so far must, first and foremost, be found in the high raw material prices on one side and a refusal to raise prices on the other."[40] Despite increasing sales, profits on pharmaceutical products were still hard to achieve. As is shown by Table 2.4, the net operating profit decreased from 13 percent in 1945 to less than half of that in 1946. Profit before extraordinary items showed the same tendency.[41] The same problem can be observed in the other company where this matter was investigated, A/S Farmaceutisk Industri.[42]

Sinking profitability was not just due to the price situation after the war. The high wartime profits had been artificial since there had been no new investments in the company whatsoever. A second factor was that Nyegaard's ambitious undertakings entailed the hiring of many new employees. There

[39] NFR, 11, A-møter: meeting, March 1, 1948.
[40] NFR, 11, A-møter: meeting January 9, 1948.
[41] NAFI, 711, ØK, 1918–1965: yearly reports, 1945–1948.
[42] Ibid.

were about 130–140 employees in the latter years of the war, and this number increased to as high as 190 in 1949 to deal with all the new opportunities and challenges. However, the price problem persisted, and it demonstrated that Karl Evang had no inclination to help the Norwegian pharmaceutical industry.

The penicillin path could have been a way forward. It was certainly the drug of the time. A collaborative attitude on the part of Nyegaard & Co. could have been the means with which to forge the same kind of fruitful relationship with the government as other and larger industrial corporations did at the time. Building a new plant with certain tax and financial preferences would have been just one possible outcome, benefitting like other private enterprises that showed trust and national commitment to political authority. Given preferences to prioritized industry was part of the new active policy of the Labour government (Sogner, 2003). Nyegaard had young engineers who could work on the project. Just how much keeping the good relationship with Glaxo mattered when Nyegaard chose to withdraw is difficult to say, but chances are that the ingrained skepticism against the Labour government—especially when seen through an Evang lens—was difficult to bypass. Pharmaceuticals was different from other industrial sectors and perhaps even more so just after a long war.

Karl Evang's pharmaceutical policy did not aim to facilitate commercial successes for the Norwegian pharmaceutical industry. He was not interested in building a common platform with a new science-based industry that was gradually emerging elsewhere. No policy of adjustment was developed to avail of the enormous opportunities for strengthening a new research-based industry; as was noted by the Ministry of Industry a few years later.[43] Evang's policy damaged the industry that had already developed in Norway and undercut the effort to build an even stronger industry in the future. The political environment sapped the morale at Nyegaard.

Sverre Blix, the patriarch

In describing a small company in an age when written justifications for decisions were few, an historian needs to employ a bit of cautious guess work. Inference suggests that the dual character of Nyegaard & Co.—enormously

---

[43] RA, I-dep, I-avdelingen, Farmsøytiske artikler: note by ØH, August 22, 1952.

inspired by research on the one hand, extremely frightened of the Labour government on the other—reflected deep-grained beliefs by the two directors, Laland and Steen, respectively. It is certain, however, that the man who made final decisions, CEO Sverre Blix, had his own particular agenda that explains why certain final choices were made. Blix directed the company with a firm hand. From the outside, managerial responsibility seemed to be shared by the company's three directors. Both Co-director Fredrik Steen and Technical Director Per Laland maintained a highly visible public profile. Yet, Sverre Blix assumed command whenever he deemed it necessary.[44]

Written sources which cast light on Blix as an individual or as a director of Nyegaard & Co. are scant. This reflects Blix's own priorities. He was not a man of eloquence and impressive words but a man of action who allowed his decisions to speak for themselves. The company he sought to develop in the 1940s was a research-based pharmaceutical company with a sound financial foundation. Blix must have seen this as *one* goal. A sound financial foundation was a necessity for a research-based pharmaceutical company. In reality, he had set himself a daunting task.

Blix's most important administrative tool was the company's financial system; management and finance thus steered Nyegaard & Co. in the 1930s and 1940s. With two distinct business activities, the pharmaceutical plant and a shipping business, it could place its capital in whichever of these yielded the higher profit. These two branches were covered by the same accounting system, and this helped toward efficient tax planning. Although pharmacy and shipping had little in common, maintaining this dual operation was Sverre Blix's personal strategy for leading the company into the future. His guiding principle was the financial result.

The shipping business had started in 1938. It is difficult to definitively determine the reasoning behind this decision, but the main motive seems to have been financial security. According to a former Nyegaard employee, the Labour party's accession to government in 1935 made the company fear that the pharmaceutical industry would be nationalized. To enter the shipping business might thus have been a way of spreading risks. The conditions which laid the groundwork for the decision to enter shipping are clear. In 1938, the company was fairly wealthy, and Sverre Blix probably had a privileged insight into shipping through his close friend Sverre Lie, a

---

[44] Interviews with Bjørn Sinding-Larsen, December 10, 1991, Fridtjov Rakli (several), Olav Bjørnson, February 11 and 25, 1991.

director of the important shipping company Fearnley & Eger. The written sources state the reason for this involvement to be simply a financial invest-ment. The importance of shipping for Nyegaard was confirmed in January 1941, when Sverre Blix contracted for a new ship (Amdam and Sogner, 1994: 55f).

In this period, the company constructed a new system for financial con-trol. During the early war years, Bernhard Hellern from the Norwegian Office for Industrial Rationalization (IRAS), who had consulted for the company since 1935, revised the accounting system in order to enable Blix to assess the profitability of each individual product (Amdam and Sogner, 1994: 61). This was a major task in view of the large number of products, but it facilitated detailed follow-up calculations of profitability.[45] Bjørn Sinding-Larsen, hired in 1937 to oversee company finances, further im-proved this accounting system, and Blix insisted that he establish a separate budget which gave an even more comprehensive picture of the business. Nyegaard was one of the first Norwegian companies to initiate this kind of modern financial control. For many years, Blix was the only one who re-ceived these budgets, but in the late 1950s, the company put them to general use.[46]

Sverre Blix planned for the very long term when he developed the com-pany's personnel policy. He considered it an important part of his strategy for innovation to create a competent and permanent staff. The personnel policy was a centralized system on the same line as the so-called func-tional system which pervaded the company. Blix used the same personnel policy for the entire company. As head of personnel, Halvorsen said in 1941: "When rationalizing a company, one should not only consider purely technical and organizational factors, but also include social rationalization: personnel management and leadership is to a high degree a psychological issue" (Halvorsen, 1942: 254f).

Psychological leadership was a philosophy that was typical of that time (Maier, 1988: 53–69). It is doubtful whether this was enforced with any great consequence, but Halvorsen formulated a strongly articulated pro-gram.[47] The philosophy of that program fitted into the company's hierar-chal structure and Blix's goal of having a talented and satisfied staff. Welfare services for employees had been expanded during the war, and in 1944, the

[45] NADM, IRAS-rapp: reports from May 1, 1940–February 3, 1942.
[46] NFR, 4: note by B. Sinding-Larsen, June 1989; NAA, 1001: "Salgs- og reklamestatistikker 1945–1964."
[47] Sinding-Larsen to Sogner, February 6, 1994.

business increased its collective pension fund so that retirement pensions represented 40 percent of an employee's basic wage.[48] In 1941, the company established new medical and dental programs and in 1947 published the first issue of its in-house newspaper, *Nyco-Mix*.[49] Nyegaard was not a pioneer in personnel policies, but it was among the forerunners when this began to be common practice in Norway.

For Blix, the test for these new policies was the performance of the company as a research-based industrial complex. It had decided to manufacture its own products rather than to be a passive distribution link for foreign companies.[50] It had sought a closer affiliation with Glaxo with that in mind.[51] Blix and Glaxo's CEO, Harry Jephcott, had similar backgrounds in pharmacy, but Jephcott seems to have been less inspired than Blix by using in-house basic scientific research as a tool going forward (Jones, 2001). Jephcott wanted to access governmental research results and build commercially on those foundations. Blix, whose son went to Birmingham to do a PhD in biochemistry, clearly had ambitions for his own company's research. Yet he was no dreamer, and, in 1949, it became pretty clear that the research euphoria of recent years had to be put on the shelf.

A dualistic government

Although Nyegaard & Co. had a sound financial basis, it was not at all clear that it could be successful only as a pharmaceutical firm in the competitive global industry. There was little the company could do, for instance, to reduce pharmaceutical costs in the short term. To address the problem of overemployment, rationalization processes began in 1948 and continued the year after.[52]

Even with an excellent insight into the company's cost structure, cutting costs was difficult.[53] The problem was two-fold. The company was still oriented toward two pre-war major products: Globoid and Nyco Fruktsalt. Their revenue was important. On the other hand, the company had many products which were far more important from a medicinal point of

---

[48] Board meeting, December 21, 1944; "Vårt firmas 75-års jubileum." *Nyco-Mix*, 1, 1950; "Sosial-medisinske tiltak ved Nyco" by Natvig, *Nyco-Mix*, 2, 1947.
[49] "Sosial-medisinske tiltak ved Nyco" by Natvig, *Nyco-Mix*, 2, 1947; *Nyco Mix*, 1, 1, 1947.
[50] Board meeting, November 30, 1945.
[51] Board meeting, June 9, 1947.
[52] NFR, 11, A-møter: meeting, June 22, 1948 and January 13, 1949.
[53] NFR, 11, A-møter: meeting, May 23, 1949.

view. Although they generated little profit, their continued production was desirable, not least for possible future growth. The number of employees could not easily be reduced; their presence represented optimism about the future. Meanwhile, investment in equipment renewal and maintenance after the wear and tear of the war years was necessary.[54] The final key to improving the financial situation was the decision to increase production:

> It may be necessary to modify our production somewhat, so that we can produce more of the absolutely life-saving preparations—or more correctly, those that are defined as such by the Directorate of Health. In this case, we could set such large raw-material requirements that we could produce for export sales in substance form, and thereby compensate for the less important products for which we are refused raw materials.[55]

The opportunity to sell primary or semi-finished products did not, however, materialize in 1948 due to the uncertain supply of raw materials.[56] When it did come a year later, the strategy was successful, but it was not a long-term solution to the enterprise's problems:

> When we started exporting in 1949, the intention was primarily to utilize our production capacity to the greatest possible degree [...] Demand for exports was high, and we quickly reached the point where we could not accept further orders without increasing production. However, steps were not taken in this direction.[57]

Nyegaard had the opportunity to become subcontractors for chemical syntheses but turned it down. This could have led to a chemical-industrial leap into the future, but two factors contributed to the discontinuation of export activities. First, the world market was wrought with uncertainty. Nyegaard's syntheses could be exported, but their profitability was not guaranteed. Prices for testosterone, for example, a product which young Nyegaard & Co. chemists successfully synthesized, plummeted after the war. The same was true of the price for vitamin B_1.[58] None of the newer substances were particularly profitable when compared with calculations

---

[54] NFR, 11, A-møter: meeting, January 9, 1948, October 26, 1949, and January 18, 1950.
[55] NFR, 11, A-møter: meeting, January 9, 1948.
[56] NFR, 11, A-møter: meeting, March 1, 1948.
[57] NFR, 11, A-møter: meeting January 19, 1951.
[58] NADM, Økonomi, skatt 1937–1949: "Ad bokettersyn," note by Bjørn Sinding-Larsen, May 16, 1949.

Table 2.5 Income Globoid and Fruktsalt, 1945–1949

Year	Globoid	Fruktsalt	Other
1945	414	18	2,182
1946	1,793	468	1,946
1947	1,706	649	3,116
1948	1,706	657	3,527
1949	1,860	976	3,358

Note: Current prices in 1,000 kroner.
Source: NADM, Øk.20: yearly accounts, 1918–1958.

for Globoid and Nyco Fruktsalt. As is shown in Table 2.5, these two veteran brands were responsible for increased sales after the war.

Second, the company's shipping activity diverted attention from pharmaceuticals. After the war, Nyegaard & Co. received a large payment on account of D/S Nyco's contribution to Nortraship during the war.[59] The vessel was then sold for about three million kroner in 1947. These funds could have been devoted to pharmaceutical undertakings but were instead set aside for investment in a new ship. While extreme fluctuations in prices and demand caused uncertainty on the international pharmaceutical market, and the Labour Party's policy spread additional uncertainty in Norwegian pharmaceutical circles, the shipping industry enjoyed favorable tax legislation. Nyegaard was able to reduce its taxable income from Nortraship by writing off the book value of a new shipbuilding contract. Income from the sale of the original vessel could be set aside, untaxed, if it was reinvested in a new ship. Shipping was thus a very profitable area for investment and was more predictable than pharmaceuticals. The decisions at Nyegaard reflected this fact. These were strong incentives to continue to invest in shipping.

The emigration of three young chemical engineers to the United States in 1948 and 1949 was significant in this regard. Torleif Utne, Bjarte Løken, and Sigurd Jermstad were chemists who worked at Nyegaard under the supervision of pharmacists. They were expected to produce pharmaceuticals because these were deemed necessary. Their chemical expertise was not seen as a basis for new activities, either in exporting or in the sale of newly developed chemical substances. When they left, their positions were

---

[59] Nortraship was a governmental organization running Norwegian-owned ships outside of Norway during the Second World War. Due to Norway's large shipping sector, this was a huge undertaking and important in the Allied war effort.

not immediately filled.[60] All three went on to careers in American pharmaceutical companies because there appeared to be no room for them in the Norwegian industry.[61] Blix's determination to develop a research-oriented company was thus constrained by the short-term analysis of Nyegaard's balance sheet.

The lack of support for research was especially noticeable compared to what was happening in Sweden. Swedish companies enjoyed greater profitability than their Norwegian counterparts. This furnished them with the resources to begin collaboration with public research institutions. Professor Nils Norman, who from 1959 led one such institution in Norway, the laboratory for hormone research at Oslo's Aker Hospital, felt this to be especially important.[62] He attributed the difference between his own situation and that of his Swedish colleague Leif Wide to the respective national industry's *financial strength*. The Norwegian industry was unable to contribute financially to collaboration with hospitals. Pharmacia in Sweden could fund and expand Wide's activities in Uppsala, Sweden.

Talks between the Norwegian and Swedish pharmaceutical industry around 1950 brought out the differences in their respective home conditions. While the Norwegian industry despaired, the Swedish one was well satisfied. The state engaged in price controls in Sweden as in Norway, but the price calculations for medicines in Sweden worked to the industry's advantage. The Swedish industry found the social democratic government to be supportive to the pharmaceutical industry—not least in its relations with producing pharmacies.[63]

Pharmacia's research and development staff was similar in size to that of Nyegaard around 1950, before the three Norwegian chemical engineers emigrated. Five civil engineers were employed with synthetic product development. But instead of reducing the number of civil engineers, as Nyegaard did in 1949, Pharmacia expanded this activity by taking on new people. Moreover, the company was able to utilize a product developed at Uppsala University known as Macrodex. The company not only sold this product but it also moved to Uppsala in order to be nearer to the University, and it built a new research team around this product area (Norgren, 1989: 119–129).

[60] NFR, 11, A-møter: meeting, March 16 and June 22, 1948, January 13, and March 14, 1949, January 18, 1950.
[61] Interview with Bjarte Løken, May 12 and June 1, 1992 and interview with Torleif Utne, June 30, 1992.
[62] Interview with Nils Norman, January 3, 1994.
[63] NAFI, No-Fa-Ki, 739: G.A. Rising to No-Fa-Ki, March 2, 1950; notes in shorthand from inter-Nordic meeting of pharmaceutical producers in Oslo, May 31–June 1, 1950 (Rising's talk).

By contrast, Nyegaard did not expand in pharmaceuticals; instead, it maintained its activities in shipping. The Swedish case illustrates the factors which could have brought Nyegaard to devote more money to pharmaceuticals: the main one was higher earnings. Arguably, the Swedish companies drew other advantages from a larger home market, a friendlier government, and a more fruitful state-sponsored research activity. In any event, Nyegaard's earnings were not large enough to support a bigger research effort. On the contrary, the company scaled down research. Nyegaard and the Norwegian industry thus ended up on the sidelines when the post-war pharmaceutical revolution was getting fully underway.

Conclusion

A new vision of creating a science-based corporation through reorienting the old-style pharmaceutical company Nyegaard & Co. was born and acted upon in the 1940s. This was an international vision, which had already started to be formulated in the 1930s, but it gained momentum during the war. The continued progress of medical science and pharmaceutical innovation in the United States—and the impact of penicillin in particular—opened up new opportunities for Scandinavian firms. In a fairly wealthy nation like Norway, young and gifted men planned careers in this promising revival of an old pharmacy industry. Some of them were hired by Nyegaard, where plans to transform the company were already underway.

But the Norwegian industry failed to make a decisive move to take advantage of the new opportunities arising in pharmaceuticals. The producing companies were constrained by a small national market, they needed all the new copy products they could muster, and they saw the ruling Labour government as a barrier to progress. Norway's political leaders were not yet able to apply the modern Scandinavian social democratic ideology that favored innovative enterprises in all relevant fields of industry. In Norway, the pharmaceutical industry was partially governed by a Health Director who seemed determined to keep pharmaceuticals very much as they had existed before the war. Nyegaard's leadership reacted to this situation by retracting somewhat from its initial optimism. It decided to invest in shipping—made a progressive force by the same government that did not remove the regulatory bottleneck in pharmaceuticals—rather than take its chances on uncertain investments in new pharmaceutical ventures.

There were political developments in Norway that a stronger and more pragmatic leadership with a long-term strategy in mind might have exploited to its advantage. The favorable shipping opportunities it used instead were clearly an example of what a broader pro-government attitude might have achieved. The government-supported penicillin plant that Nyegaard & Co. killed was one obvious missed opportunity to establish the company as a friend of a common collaborate national business strategy. Nyegaard decided instead to follow its British ally Glaxo in this matter and turn the penicillin venture with the state down, a conservative decision consistent in many ways with other decisions that Blix made at this crucial juncture.

Nyegaard & Co. was thus similar to British Glaxo at this time. Even if they were of different sizes, they seem to have had much the same approach to corporate strategy. Both had positive experiences stemming from their own research results, yet Glaxo and Nyegaard were both cautious in their attempts to embrace the pharmaceutical revolution. There were several companies in the United States at this time that directed their research in a manner that would establish a new industry standard for systematic research for patentable new chemical entities. But Glaxo would not go down that road for many years. Nyegaard too was slow to get involved in this type of research and development.

The fortunes of Norway and Sweden diverted in these years. Sweden followed the path of Denmark into sustained innovation. Nyegaard lagged behind, not because it was a small company but because it was cautious and risk averse—partly for very legitimate reasons. During these important years, the global pharmaceutical industry made great strides, and small companies were often prominent in the development of new products. Nyegaard had the financial resources to fund stronger pharmaceutical activities, but it continued to be cautious—maybe even paranoid—about its political context. It was inexperienced and insecure about the way forward in the new and exciting international world of the pharmaceutical revolution. It was most certainly not helped by its national political-institutional environment.

References

Amdam, R. P. and Sogner, K. 1994. *Wealth of Contrasts: Nyegaard & Co—a Norwegian Pharmaceutical Company 1874–1985*. Oslo: Ad notam Gyldendal.

Amdam, R. P., Hagberg, A. E., and Sissener, E. W. 2003. *A.L. 1903–2003: Internasjonalisering med lånte penger*. Oslo: A.L. industrier.

Benterud, A. 1958. *Collett & Co. AS. En beretning om de første 25 år 1933–1958.* Oslo: Collett & Co.

Bjørnson, O. 1974. "Nyegaard & Co 100 år." Oslo, private publication.

Carpenter, K. C. 1986. *The History of Scurvy and Vitamin C.* New York: Cambridge University Press.

Galambos, L. 1991. "Values." *In*: Sturchio, J. L. (ed.) *Values & Visions: A Merck Century.* Rahway, NJ: Merck, Sharp and Dohme, pp. 5–156.

Halvorsen, A. 1942. "Personalforvaltning." Norges Apotekerforenings Tidsskrift, 50, 15.

Holtermann, H. 1951. "Studies on Saturated Alicylic Ketones Related to the Sterol." Unpublished DPhil thesis, Oriel College, University of Oxford.

Johannessen, F. E., Skeie, J., and Norsk Farmasihistorisk, M. 1995. *Bitre piller og sterke dråper: norske apotek gjennom 400 år, 1595–1995.* Oslo: Norsk Farmasihistorisk Museum.

Jones, E. 2001. *The Business of Medicine. The Extraordinary History of Glaxo, a Baby Food Producer, which Became One of the World's Most Successful Pharmaceutical Companies.* London: Profile Books.

Maier, C. S. 1988. *In Search of Stability: Explorations in Historical Political Economy.* Cambridge: Cambridge University Press.

Norgren, L. 1989. *Kunskapsöverföring från universitet till företag: en studie av universitetsforskningens betydelse för de svenska läkemedelsföretagens produktlanseringar 1945–1984.* Stockholm: Allmänna förlaget.

Ødegaard, N. K. 1981. "Apotekenes legemiddelproduksjon og utvikling av den sentrale produksjon." *In*: Hopstock, A., Reizer, S., and Torud, Y. (eds) *Apotekfarmasi gjennom 100 år.* Oslo: Farmasøytisk Institutt, pp. 91–150.

Olsen, K. A. 1955. *Norsk Hydro gjennom 50 år: et eventyr fra realitetenes verden: 1905–1955.* Oslo: Norsk Hydro.

Palmer, H. 1992. *Utviklingen av den kliniske kjemi i Norge.* Oslo: Norsk selskap for klinisk kjemi og klinisk fysiologi.

Sevje, S. 1977. *En uheldig hund i keglespill: Studieselskapet for norsk industri.* Oslo: Master Master.

Sindbæk, H. 2019. *De renfærdige. Fortellingen om Novo-Nordisk.* Copenhagen: Politikens forlag.

Sogner, K. 2003. *Skaperkraft: Elkem gjennom 100 år, 1904–2004.* Oslo: Messel forl.

Todd, L. and Cornforth, J. W. 1976. "Robert Robinson. 13 September 1886—8 February 1975." *Biographical Memoirs of Fellows of the Royal Society*, 22, 414–527.

Tweedale, G. 1990. *At the Sign of The Plough: 275 Years of Allen & Hanburys and the British Pharmaceutical Industry 1715–1990.* London: John Murray Publishers Ltd.

3
The Sources of Entrepreneurial Hesitancy, 1950–1958

The 1950s provided a world of opportunities and challenges for the pharmaceutical industry in Scandinavia. While the 1940s saw the development of penicillin, in the 1950s, hormones and steroids came to the fore. The Danish industry was an early achiever in antibiotics, and during the 1950s, antibiotics came to be an export product even more important than insulin. This advance confirmed Denmark's place among the progressive countries (Hyldtoft and Johansen, 2005: 1–18). The Swedish industry was already on a positive path, and the 1950s was the decade when those new products developed in the 1940s proved viable on the international market. The Swedish export ratio grew from 5 percent in 1940 to between 15 and 20 percent around 1960, while the industry held its position in the home market. In the same period, the Norwegian export ratio—bolstered by transitory vitamin sales—decreased from around 40 percent in 1950 to around 20 percent in 1960 with the fall of vitamin sales. The Norwegian industry also had a much smaller share of its home market than did the Swedish industry in 1960.

Nyegaard developed new products but none that was any great commercial value. The company had doubled the real value of its turnover in the decade from 1940 to 1949 but could not match this from 1950–1958. Turnover stagnated. Other areas were also at a standstill: export activity was minimal, and the company built up no significant sales for new products. To the outside observer, the company seemed to be losing ground, despite intense efforts to improve its situation. In contrast to Norway, the innovative pharmaceutical firms in the four main countries—the United States, Great Britain, Germany, and Switzerland—benefitted not only from their participation in scientific networks but also from a broader industrial policy that included high relative prices and strict regulatory practices; corporate size also seemed to give their firms an advantage (Lacy Glenn Thomas, 1996). Those countries had a registration policy that gave new, innovative, ordinarily patented drugs the opportunity to be sold at fairly

Norway's Pharmaceutical Revolution. Knut Sogner, Oxford University Press.
© Knut Sogner (2022). DOI: 10.1093/oso/9780192869005.003.0003

high prices in order for the innovative firm to appropriate solid profits from its discovery. Obviously, having an academic sector of high standards and emphasis on deep understanding of scientific discovery was also advantageous.

This chapter probes the continued difficult interplay between a research-ambitious small company and the Norwegian regulatory system. A comparison with the situations in Denmark and Sweden will highlight some of the problems in Norway. As the chapter shows, state policies were certainly not converging to "best international practice." The company's interpretations of these Norwegian policies may have been a problem too, especially as there were signs of improving research results as time went on.

Developing a scientific community

The decision in Nyegaard to emphasize new research projects in the summer of 1950 had several causes. The candidates sent to England for additional education were starting to come back. The war was left behind and there was a return to a more normal life in the whole of Norway. Meanwhile, the international economy was opening up. But more than anything, there was an appreciation in the firm of the good work done by Laland and Klem in coming close to isolating vitamin B_{12} in the interwar period. As the Board stated in June 1950:

> In the future, special tasks will be given to our researchers so that we do not spread ourselves too much. For example, if the war had not prevented Laland and Klem from continuing their research in liver, we might possibly have found B_{12} many years ago.[1]

The influence of a new generation began to be felt. Ulf Blix, Hugo Holtermann, and Søren Gustav Laland each received their doctorates in the early 1950s and were three of the five men with whom Per Laland worked most closely. Ulf Blix, having been singled out for key administrative duties in the future, became technical director Laland's secretary. In Hugo Holtermann and Søren Gustav Laland, Nyegaard had acquired the services of two of Norway's best young chemists. Holtermann was rather quickly appointed as head of the company's Research Department in 1954. Søren

---

[1] Board meeting, June 2, 1950.

Gustav Laland stayed in close contact with the company but preferred to pursue his academic ambitions. In 1956, at only 34 years of age, he was appointed the University of Oslo's first Professor of Biochemistry.[2]

The two other members of Per Laland's scientific group were Pharmacist Olav Bjørnson and Laland's good friend, Associate Professor Jens Dedichen, MD, PhD. In 1950, Bjørnson became Assistant Technical Manager. By then, he had been with the company more than 10 years, and had held the position of production manager. His main work had been in running the company's external public relations. During the 1940s, he and Laland had the key task of maintaining contact with physicians.[3] He also played an important role in Nyegaard's production policy as a member of the Preparation Council. He edited the company journal, *Farmakoterapi*, an important communication link with the outside world. Many pharmacists occupied key positions, often in either specialized or administrative functions. In the 1950s, Bjørnson became the company's leading pharmacist. Per Laland's good friend Jens Dedichen, a physician involved in liver research before the war, was a consultant from 1948 (Dedichen, 1974).[4] While Laland was working mainly on the isolation of the substance in liver that was effective against pernicious anemia, Dedichen searched for a different medically active substance in liver. Dedichen's doctoral thesis dealt with the "L-Factor" (L for leucocytosis), a factor which, when injected into humans and animals, increased the number of white blood cells (leukocytes).

This rebuilding and reorientation of resources still left the Norwegian enterprise in a challenging situation. In 1950, on his return from England, Hugo Holtermann had expected to find an environment supportive of organic-synthetic research. Instead, he found himself more or less alone as an organic chemist after Jermstad, Løken, and Utne left for the United States.[5] As the board stated in the summer of 1950: "We are, in spite of everything, a small operation, and we should rather concentrate on taking over methods from foreign factories which we cooperate with."[6] Nevertheless, in 1951, they devoted time to the search for a new cortisone synthesis. This was an area the pharmaceutical industry had invested heavily in; cortisone could be synthesized, but the process was extremely complicated.

---

[2] Interview with Søren Gustav Laland, August 11, 1992.
[3] Olav Bjørnson's CV, kept by the author. On physicians, see: NFR, 11, Sulfazol: meeting nr 10, December 2, 1943.
[4] NFR, 3, 52, Prep.råd: meeting, September 3, 1948.
[5] Interview with Hugo Holtermann, August 5, August 10, and December 13, 1991.
[6] Board meeting, June 2, 1950.

Glaxo entered this field in 1950 (Tweedale, 1990: 190; Schwartzman, 1976), but Nyegaard discontinued its cortisone project when Syntex in Mexico published a new process.

Rather than continuing its work on cortisone as Glaxo did (Davenport-Hines and Slinn, 1992),[7] Nyegaard redirected its efforts to a related field: ACTH, the adrenocorticotropic hormone formed in the anterior lobe of the pituitary gland. This was a captivating product with extraordinarily effective properties. Like the hormone preparation cortisone, ACTH was especially effective in treating rheumatism and rheumatoid arthritis. Persons who had been crippled and unable to lead normal lives experienced dramatically renewed mobility. Among other positive effects, ACTH was very effective in treating burns. Cortisone was a single, isolated hormone from the adrenal cortex with a direct replacement effect on tissue. ACTH stimulated the adrenal glands, activating the body's own production of a wide range of hormones, one of which was cortisone.[8]

When the effects of ACTH were discovered in 1948, the potential importance of the product was quickly recognized. In March 1951, the Norwegian government accorded ACTH almost as much attention as penicillin in that a separate "Cortisone Council" was established.[9] Its function was to distribute these scarce but vitally important medicines. ACTH promised to improve the quality of life for a great number of people and constituted a major opportunity for the company and Norway. Internationally, the hormone had been isolated from pigs' pituitary glands. Nyegaard, however, worked on isolating it from the pituitary glands of whales, which had a much higher ACTH content. The Norwegian whaling industry supplied the glands.

The research program was comprehensive and depended on extensive cooperation with Norwegian physicians; Olaf Rømcke (Drammen Hospital), Jan Solem (Bærum Hospital), and Vilhelm Forbech (Oslo Rheumatism Hospital) were especially active participants. The physicians provided medical expertise, product trials, and comparisons of Nyegaard's ACTH with that of other companies.[10] In this way, Nyegaard gathered

[7] NFR, 14, Glaxo (1949–1951): Laland to Walker, November 12, 1951; also Laland to Macrae, July 12, 1951.
[8] NFR, 14, ACTH (1949–1951): "Cortison-Corticotropin" by Roald Rinvik (chief physician).
[9] RA, Sd, Hd, Ak, box 534 (Cortison og ACTH): Totland (Ak) to Budsjett-og Personalkontoret, September 18, 1952.
[10] NFR, 14, div.rapp: "Situasjonsr." by Olav Bjørnson, May 4, 1951; "Ad ... Cortico-Depot etc...," Holtermann to Laland, June 9, 1953; "... konferanse med dr. Solem ...," Holtermann to Laland, October 9, 1953.

the information necessary for developing a slow-working ACTH, a user-friendly product requiring fewer injections. Holtermann developed and patented this "depot principle." Marketed under the name Cortico-Depot, it was Nyegaard's first patented, independently developed, therapeutic product.[11] It was a tangible result of the firm's newly strengthened scientific orientation.

ACTH was a technical success for Nyegaard & Co., but problems with its use soon arose. The US hormone researcher Philip Hench received the Nobel Prize in Medicine in 1950 for his discovery of ACTH's effect on rheumatic diseases. In his Nobel acceptance speech, he made use of an analogy to fire. ACTH and cortisone seemed to work like flame retardants and fire walls, but they neither extinguished the flames nor had any corrective effect. ACTH had no curative effect.[12] Furthermore, its strong impact on the adrenal glands created a number of side effects, which resulted in the product being used less frequently than cortisone. As a result, ACTH sales peaked in 1952, the year after it was introduced; sales then dwindled slowly but steadily for Nyegaard and its numerous competitors, including two in Sweden (Norgren, 1989).[13]

As it turned out, Per Laland's liver project was the company's most important undertaking (Dedichen, 1974). The isolation of vitamin B_{12} in 1948 showed that Laland had been on the trail of a scientific breakthrough in the 1930s, and it also shed new light on Jens Dedichen's doctoral studies from that time. Dedichen had been working with the liver fractions that Laland and Klem had isolated while searching for a cure for pernicious anemia. He injected these fractions into humans and found that they stimulated the body's production of white blood cells. As soon as Dedichen and Laland obtained pure vitamin B_{12}, they went to work to discover whether B_{12} also stimulated the production of white blood cells, as Klem and Laland's fractions had. This vitamin did *not* stimulate white blood cell production; therefore, the liver fractions that had been isolated in the 1930s were likely to contain an additional substance not yet discovered that stimulated the production of white cells. A new research project was born. If this L-Factor could be isolated, it might be of major therapeutic importance.

By 1954, the project's results were promising enough for the company to collaborate with one of the men who had isolated vitamin B_{12}, Karl Folkers from Merck. Both companies would continue to work on isolating

[11] Interview with Hugo Holtermann, August 5, 1991.
[12] NFR, 14, ACTH (1949–1951): "Langsomtvirkende ACTH" by Jan Solem.
[13] Board meeting, March 24, 1953.

substances. In addition, Merck would be responsible for screening the substance's pharmaceutical properties, and Nyegaard would perform tests on healthy human volunteers (Dedichen, 1974). This project brought the Norwegian firm into contact with a renowned researcher from one of the world's leading industrial pharmaceutical companies. As Merck's historian noted, "Karl Folkers was becoming the company's leader in basic research" (Galambos, 1991: 73). The L-Factor project, named by Folkers, was pure scientific research, shrouded in secrecy. In 1956, in a letter to Per Laland, Olav Bjørnson wrote after meeting with Karl Folkers:

> He is of the opinion that your group and his are probably in possession of a very important substance, but that it is highly possible that others might be on the trail. The key is to be first.[14]

Then suddenly, they had to shelve the L-Factor project. It was demonstrated that the increase in white blood cells which occurred after L-Factor injections was in all probability caused by an impurity—pyrogens—rather than a useful new chemical substance. Merck abruptly withdrew from the project (Dedichen, 1974).[15]

These two failed projects illustrated the pitfalls of industrial research undertaken by a firm with limited resources. In the ACTH project, Holtermann had been assisted by a newly employed engineer, Carl Haug, but no further expert personnel was available. The L-Factor project was also poorly staffed. Although it was an extensive project by Norwegian standards, the invested resources were small compared to the research programs of foreign companies. To a certain extent, the project was a part-time occupation for Jens Dedichen, Per and Søren Gustav Laland, while only technician Nils Thorsdalen worked on it full time.

There were, however, some positive aspects to savor: By the mid-1950s, Nyegaard had involved itself deeply in scientific activities with key physicians in Norway and central figures in the international industrial research community. By building up new internal competence, Per Laland had created a scientific atmosphere in the company that was strong enough to warrant the establishment of external ties. His concentration on research also fitted in with the government's general objectives of using research to achieve economic growth, yet this objective was less clear within the pharmaceutical sector.

---

[14] NFR, 15, reiserapp.div: Bjørnson to Laland, March 17, 1956.
[15] NFR, 3, 23, L-Faktor: Folkers to Laland, undated, 1956.

Toward a new government policy

As late as the 1950s, there was no Norwegian industrial policy directed at the pharmaceutical industry that was consciously pursued as such. Yet, the configuration of measures from the government, the Parliament and the Directorate of Health had complex policy implications for the industry's firms. The major dominating force was Director General of Health, Karl Evang. He implemented and aimed to sustain a physician-led national medicinal supply policy that included the Norwegian pharmaceutical industry as providers. He was not concerned with innovation, exports, or other contributions to the wealth of the nation. The government had had some such inclinations, but during the early 1950s, Evang took control of the situation. The Labour government thus came to build a new framework around Norwegian pharmacies and the pharmaceutical industry. This policy helped to secure the status quo in the organizational structure of the pharmaceutical supply system and precluded government support for further development of this industry.

The new framework was expressed in Storting's decision in 1953 to establish the Norwegian Medicinal Depot—a state wholesale monopoly for pharmaceuticals. The Labour Party *considered* such a monopoly as part of a constructive, post-war pharmaceutical policy. The Minister of Health and Social Affairs, Sven Oftedal, supported the proposal for a Norwegian penicillin plant in 1946, and he planned to strengthen Norwegian pharmaceutical production by establishing a government-controlled medicinal depot. These supportive elements disappeared with Oftedal's unexpected death in 1948. It has been pointed out that Oftedal, in contrast to Health Director Evang, followed Labour Party policy and gave priority to increasing production (even though this conflicted with the party's socio-political objectives) (Nordby, 1989). The three main factors that had contributed to the government's ineffective role in the development of the Norwegian pharmaceutical industry in the 1940s thus carried forward into the 1950s; they included the strong tradition of regulation in the pharmaceutical sector, the antagonism between the Labour Party and the pharmacies and the pharmaceutical industry, and Karl Evang's lack of interest in modernizing this sector. Thus, the pharmaceutical industry was supposed to supply the Norwegian market, making do with a national rather than an international status.

There was some reason to believe that industry would be given priority over pharmacies. Oftedal probably thought along these lines. Clearly, it was economically unwise to continue to have a large portion of pharmaceutical production dispersed among many small pharmacies rather than concentrated in a few industrial facilities in or around the capital Oslo. Oftedal's support of a penicillin plant in 1946 can be interpreted as an invitation from the government for cooperation with the industry. But Nyegaard decisively opposed a project in which the government would wield the most power in its role as partial owner and regulatory authority.

The Norwegian Medicinal Depot (NMD) Act illustrates this clearly. There are few areas in which the Labour Party worked as strongly toward nationalization as in the field of pharmaceutical supply. The decision to establish the NMD in 1953 resulted in the nationalization of wholesale pharmaceutical operations. Pharmacies and industry had a perfectly reasonable fear that they would be next. The Labour Party majority signaled as much in Storting's Social Committee's commentary on the establishment of the Norwegian Medicinal Depot in 1953:

> The committee majority presupposes that the question of the public operation of the pharmacy system as a whole will be the subject of further discussion when the Norwegian Medicinal Depot is in operation, and some experience has been gained concerning how the system works. The committee views the present recommendation for initiating the Norwegian Medicinal Depot as a first step toward placing all supply of pharmaceutical products under public authority
>
> (Innst. O. I., 1953).

The Labour Party left no room for doubt that its goal was to obtain strong government control, and it appeared willing to use a variety of measures to achieve its objective. The undertaking had a socio-political motive, but this was only part of the argumentation originally put forward by Health and Social Affairs Minister, Oftedal. Oftedal considered this to be one stage in a government-initiated modernization policy, one that had its primary objective to increase Norwegian living standards. The Labour Party attitude toward state ownership was complex and included anti-capitalist sentiments (Grønlie, 1989). The stance in the pharmaceutical sector reflects that. Prime minister Gerhardsen, Oftedal, and the dominating politicians in the party had a more pragmatic view and one that was influenced by the trust-forging relations that had developed primarily through the common and broad national resistance against the German occupation (Lange, 1991). Although Norwegian Labour Party attitudes toward nationalization stemmed from the common European socialist background, as in other countries like Great Britain, the actual examples of nationalization in Norway just after the war came primarily through state take-over of German ownership positions.

There was also another aborted state-involved attempt to initiate the production of penicillin in Norway, this time in 1948. Apothekernes Laboratorium (AL), with support from the Ministry of Trade and the Directorate for Industry, tried to initiate production on the basis of Danish technical methods. Their intention was to use Norwegian raw materials and to render Norway self-sufficient in this important antibiotic, but the project met with severe technical difficulties. In 1950, a foreign currency permit was required for the purchase of production equipment. The permit application passed through the Directorate of Health, whose Director General, Karl Evang, disliked the fact that additional ministries and directorates had become involved in his domain. He called for a meeting with representatives from the Ministry of Trade and the Directorate for Industry.[16] The meeting confirms the viewpoint that Evang did not see it as his task to modernize Norway's pharmaceutical supply system.

In fact, Evang was negative about any plans for expansion of the Norwegian pharmaceutical industry. He emphasized the "difficulties" the Directorate of Health faced, "in that different government authorities are positive about expansions and new activities in our various pharmaceutical companies."[17] AL's intention to start up penicillin production was one example. Difficulties arose because it was the Director of Health who made the final decision on which products were to be allowed on the Norwegian market and at what price these could be sold. AL is said to have anticipated a monopoly on penicillin and a profitable price level, both of which Evang, through the Proprietary Medicines Board, was authorized to grant. But Evang was not in favor of giving this authorization. He "appealed" to other governmental departments to agree that in future cases dealing with the pharmaceutical industry, all concerned departments were to be in agreement. In short, other governmental departments were to submit to his administrative objectives.

Evang's stubborn attitude was based on lack of interest in the pharmaceutical industry's activities rather than animosity toward the sector. In principle, Evang wanted to reduce Norway's general consumption of

---

[16] RA, Sd, Hd, Ak, box 589, tilv. 1950: "Møteref. i anl. . . . ekspansjon av landets farmasøytiske industri 14.1.50."
[17] Ibid.

medicines rather than develop greater production capacity.[18] Therefore, *he* was not concerned with using governmental power to industrialize and modernize Norwegian medicinal supply systems. This may also explain his lack of interest in the nationalization of the sector.[19] Although pharmaceutical plants feared impending nationalization during the 1940s and 1950s, this was not Evang's primary objective. He had said this to Sverre Blix as early as March of 1947. In Evang's view, the issue was *inappropriate*.[20] Evang could achieve *his* goals by regulating the pharmaceutical industry.

The Labour Party government's policy in this area seems to have been somewhat two-sided. On the one hand, it set up a power apparatus to modernize, among other things, the pharmaceutical supply system. On the other hand, Karl Evang, Director General of Health, had other interests to protect. The pharmaceutical industry's aversion to government-directed modernization actually forced it to cooperate with Karl Evang and the pharmacies, as became evident when, in 1949, a Committee for Pharmacy and Industry was formed in response to Henning Bødtker's 1946 letter about the need to modernize the pharmaceutical industry. Bødtker's letter called for a modernization of pharmaceutical supply in lines that were consistent with the then minister Oftedal's take on Labour Party politics.

But even as the committee was being set up, the concept of a consensus solution between the industry and the pharmacies was gathering strength. Two of the six members of the committee were pharmacists, two came from industry (Fredrik Steen and Olaf Weider), and the remaining two represented the Directorate of Health and the Proprietary Medicines Board, respectively. In principle, the committee in 1951 agreed with Bødtker's argument for the necessity of an independent Norwegian industry, but it also specified that it was important to continue production in the pharmacies. The committee recommendation in 1951 can be given "credit" for re-establishing peace between the pharmacies and Norwegian industry. The two factions again accepted one another's existence.[21] The committee also encouraged an atmosphere of understanding between the health authorities and manufacturers, and this may have helped to guarantee the continued existence of private industrial ownership in Norway. The consensus solution was based on a pre-war model, and the Pharmacy and

---

[18] RA, Sd, H7, box 794: Evang to Oftedal, December 30, 1946.
[19] In a conversation on April 2, 1992, former Minister of Social Affairs Rakel Seweriin said that Evang was not a "nationalization man."
[20] NFR, 14, No-Fa-Ki 1947–1952: minutes of annual meeting, March 10, 1947.
[21] Report Pharmacy-Industry committee, June 21, 1951.

Industry Committee's recommendation in 1951 contained a number of viewpoints that Karl Evang later supported in relation to the supply of pharmaceuticals.

Both the committee and Evang focused on *distribution*. Evang was concerned with the scope of health services; to include everyone, health was to be defined in broad terms and high standards were set (Nordby, 1989; Evang, 1955). The Pharmacy and Industry Committee recommendation emphasized the question of supply and so did Evang. Before and after the war, the government wanted to ensure Norwegian production and to build up a reserve supply of medicines. In 1947, Nyegaard was allocated foreign exchange for purchasing machinery after meeting with Evang, subject to the stipulation that it was to cover *Norwegian* requirements.[22] The allocation was part of a "package" in which the company sent to the Director of Health an outline of the products it synthesized and of those which it could take responsibility for manufacturing in a time of crisis (without consideration of profitability).

At the time, Evang was working on the creation of an emergency stockpile of pharmaceutical products.[23] He, the pharmacies, and the Norwegian industry had the common goal of increasing—or, rather, streamlining—Norwegian production capacity. This involved a policy aimed at creating and maintaining a *broad* range of Norwegian-made products. Through his power in the Proprietary Medicines Board, Evang enforced strict controls on market authorization; in 1955, there were only about 1,300 registered medicines in Norway as opposed to almost 30,000 in some other countries (Evang, 1955). A consequence of the intention to establish a broad range of production in Norway (with a limited number of total products) was that many foreign products were denied registration. Although Norwegian products were also denied registration, the system protected the Norwegian pharmaceutical industry in its domestic market.

This conservative protective policy had many other aspects. It was implemented in agreement with the Norwegian industry, which actively sought to protect itself from foreign manufacturers. Norwegian companies were working to keep their prices below foreign price levels.[24] The industry also attempted to reduce competition among Norwegian companies by dividing the Norwegian market among themselves. By 1950, this arrangement

---

[22] Board meeting, October 2, 1947 (my emphasis).
[23] Board meeting, October 2, 1947; NFR, 14, No-Fa-Ki 1947–1952: meeting, December 4, 1948.
[24] NFR, 14.No-Fa-Ki 1944–1948: meeting, April 19, 1944.

had the explicit approval of the government.[25] The Directorate of Health had detailed, up-to-date knowledge of production at each industrial plant. In 1953, the Directorate of Health compiled a list showing that Nyegaard & Co. produced 86 important products but that in only 12 did it compete with other Norwegian companies.[26] The agreement promoted a division of labor, and eventually the Proprietary Medicines Board set its affairs in order. The first foreign proprietary products and Norway's first copy products were registered. The Norwegian patent law covering the production process rather than the chemical entity made circumvention of patents not only doable but also part of state policy. The enforcement of the Need Clause then barred new variations from Norwegian and foreign competitors.[27]

Up to this point, there was complete agreement among the interested parties: Karl Evang, industry, and the pharmacies. They had reached a consensus based on a continuation of pre-war policies. However, two elements in the post-war policy were new, and both created problems for the Norwegian pharmaceutical industry. The first, which can be attributed to Karl Evang, concerned the price level for pharmaceuticals that would be decided by the Evang-led Proprietary Medicines Board. As Evang concluded: "The system has greatly simplified the sale of pharmaceuticals, and ensured access to medicines to the Norwegian people and their doctors at prices that are lower than in most other areas of the world" (Evang, 1955). The problem for Norwegian companies was to cover the needs of the Norwegian market while simultaneously maintaining prices that were lower than in other countries. Germany protested against Norway's low pharmaceutical prices to the Organisation for European Economic Co-operation (OEEC) chemistry committee, maintaining that these low prices obstructed fair trade (Ot. Prp. Nr 28, 1963–1964: 13)! It goes without saying that a company like Nyegaard, with about 100 products and 200 employees, did not have the advantage of the cost-lowering, large-scale production enjoyed by foreign companies. They had both larger domestic markets and significant export businesses.

Evang was clearly acting in a well-established Norwegian tradition. In Sweden, the price policy was favorable toward growth in the pharmaceutical industry. In Norway, there was precedent to place the interests

---

[25] NFR, 14.No-Fa-Ki 1947–1952: meeting No-Fa-Ki, March 7, 1950; apotek-industri-komiteen, June 21, 1951.

[26] RA, Sd, Hd, Ak, eske 534: undated (c.1953).

[27] RA, I-dep, I-avd., Farm.Ind. 1951–1966: "Redegjørelse . . ." by Olaf Weider, June 3, 1954.

of business below the interests of domestic consumers. Pharmaceuticals was not the only industry controlled in this manner. Even though Norway had large hydro-electric power resources, and although facilities for exploiting these resources were being built at great speed from the turn of the twentieth century, the state acted to ensure that the new electrical power supply enriched the general population and the small-business sector. The priority was cheap energy for the many, rather than cheap energy for a new, power-hungry big business (Thue, 1994). As befitted the coming of the Second Industrial Revolution, Norway gained its share of bigger companies, but not as many as it would have had if freer market forces reigned. Evang imposed on pharmaceuticals a regime that did not promote vigorous innovation targeted on global markets.

The second problem concerned the new power structure. The NMD Act created a new post-war power structure which did little to strengthen the Norwegian pharmaceutical industry. The industry was understandably concerned and regarded one particular feature of the NMD Act—the state export monopoly—as particularly dangerous. As this last brick fell into place, it gave the government near-total control of the industry. The Proprietary Medicines Board gave the government the power to refuse approval of products or renewal of their approval. With the NMD, the government gained control over imports as well as exports. The export terms were never put into practice, and industry exported on the basis of temporary approvals. Nevertheless, the health authorities had obtained a great deal of authority, and industry felt increasingly uncertain about the future role of private enterprise in Norway.[28]

The nation's pharmaceutical companies were in an ambivalent position. Insofar as pre-war policies were continued, both industry and the pharmacies took part in supplying the country's pharmaceuticals. Yet, both were subordinate to a state power structure. While pharmacies and industry agreed among themselves, the Directorate of Health pressured industry to maintain a wide range of products. The order of the day was that export sales should not begin until the companies had fulfilled their obligations as pharmaceutical *suppliers* in Norway. In effect, this treated the industry like a productive pharmacy—as long as it catered for the national supply, it could maintain its formal freedom. During the 1950s, the Directorate of

---

[28] RA, Sd, Hd, H7, box 9, Apoteklovg. av 1954: innkomne brev fra andre enn komitémedlemmene, No-Fa-Ki to Department of Social Affairs, August 28, 1958.

Health aimed for a supply system that consisted of dispensing pharmacies, producing pharmacies, and an industry treated as a pharmacy, albeit a large one, without its own sales outlets.

The new policy was an expression of the traditional organization of Norwegian pharmaceutical supply. It created a system which had not really been planned. The power structure arising from the NMD Act was in part a tool facilitating the modernization of pharmaceutical supply, a goal in which Karl Evang had little interest. Since the state was closely involved in the modernization process, industry, which was a proponent of modernization, decided to cooperate with Evang and the pharmacies. Pharmacies and industry had the common goal of avoiding nationalization and tried to make the best of Karl Evang's regulatory regime. In a sense, the postwar control of the Norwegian pharmaceutical industry resembled the old, mercantilistic policy of privilege. Industry's role was as an effective manufacturer operating with a high level of safety and standardization. Industry and pharmacy were part of one system, which itself was a response to the sparse Norwegian population. The state policy was not concerned with encouraging industry to develop improved or less expensive medicines.

There is something unique about the Norwegian regulatory system. On the one hand, and in practice, Norway falls in line with those countries like Canada, Austria, and Spain with low drug prices (Lacy Glenn Thomas, 1996). That was a hindrance to development. That the companies were handed a role as official copycats in order to maintain a state-of-the-art national production capacity further cemented the industry in a small-scale and low-profitability model. Norway sharply differed, however, from countries like France, Italy, and Japan that had a regulatory system that was quite lenient when it came to registering new drugs, and which therefore developed national industries that both copied, and in addition were satisfied with, developing patentable pharmaceuticals. The Norwegian industry was really only a copycat when it came to being part of a supply system. For Evang, drugs should be necessary and potent. Not for him to allow patentable drugs that were only variations of existing drugs. Nyegaard, too, looked upon drug discovery as scientific and globally important, as schooled by the Anglo–American–German science ideal. One should have thought that Evang and the industry saw eye to eye, and in this scientific sense they did. But there was a gulf between them when it came to how they saw the whole system of drug regulations should function.

Evang was more aligned with Norwegian traditions than with hegemonic Labour Party politics. The Norwegian Labour-led state promoted the modernization of society through industrialization. The state was the driving force of an approach for "participatory capitalism," in which the top people in the state apparatus and among organized interest groups arrived at a consensus. The state and private industry could follow a common goal, economic growth. The contours of such a policy can be seen in the pharmaceutical sector prior to Sven Oftedal's sudden death in 1948. The modernization of the entire health sector, including pharmaceutical production, was deemed important. But this kind of consensus did not materialize between Karl Evang and the industry; instead, antagonism reigned over Evang's strong and consistent drive for cheap medicines.

The consumers won out in the 1940s and 1950s both because of Evang's powerful leadership and because of the strong position of the pharmacies in Norway. In the post-war world, the pharmacies had little new to offer in Norway. They were the main target of social democratic nationalization plans. However, they were well able to mobilize support due to their locations throughout the country and their links to industry in opposition to nationalization. Industry chose this path, instead of seeking a new relationship with the state. Industry and the state tended to see each other in old, ideological terms. Since Karl Evang was not interested in promoting the private pharmaceutical industry, the industry tended to see him as a quintessential socialist. Nyegaard was a paternalistic company, but Evang saw it as quintessentially capitalist. Neither side was prepared to search for a new common platform. The pre-war system of pharmaceutical production continued after the war, hindering the development of a new, growth-oriented industry.

These developments resembled what Francis Sejersted has labeled "democratic capitalism." Oslo-based industry had to coexist with dispersed and localized production by the Norwegian pharmacies. The pharmacies were rooted in local communities just as savings banks, dairies, and power companies were. The pharmaceutical industry and Evang adapted to this pattern in the 1950s and thus the political setting opposed Nyegaard's effort to become a progressive, research-based company.

A slow turnaround

There was no sudden, radical shift in Nyegaard's orientation at the beginning of the 1950s: The research effort went hand in hand with deep skepticism about the state and a strong, short-term financial orientation.

Some efforts during the 1950s were backward-looking, but the trend in the second half of the decade favored optimism. This was encouraged when some of the previous efforts to become more scientifically inclined started to pay off.

The change was in large part a result of Per Laland's leadership. He had plenty of ideas, but since resources were lacking, the company did not have the capacity to adequately pursue the best of them.[29] But Nyegaard's technical director succeeded in creating an open and generous scientific environment while adhering to a policy embracing a broad range of products.[30] The prospects of success were hampered by the lack of concentration on a smaller number of projects. Even more decisive was the scarcity of resources at Laland's disposal. Since he was open to new ideas, there was always room for including new undertakings. For this reason, it was possible to create a totally new line of products in response to government regulations. The board of directors' policy statement for 1955 reflects this goal:

> We have already worked for many years to seek products that can be sold freely in an attempt to become less dependent on the medicinal products which fall under the unreasonable and limiting rulings of the Proprietary Medicines Board.[31]

As this statement indicated, the company was spending a great deal of time trying to avoid governmental control of specialty pharmaceuticals. The company had developed a line of "technical products" which did not fall under the authority of the Proprietary Medicines Board. These "free trade products," as they were called,[32] were a potential safeguard if the pharmaceutical industry were to be nationalized. The company already had Nyco Fruktsalt and, in 1955, it launched a tooth powder, Nyx, which Per Laland had started to develop during the war. "We hope that we can gradually market other technical products,"[33] was a watchword for the future. The

---

[29] In interviews, the following have given information about Laland: Bjørn Sinding-Larsen (Nyco from 1937) on December 10, 1991; Olav Bjørnson (from 1939) on February 11 and 25, 1991; Fridtjov Rakli (from 1940) several times; and Hugo Holtermann (from 1946) on August 5 and 10 and December 13, 1991.

[30] Interview with Holtermann, August 5 and 10, 1991.

[31] Board meeting, March 21, 1955.

[32] NFR, 17.B, 1. skuff. PM ex. 1952/1962: Holtermann to Laland, September 15, 1953; board meeting, March 21, 1955.

[33] Board meeting, March 21, 1955.

company worked on everything from shoe creams, silver polish, and fertilizers to wood-impregnation chemicals. Throughout the 1960s, the wood treatment product enjoyed some success, as did Nyx and its successor, Nyxident, but they never became a major source of income. Marketing became a problem: "Trying to win public favor through mass advertisements, or more correctly, through advertising mass products appears to be a costly luxury," summarized Sinding-Larsen in 1961.[34]

These attempts to get around government control received a great deal of corporate attention in the 1950s. They had little positive effect, and they diverted attention from more important activities. When, in 1957, the question arose of concentrating on a fertilizer, Gibberella, Holtermann warned against doing this without hiring more people. It would pull virtually all of Nyegaard's research capacity into one field of technical products.[35] There were strong similarities between concentrating on a broad range of pharmaceutical/medicinal products and concentrating on technical products. Both involved strategies expanding the number of products, and both were aimed at the domestic market. Furthermore, they were both influenced by government policies, though for different reasons. The pharmaceutical and medicinal target area had grown from a policy that Nyegaard and the government had in common. Concentrating on "free trade" products was, however, the result of conflict with the government. Since Nyegaard did not follow a single, clearly defined strategy and had meager resources, the final strategy was in effect primarily a result of the firm's relationship with the government. The company ended up with an increased range of products for the home market but with too little depth in its research. As early as 1951, internal criticism of diversified production began to arise:

> Bjørnson ... thought that the company should not spread its activities at present in consideration of new projects that are underway.... If we take on too much, it will influence the larger projects ...[36]

When Hugo Holtermann in 1954 presented his departmental report to Per Laland, he listed 40 activities that were carried out by himself, Engineer Haug, a technician, and two assistants. Holtermann also had administrative

---

[34] NFR, 1, 69, PM: PM by Sinding-Larsen, June 26, 1961.
[35] NFR, 11, Gibberella: "Expose Gibberella" by Hugo Holtermann, May 20, 1957 (with Erik Onarheim).
[36] NFR, 3, 53, Preparatrådsmøter: meeting, September 28, 1951.

responsibility and was required to keep abreast of current developments in organic chemistry.[37] The research department did not hire a new engineer until 1955, when Leif G. Haugen joined the company. When a new and exciting project was launched in 1957, Holtermann was explicit about the problem of priorities:

> To transfer people from another project would affect our work in the medicinal field. Considering our small research staff, one cannot assume that over a period of time a staff reduction will not noticeably diminish the area from which personnel has been removed.[38]

Despite these concerns, the work of Bjørnson, Holtermann, and others started to pay off. The long-term result of the ACTH undertaking was an agreement with the US Schering Corporation. Through Head Physician Forbech's private correspondence with Philip Hench, Nyegaard learned that Schering had launched new and greatly improved cortisone preparations. The company had a basis for negotiating with Schering in that it had links to Forbech, Rømcke, and Solem, the best Norwegian medical contacts in this field. As a result, Nyegaard was given the contract to distribute Schering's top-of-the-line products in Norway, ahead of AL.[39] With the inclusion of the income from the Schering products (from 1956), Nyegaard's profitability improved.

Table 3.1 shows that there was no growth in turnover in the 1950s. Sales at fixed prices reached the highest level ever in 1950, but this figure was not matched until 1957. The fact that sales for 1957–1959 stabilized at a higher level than before was due to the Schering products. Nyegaard never operated at a loss but only because of its shipping operations. The pharmaceutical activities lost money in 1951 and 1952.[40] Table 3.2 shows this indirectly, in that net operating profits of pharmaceuticals were only 2–3 percent of operating revenues during these years and in 1956. The net result is negative if financial expenses are taken into account.

[37] NFR, 14, div.rapp: "Arbeidet ved Biokjemisk avdeling pr. 25. februar 1954," Holtermann to Laland; also "Oversikt over arbeidsprogram ved Biokjemisk avdeling i september, 1953," Holtermann to Laland, September 15, 1953.
[38] NFR, 11, Gibberella: "Expose Gibberella" by Hugo Holtermann, May 20, 1957 (with Erik Onarheim).
[39] NFR, 14, div.rapp: "Ad. Metacortandracine og Metacortandralone," Holtermann to Bjørnson, March 2, 1955; NFR, 20.26, Schering: Steen/Bjørnson to Schering, March 7, 1955.
[40] NADM, økonomi, skatt 1950–1955: "Ad regnskapet for 1953" by Bjørn Sinding Sinding-Larsen, March 5, 1954.

Table 3.1 Operating revenues in
million kroner, 1950–1958; fixed prices:
1985= 100 (SSB consumer price index)

1950	61
1951	50
1952	57
1953	51
1954	49
1955	57
1956	59
1957	68
1958	61

Source: NADM, Øk.20: yearly accounts,
1918–1958.

Table 3.2 Net operating profit pharmaceuticals (NOP) and income before taxes
(IBT) in percent of operating revenue; solidity (SOL) in percent, 1950–1958

	1951	1952	1953	1954	1955	1956	1957	1958
NOP	3	2	8	6	8	3	8	8
IBT	6	10	3	6	10	9	8	6
SOL	23	22	25	27	28	21	32	23

Source: NADM, Øk.20: yearly accounts, 1918–1958.

Increased efforts at "rationalizing" company operations led to a gradual improvement in profits. Production of Globoid and Nyco Fruktsalt was transferred to a new plant in Lillestrøm outside Oslo in 1952. The resulting improvement in production efficiency contributed to the results in 1953 surpassing those of the previous year. The rationalization measures enforced after the move did not involve reduction of manpower.[41] Not until 1953, a year in which shipping—a traditional source of profit for Nyegaard—did poorly, was there a significant reduction in the number of employees. In the course of the year, the number of employees fell from 193 to 170.[42]

Clearly, Nyegaard & Co. benefitted greatly from its financial control system in the years between 1946 and 1958. Operating profits were so weak that any mistake could put the company in serious trouble. No important new products emerged from in-house activities, and the product range

[41] Interview with Bjørn Sinding-Larsen, December 10, 1991.
[42] Board meetings, March 29, 1954 and March 21, 1955.

was not cut—it was there partly to accommodate its supply function for the Norwegian market. Apart from relocating production of Globoid and Nyco Fruktsalt, the key to slightly improved financial results seems to have been the financial department's overview of product profitability. Basing operations on these key figures, pressuring the government to grant price increases, economizing production, discontinuing certain product lines, focusing more on the sale of a few special products, and launching new copy products all helped toward stable and slightly improved profitability.

In the area of financial control, Sverre Blix was still an influential figure. He was not involved as actively in the everyday administration of the company and was no longer its driving force. But he still participated in many board meetings.[43] After 1948, his eldest son Nils became increasingly involved in both the administration and the board. Bjørn Sinding-Larsen, who was responsible for finances, followed Sverre Blix's instructions. When Blix withdrew from the company in May 1949, "Sinding-Larsen was given the authority to ensure and enable compliance with present and future guidelines for organization and internal control."[44] This clearly limited the activities of Directors Fredrik Steen and Per Laland.

Although the firm was not successful in bringing in increased turnover and income in the bulk of the 1950s, it succeeded in changing its pharmaceutical course. The stunted research effort that brought few results in terms of new products nevertheless created new external networks that brought a short collaboration with Merck and a licensing agreement with Schering. Research was one part of an integrated, scientific concentration in the fields of chemistry, pharmacy, and medicine, and it now provided the company with two new opportunities of great significance.

Finally something to believe in

At the end of the 1950s, Nyegaard acquired two new products that were to reshape the future of the company. Thrombotest and Isopaque were products of the scientific culture nurtured after the war and the company's evolving networks. External contacts, highly competent personnel, and a pro-active policy based on medicinal and pharmaceutical considerations

---

[43] Interviews with Olav Bjørnson, February 11 and 25, 1991 and with Bjørn Sinding-Larsen, December 10, 1991.
[44] NADM, 4, Bilag styreprot. 1949–1971: minutes from meeting with dir. Blix, May 21, 1949 (S. Blix, N. Blix, og B. Sinding-Larsen); interview with Bjørn Sinding-Larsen, December 10, 1991.

were the three factors that played a decisive role in the development of these new products.

Thrombotest came first. In February 1958, Per Laland related important news to Olav Bjørnson, who was then in the United States. The world-famous Norwegian professor, Paul Owren, had developed a freeze-dried prothrombin reagent, a blood coagulation test. "It looks wonderful. We have the chance to get this for the whole world, and he wants, either him-self or through us, to license or export it to America."[45] Laland wrote to Bjørnson about the coagulation test so that Bjørnson could use it to at-tract interest from US companies. Little came of that effort, though Paul Owren's product became vital to the company. Tests of this type are im-portant tools in the treatment of heart attacks and blood clots, which are often caused by acute coagulation in an area where the artery has become calcified. Little could be done to treat these blockages, but there were sub-stances that prevented the blood from coagulating. The coagulation tests could measure how the anti-coagulation treatment was working. Owren was a key figure in this field, both in Norway and internationally, and his paper "The Coagulation of the Blood. Investigation of a new Clot-ting Factor" had received widespread international recognition (Schmidt, 1982).[46]

Owren had approached Nyegaard because he and Per Laland had known each other for many years. They had neighboring summer cabins in an area in southern Norway where many other medical professors also holi-dayed.[47] Owren's first product, an earlier test for controlling the clotting tendencies of blood, had been marketed by Nyegaard since 1954. Sales of the first version were modest (less than NOK 150,000 in 1958)[48] but Owren continued his research, which, after 1956, was conducted at the new University Institute for Thrombosis Research at the National Hos-pital (Larsen, 1989). In 1958, he completed the reagent for control of anticoagulation treatment, which was to be called Thrombotest. At the time, it was the most advanced test in its field. Thrombotest was the first reagent to single out and control only those coagulation factors which had been reduced by anticoagulation treatment. The test was relatively easy to administer, and after Owren published his results in *The Lancet*, they quickly attracted international attention. Thrombotest was a stable,

[45] NFR, 15, reiserapp.div: Laland to Bjørnson, February 8, 1958.
[46] *In*: 1947. *Acta Medica Scandinavica*, suppl. 194.
[47] Interview with Ole Jacob Broch, September 27, 1993.
[48] NAA, 1001: Sales and marketing statistics, 1945–1964.

freeze-dried, standardized, and patentable product that clearly had export potential.[49]

The second product that marked a new course for Nyegaard, Isopaque, came directly out of the enterprise's ongoing search for new products. In 1956 and 1957, it became evident that contrast agent Nycotrast was ripe for replacement. X-ray contrast agents were mostly iodine-containing liquids injected into the body so that the vascular system and body cavities stood out in an X-ray examination. The iodine substance in the contrast medium absorbs the X-ray, with the result that the blood vessel or body cavity in the area where the contrast medium is present is outlined. X-ray contrast media make it possible to see inside the body without any surgical procedures. The use of diagnostic X-ray contrast media was an integral part of the therapeutic revolution that started in the 1930s. Nyegaard had sold contrast agents ever since 1934. Its first was Urotrast; Cholotrast and Oleotrast appeared in 1936 and 1938. In 1947, it added Nycotrast to its portfolio (Rakli, undated). None of the four were original products. Nycotrast had an annual turnover of less than NOK 100,000 at the end of the 1950s, a level similar to that of Owren's first test method. The two products comprised about 2 percent of turnover in 1957[50] and were part of the company's broad product range for the Norwegian market.

It was only natural, then, for the firm to launch *Nycopaque*, a product based on the molecule diatrizoate, which was far superior to the existing products (Grainger, 1982: 1–18). According to Nyegaard's findings, the product was not patented in Norway and was thus registered with the production methods made public by its US originator, Sterling Drug. Nyegaard registered Nycopaque with the Proprietary Medicines Board in July 1957 and launched the new product. The company soon learned, however, that Nycopaque would have to be withdrawn from the market. The patent office had erred in replying to Nyegaard's inquiry.[51] In November 1958, Sterling Drug's German licensees, Schering AG (not the same company as Nyegaard's licensor, the US Schering Corporation!),[52] pointed out that Nyegaard & Co. had broken the patent law: "You are thus infringing the

---

[49] NFR, 20, 1, reiserapp: Olav Bjørnson's travel to Sweden January 7–8 and 12–13, 1959 and travel to Finland January 9–10, 1959; interview with Bjørnson, February 11 and 25, 1991.

[50] NAA, 1001: Sales and marketing statistics, 1945–1964.

[51] NFR, 20.20, Sverige-Tyskland, Schering 1958–1962: Nyegaard & Co. to Schering, November 29, 1958.

[52] The US companies Schering and Merck were subsidiary companies of the German pharmaceutical companies Schering and Merck, which, in connection with the Second World War and the First World War, respectively, were taken over by US owners.

Norwegian patent No. 87.936. We have been granted an exclusive license under this patent by Messrs. Sterling Drug, who have authorized us to claim the rights under this patent."[53]

However, this defeat had a successful ending: the discovery of Isopaque, Nyegaard's first original contrast agent.[54] Diatrizoate was protected in Norway by a "process patent," which meant that the compound could be manufactured and sold if a company developed a new, unpatented method for its manufacture. When Nyegaard's researchers thought they had achieved just that, they noted that the compound they believed was diatrizoate acted strangely. Closer analysis revealed that the synthesis had resulted in a mixture of three substances, diatrizoate and two other substances, x- and y-acid. X-acid had notable similarities with diatrizoate, and for a time it was speculated that x-acid and diatrizoate had identical chemical compositions but different geometric structures. X-acid thus seemed a potential X-ray contrast agent. As it happened, x-acid was even more promising. It was a new molecule, a substance that could be used as a contrast medium and patented both domestically and internationally. This was a fantastic breakthrough that led Nyegaard into the contrast agent field with a new, patentable substance.

The researchers gave X-acid the generic name metrizoic acid and it was later sold under the brand name Isopaque. Isopaque bore testimony to the success of Nyegaard's continuing ventures into scientific research in the 1950s even though new contrast agents had not been a specific part of the company's strategy and the discovery of the new product was coincidental. That Nyegaard discovered something new was no coincidence, however. The competence necessary for discovering new substances had been built up within the company.

Thrombotest and Isopaque were thus both results of the company's concentration on scientific activity and the relationships it produced. Both new products were logical consequences of the policies that Per Laland had set in motion. Nyegaard & Co. now had two products for the export market, products which could become the basis for further expansion.

[53] NFR, 20.20, Sverige-Tyskland, Schering 1958–1962: Schering to Nyegaard & Co., November 25, 1958. Diatrizoate, the compound's *generic* name, was sold by Sterling Drug in the United States under the brand name Hypaque and by the German Schering AG under the brand name Urografin in Europe and Japan. It was sold by AFI in Norway.
[54] NFR, 5, 12: "Det var slik det begynte," manuscript by Leif G. Haugen, April 1986; interview with Hugo Holtermann, August 5 and 10, 1991 and December 13, 1991.

Conclusion

Nyegaard's performance during the 1950s stemmed from a mixed bag of skills, incentives, and culture: Although skilled from an old pharmaceutical point of view, the organization set out to build a new research organization more of less from scratch. As noted in this chapter, the political context did not favor this new undertaking. Indeed, it discouraged such a bold initiative. Understandably, the company began this uphill struggle in a half-hearted way while it was being pushed to remain a mere supplier of products from other countries. Given that context, the modernizing results were as good as could be expected. Two new, as yet unproven, products had emerged at the end of the decade as consequences of the company's new capabilities and its involvement in the Norwegian medical and scientific ecosystem. The chance to represent Schering Corporation in the Norwegian market had been a sign of progress too. But at the end of the decade, Nyegaard's strategy was still dominated by its role as a supplier of a large portfolio of small-batch production of generic—and branded generic—products to a small national market.

Nyegaard's fortunes were shaped more by a pre war regulatory practice than the new, forward-looking policies for growth the company could have expected from the Labour government. The regulatory practice commanded by Director of Health Karl Evang was particular to the pharmaceutical field, yet it also reflected a national pattern emphasizing the need to construct the nation's drug supply on decentralized production units making low priced and necessary products. The regulatory practice did modernize, as is indicated by Norway's eagerness to register new and important pharmaceuticals and build national capacity to provide these same new products. Thus the industry's political context stressed three goals: upgrading the generic portfolio, filling a need in the Norwegian market, and selling at low prices. Not for Norway to put the national industry in any financial position to do extensive research like the big four (United States, Great Britain, Germany, and Switzerland) and Sweden. Not for Norway to be lenient in the registration of numerous products as happened in Italy, France, and initially in Japan.

Could the company have changed the government's role and its performance if it had developed a more self-confident and mature scientific culture within the company? It would have been difficult. There was no way any company could have disregarded the package of incentives and disincentives that characterized the sum total of state policy. To continue to invest in shipping was, for tax incentives, much more profitable than to invest only in highly regulated pharmaceuticals. In addition, there was real danger of a coming nationalization of the whole industry, a very clear threat after the nationalization of the wholesale function in pharmaceuticals. To get out from under these regulations and the possible state takeover of the pharmaceutical business, Nyegaard had started using its scarce resources in developing so-called "technical products," toothpaste, and shoe cream, and other things not under state regulation.

Does this mean the state is to be blamed for the relative stagnation of the Norwegian pharmaceutical industry? Yes and no. Yes because its price policy had powerful negative consequences. Yes, too, because the government generated a fear of nationalization. No because there was room for interpreting the state's policies differently. It is highly likely that the state would have taken a positive attitude to greater efforts by industry to generate scientific breakthroughs. Such efforts could have been a means for attaining greater public recognition and perhaps support. But the final total places primary blame for what happened in the political sector. A glance at what was achieved by Sweden and Denmark supports this conclusion. Quite a lot could have developed differently in Norway had firms like Nyegaard had the profits needed to do more research, the incentive to direct shipping investments into pharmaceuticals, and the strong support of a government determined to gain a new position in an important science-based industry.

References

Davenport-Hines, R. P. T. and Slinn, J. 1992. *Glaxo: A History to 1962, Cambridge.* Cambridge: Cambridge University Press.

Dedichen, J. 1974. *Lege på flere måter: på spor av et nytt stoff.* Oslo: Cappelen.

Evang, K. 1955. "Helsestellets utvikling i Norge gjennom 75 år." Tidsskrift for den norske Lægeforening, Jubileumsnummer (jubilee edition), 51–70.

Galambos, L. 1991. "Values." *In*: Sturchio, J. L. (ed.) *Values & Visions: A Merck Century.* Rahway, NJ: Merck, Sharp and Dohme, pp. 5–156.

Grainger, R. G. 1982. "Intravascular Contrast Media—the Past, the Present and the Future. Mackenzie Davidson Memorial Lecture, April 1981." *British Journal of Radiology*, 55, 1–18.

Grønlie, T. 1989. *Statsdrift: staten som industrieier i Norge 1945–1963.* Oslo: TANO.

Hyldtoft, O. and Johansen, H. C. 2005. *Teknologiske forandringer i dansk industri, 1896–1972.* Odense: Syddansk universitetsforlag.

Innst. O. I. 1953. *Innstilling fra sosialkomiteen om lover om Norsk Medisinaldepot og om endringer i lovgivningen om innførsel og omsetning av apotekvarer og gifter.* Oslo: Stortinget.

Lacy Glenn Thomas, I. 1996. "Industrial Policy and International Competitiveness in the Pharmaceutical Industry." *In*: Helms, R. B. (ed.) *Competitive Strategies in the Pharmaceutical Industry.* Washington, DC: The AEI Press, pp. 107–129.

Lange, E. 1991. "Førsteopponentinnlegg, Tore Grønlies Statsdrift." *Historisk tidsskrift*, 70(3), 406–418.

Larsen, Ø. 1989. *Mangfoldig medisin : Det medisinske fakultet, Universitetet i Oslo 175 år, 1814–1989,* Oslo, Ø. Larsen, Seksjon for medisinsk historie, Universitetet i Oslo.

Nordby, T. 1989. *Karl Evang: en biografi/* Oslo: Aschehoug.

Norgren, L. 1989. *Kunskapsöverföring från universitet till företag: en studie av universitetsforskningens betydelse för de svenska läkemedelsföretagens produktlanseringar 1945–1984.* Stockholm: Allmänna förlaget.

Ot. Prp. Nr 28. 1963–1964. *Odelstingsproposisjon.* Oslo: Stortinget.

Rakli, F. Undated. *Nyco-produkter. Historisk oversikt 1914–1985.* Oslo: Nycomed.

Schmidt, V. 1982. *Klinisk kemis historie: læger og laboratorieundersøgelser.* Rødovre: Rolv forlag.

Schwartzman, D. 1976. *Innovation in the Pharmaceutical Industry.* Baltimore, MD and London: John Hopkins University Press.

Thue, L. 1994. *Statens kraft 1890–1947: kraftutbygging og samfunnsutvikling.* Oslo: Cappelen.

Tweedale, G. 1990. *At the Sign of The Plough: 275 Years of Allen & Hanburys and the British Pharmaceutical Industry 1715–1990,* London: John Murray Publishers Ltd.

4

The Long Road to a New Path, 1959–1966

The research-based pharmaceutical company was not as clear-cut an ideal as might be perceived from a cursory glance. Glaxo, for instance, was a reluctant committer to full-blown research. The two parts of Glaxo—Glaxo and its recent purchase Allen & Hanbury's—had research histories going back to the interwar period, but all through the 1950s they refrained from committing to the kind of huge innovative effort made by Merck and other US companies (Jones, 2001). Glaxo learned about the possibilities for innovative breakthroughs, however, and the new chairman of 1963, Sir Alan Wilson, finally took Glaxo firmly onto a very ambitious research route. Wilson was a scientist with an industrial background from Courtaulds, who was involved in several of the Allied collaborative research efforts during the war that came to define "big science," that is, huge, collective and directed science efforts.

The leading representatives of the Danish and Swedish pharmaceutical industries stood out as even clearer examples than Glaxo of where the forefront in providing commercially successful original research was. Novo, Nordisk, and Løven (Leo) were important Danish houses that brought antibiotics, insulin, and enzymes to the world, while Swedish Astra sold Xylocain and Pharmacia provided Macrodex (Norgren, 1989; Hyldtoft and Johansen, 2005). The Norwegian backwardness in Scandinavia was screamingly evident around 1960. In that decade, however, Norway's Nyegaard & Co. made a series of decisions that firmly put it on the road to becoming an innovative pharmaceutical company. For 1961, when leadership changed to the generation that became adults during the pharmaceutical revolution, a note in the yearly report stated bluntly that the company's goal was to build a research-based pharmaceutical house.[1]

Moving forward as a renewed company was by no means easy for a small company with many obligations and several stakeholders. Finding

---

[1] Yearly report, 1961.

Norway's Pharmaceutical Revolution. Knut Sogner, Oxford University Press.
© Knut Sogner (2022). DOI: 10.1093/oso/9780192869005.003.0004

the specific research paths, and committing strongly to them, was difficult and reminiscent of the 1950s. This prompted internal conflict over use of scarce resources. The decision in the spring of 1967 to concentrate research on contrast media finally released some of the tension and alleviated further internal strife. Nyegaard had made a succession of difficult choices in a few years: selling original products, strengthening research, and focusing on contrast media (which may have been the most difficult decision to make).

From a large pharmacy to an industrial plant

It was a complex, risky undertaking to transform an organization with a strong tradition of locally oriented operations. But the new leadership nevertheless commenced the 1960s with an optimistic and youthful thrust. The opportunities inherited from the 1950s were taken with as much gusto as the small company could muster. Export organizations needed to be built, new production lines constructed, documentation of new products procured: the company committed itself to a new logic.

New President Nils and new Technical Director Ulf—both Blix—knew the company well. Nils had been involved in general operations and in particular in shipping activities since the 1940s. The company thus maintained its shipping investments (a hedge against a failure in pharmaceutical innovation), although the shipping markets had been weak and unstable since 1958.[2] Ulf had a doctorate in biochemistry and had worked alongside Per Laland. The two brothers represented Nyegaard's two branches of activity: shipping and pharmaceuticals. As representatives of the majority-owning family, their positions had a certain legitimacy among the board of directors. The Blix brothers replaced retiring Fredrik Steen and Per Laland. The new "administration" also consisted of Olav Bjørnson and Bjørn Sinding-Larsen.[3] In 1965, the board of directors consisted of these four representatives from the administration, as well as Sverre Blix MD, PhD, brother of Nils and Ulf, and Per Laland's son, Søren Gustav Laland. Sinding-Larsen retired in 1970, but otherwise this constellation remained unchanged until 1979.

[2] Yearly reports, 1958–1959: 61–70.
[3] Board meeting, November 12, 1962.

The firm put Thrombotest on the Norwegian market in May 1959 and launched it later in the year in Sweden, Denmark, and Finland.[4] The company gathered information on credit ratings of pharmaceutical distributors throughout Europe and the United States in order to choose the best partners. Comprehensive testing was envisaged "in recognized laboratories and hospitals" in the countries that Nyegaard had targeted. Inventor Paul Owren often contacted the most important research and medical centers himself. This enabled documentation to be compiled on Thrombotest's results, an important step toward the presentation of the product as a fully developed international standard for coagulation testing. Nyegaard then marketed the product through its own distributors.[5]

An extensive network was established. In Scandinavia, Nyegaard used its former distributor, Erco in Sweden and Ercopharm in Denmark. In Finland, Medica was chosen as the company's agent. The years 1960–1962 were spent in establishing a far-reaching European sales network. Delforge in Belgium, Pharmachemie in the Netherlands, and Delagrange in France all became important partners. Nyegaard also contracted with established distributors in the large Japanese and US markets (Eisai (1961) and B-D Laboratories (1962), respectively).[6]

As shown in Table 4.1, company export figures tripled from 1959 to 1960; from 1959 to 1961, they increased fivefold. Between 1960 and 1963, Thrombotest alone represented 60–70 percent of all Nyegaard's exports. In 1959, the company's two export markets were Sweden and Denmark. In 1960 and 1961, it increased the number of foreign markets significantly. Thrombotest was not a product with high sales in one single country, but it sold in many different markets, as is apparent in box 4.1. To increase sales volume, a major price decrease was announced in 1961: "We have now reached the stage at which, after the initial introduction, it could be expedient to offer price reductions as an extra incentive to change over to the technical equipment that is necessary for using Thrombotest." The company now had its eyes on the world market.[7]

---

[4] NTA, "Trombotest eksploatering – Europa" by Olav Bjørnson, May 20, 1960.
[5] NTA, "Trombotest-exploiteringsplan for 1960" by Olav Bjørnson, November 27, 1959; "Situasjonsrapport" by Bjørnson, July 1, 1959; "Trombotest eksploatering – Europa" by Bjørnson, May 20, 1960; board meeting, June 19, 1961.
[6] Board meetings December 14, 1960, April 12 and December 12, 1961, and June 6 and November 12, 1962.
[7] Board meeting, June 19, 1961.

Table 4.1 Sales of licensed products and exports in 1,000 kroner, 1955–1963; fixed prices: 1961 = 100 (SSB wholesale price index)

Year	Licensed products	Exports
1955	112	308
1956	827	372
1957	1,106	417
1958	1,140	350
1959	2,238	292
1960	2,187	878
1961	2,575	1,576
1962	3,160	2,505
1963	3,313	2,383

Source: NAA, 1001: Salgs- og reklamestatistikker, 1945–1964.

Box 4.1 Nyegaard & Co.'s export markets (Thrombotest), 1959–1961

1959	1960	1961
Sweden	Sweden	Sweden
Denmark	Denmark	Denmark
	Canada	Canada
	Great Britain	Great Britain
		Belgium
		France
		Italy
		Japan
		Holland
		Spain
		Portugal
		West-Germany
		Switzerland
		Austria

Source: Nycomed.

"This has given us valuable experience for the future," the board stated about the extensive marketing and information campaign behind the launch of Thrombotest.[8] And now Nyegaard had another trump card at hand: Isopaque, "an X-ray contrast medium which in higher concentrations proves to be better than the present ones."[9] Launching Isopaque on the export market required substantial financial investments which consumed a large portion of the 1962 profit; the Board justified the expenses with the comment that "one considers this year a year of transition before profits from the intense research on X-ray contrast media begin to materialize."[10]

Emphasis on exports was part of a comprehensive concentration on original products. At first, this allowed for the continued sale of licensed products on the domestic market. But in 1961, the Board made a landmark policy decision to stop copying products.[11] The licensed products and those developed by the company were original. The company sold its own original products on the export market and represented other products from foreign firms on the Norwegian market. Since the company aimed at selling its own products abroad, it was important to avoid competing on its domestic market with products copied from foreign companies.

Since the signing of the contract with the Schering Corporation in 1955, licensed products had become steadily more important to Nyegaard. The agreement with Schering coincided with increased importance of licensed products from Glaxo. Nyegaard had sold Glaxo-licensed products since the 1940s, and sales began to soar in the late 1950s. Dekadin throat lozenges, which Nyegaard produced under license from a Glaxo subsidiary, Allen & Hanbury's, sold well.[12] The licensed products' share of Nyegaard's turnover rose from 1 percent in 1955 to 17.5 percent in 1962–1963. In 1963, about 30 percent of the company's sales were generated either by licensed or exported products developed by Nyegaard. The licensed products brought in high earnings.[13] Increased sales of original products helped profitability for pharmaceutical activities in 1959 to return to the pre-1945 level (see Table 4.2). Financial results weakened in the years following 1959, mainly as a result of export costs and of investments in plant and equipment.

Isopaque, Thrombotest, and products licensed from Schering Corporation made it necessary to enlarge the facilities, and the firm built new premises for tablet production and product-control laboratories beside the

[8] Annual report, 1962.
[9] Minutes of board meeting, June 19, 1961.
[10] Board meeting, December 12, 1961.
[11] Interview with Hugo Holtermann, December 13, 1991.
[12] NAA, 1001: Salgs-og reklamestatistikker 1945–1964.
[13] Personal communication, Thor Andersen, May 21, 1992.

Table 4.2 Net operating profit pharmaceuticals (NOP) and income before taxes (IBT) in percent of operating revenue; solidity (SOL) in percent, 1959–1966

	1959	1960	1961	1962	1963	1964	1965	1966
NOP	11	10	5	12	9	4	5	10
IBT	20	15	9	13	9	8	8	12
SOL	19	23	21	19	27	19	15	20

Source: NADM, ØK.20: årsregnskap, 1956–1972.

old plant at Sandaker in Oslo. Growth in size and new products (between four and seven annually) prompted regular improvements in equipment, more precise standardization, and better control procedures. Most of them required quality production systems, testing, analysis, and biological trials. As its equipment steadily improved, Nyegaard got closer to the standards of major international companies, but the company was for a very long time reusing equipment for its small-batch production. Open containers and gaseous fumes in the production premises were not uncommon, and the safety measures, which improved during the 1950s, remained unsatisfactory for a long time.[14] Since Isopaque had the potential to become a major product, enameled reaction vessels of the highest quality were purchased for the first time; the vessels that the company had been using had created many problems by contaminating production since their surfaces were not chemically stable. The Thrombotest production process also required new freeze-drying equipment.[15]

Isopaque represented a turning point. It was a source of inspiration, an original product developed from in-house research, and a confirmation of Nyegaard & Co.'s success as a modern pharmaceutical company. For the first time, it became necessary to plan comprehensive, large-scale synthesizing procedures.[16] The formation of an Isopaque Council symbolized the arrival of a new era. Representatives from the groups involved in the product were brought together with representatives from chemical research, product development, production, pharmaceutical research, and clinical testing. They met to discuss all future plans. As a direct result of Isopaque,

---

[14] Interview with Knut Wille, December 16, 1991; Fridtjov Rakli in a letter to the author, July 1992.
[15] Interview with Knut Wille, December 16, 1991; NFR, 4: Knut Paul Brekke about his years with Nyco (1944–1975), Oslo, March 1984.
[16] NFR, 17, A, 1. skuff. Isopaque-utvalg: minutes from 1. meeting at the Isopaque group, December 21, 1962 by Knut Tjønneland, February 15, 1963); also interview with Hugo Holtermann, August 5 and 10, and December 13, 1991.

the business opened a pharmaceutical research department (1961) with special responsibility for Isopaque formulations.[17]

The company then gained an opportunity to internationalize yet another product, a reagent just like Thrombotest. Up to the 1960s, the number of hospital tests increased manifold. But many different tests existed for the same analyses, and their results could not be scientifically corroborated (Whitby, 1963). In 1960, however, 40-year-old Professor Lorentz Eldjarn established the basis for a standardized test serum for analysis control in hospital laboratories. His goal was to develop a standard reference point for clinical-chemical analyses so that results from different tests taken in different laboratories could be compared (Eldjarn, 1993).[18] The product became known as Seronorm, which could be marketed through Thrombotest's previously established sales network. Prospects for export were good, and these products required relatively few company resources.

During the 1960s, Nyegaard also began to develop medical devices. The largest and most comprehensive project involved a blood flow gauge from the Central Institute for Industrial Research (SI).[19] Soon afterward, the company acquired the rights to an "artificial kidney"—a dialysis machine—through Professor Lars Grimsrud at the Norwegian Institute of Technology (NTH).[20] On the basis of these two products, Nyegaard set up a separate company—Nycotron.[21]

By this time, the new leadership had taken an assertive grasp on a new strategy. It focused on developing new and original products in-house and through the Norwegian medical ecosystem. No longer copying other companies' innovative products, Nyegaard was indeed committed to increasing exports and licensed products in the home market.

The inclusive state

The change in government policies at this time had both positive and negative effects on the firm's transition. The state policy of the 1960s was certainly a mixed bag. In the early 1960s, a new wave of criticism hit

---

[17] Yearly report, 1961; NFR, 4: Fridtjov Rakli about his years with Nyco, 34pp., undated; Odd Fr. Ekfelt, interviewed September 6, 1985 by Rakli.
[18] NFR, 20, 13, Standardserum: Laland to Eldjarn, February 25, 1960 and PM by Olav Bjørnson, January 24, 1961; note by Odd Ekfelt, May 27, 1963.
[19] NFR, 15, Sero-SI: PM by Arne Wøien, October 21, 1963.
[20] NNY, Grimsrud. Kontr: "Dr. Grimsrud" by Arne Wøien, May 24, 1967.
[21] Board meeting, December 19, 1966; "Muntlig redegjørelse på ordinær generalforsamling den 29/3.1967 . . .," appendix to minutes of board meeting.

the pharmaceutical industry after the serious side effects of the sedative Thalidomide became public knowledge. The entire industry came under fire: "Of course we cannot trust the pharmaceutical industry. Remember, it is a commercial enterprise!" Karl Evang said in a televised debate in August 1963 (Næss, 1963). Newspapers printed numerous articles about the changing pharmacy and pharmaceutical legislation. Headlines such as: "Silent Nationalization," "A New Step on the Path to Monopoly?," "Step-by-Step Nationalization of Pharmacies" alarmed the industry.[22] The articles examined whether the Norwegian Medicinal Depot should be given an additional domain, that of running pharmacies. Parliament passed the proposal in the spring of 1963 by a vote of 19 to 18 in the Upper House.[23]

These clouds cast a shadow over the future of the industry. Nyegaard responded with determination. It refused to allow these threats to influence its research and export priorities:

> The board of directors is concerned about possible political decisions in Norway, but cannot find itself convinced that the government intends to place a lid on the work that is underway in an industry that is concentrating on research and which has proven its ability to introduce important products on the world market.[24]

Fortunately for the firm, the Directorate of Health changed its policies gradually as a reflection of Karl Evang's professional orientation. He built up a staff including both medical and pharmaceutical professionals and included these pharmacists' opinions in his considerations (Nordby, 1989). The professionals were flexible about developments in the health services. Magne Moe, who was appointed to lead the new monopoly Norwegian Medicinal Depot (NMD), and Elias Reite, new Laboratory Manager for the Proprietary Medicines Board, were both pharmacists who had been employed by the industry. Moe had been the sales director of one of the privately owned wholesale companies that the Medicinal Depot replaced. Elias Reite's background included a spell at Nyegaard. These two were not heavy-handed executors of state industrial policies.

---

[22] *Norges Handels- og Sjøfartstidende*, June 18, 1963; *Nationen*, May 18, 1963; and *Agderposten*, June 13, 1963, respectively.

[23] Lagtinget 1963, June 19, pp. 140–142.

[24] Yearly report, 1963, pp. 6 and 7.

Magne Moe received little in the way of instructions on assuming his position in the summer of 1954.[25] The sole guideline was that NMD was to function as a wholesale organ. In addition to its import-and-export monopoly, it was authorized to manufacture products. There were few formal limitations on Moe, NMD's board of directors, the Directorate of Health, or the Ministry of Health and Social Affairs. They could have acted more aggressively toward the pharmaceutical industry. While at Nyegaard & Co., Elias Reite had been extremely critical of the Proprietary Medicine Board's methods of determining price levels. He was one of the state pricing policy's strongest opponents: the system, he realized, was based on outdated rates and on the principle that unprofitable products should be financed by profitable ones.[26] In connection with legislative work in 1958, Reite and the former Laboratory Manager Åsmund Thorvik, prepared the ground for the Proprietary Medicines Board's increased flexibility of price-fixing procedures.[27] Until the early 1970s, industry was satisfied with the government's treatment of its price recommendations.[28]

Events did not turn out the way the Social Committee had suggested. The legislation sought to "place all pharmaceutical supply under public authority." But from 1962 to 1964 the government backed away from nationalization. But only just, as the majority of the Pharmacy Act Committee, the Ministry of Health and Social Affairs, and powerful forces in the Labour Party in the Storting (led by Executive Chairman Sverre Løberg), still believed *in principle* that pharmacies should be "placed under public authority." But the principle was not put into practice (Odelsting-Bill-No. 59, 1961–1962; Odelsting-Bill-No. 28, 1963–1964; Odelstinget, 1963–1964).[29]

The threat of nationalization was thus reduced dramatically after 1960, and the Recommendation from the Pharmacy Act Committee, with the Storting's revisions, was completed in 1964. This reversed the trend of the years from 1945 to 1954 toward increased governmental control of pharmaceutical supply even though the new relationship between industry and the Directorate of Health was not entirely cozy.

[25] Builds on interview with Magne Moe, March 26, 1992.
[26] NFR, 11, A-møter: meeting, March 1, 1948.
[27] HD, H7, N124, 1981: Nomi to the Health Directorate, August 27, 1981.
[28] HD, H7, N124, 1981: Nomi to the Health Directorate, August 27, 1981.
[29] Sverre Løberg's briefing in the Odelsting: 1963 Em. June 14, pp. 668–670. In an interview on April 2, 1992, Rakel Seweriin said that the pharmacies' royal privileges made the matter more complicated than the Labour Party had imagined.

Karl Evang had both praised and criticized the pharmaceutical industry at the time of the Thalidomide tragedy. While openly critical of industry on television, he also described its substantial breakthroughs (Næss, 1963). After the war, Evang had chosen to disregard industry when he developed a policy for pharmaceutical supply. Paradoxically, 15 years later, at a time when the newspapers were filled with objections to the industry, Evang's relationship with it actually improved somewhat. The many and important product breakthroughs had made industry a force to reckon with. Indeed, the research-based company was increasingly becoming an ideal in Norwegian industrial policy.

In 1962, Nyegaard responded to the beginnings of this new industrial policy. Bjørn Sinding-Larsen met with Industry Minister Kjell Holler and learned that the Ministry wanted Nyegaard to set up some of its facilities in rural Norway. In return, the government offered favorable loans and financial support. Sinding-Larsen replied that this was problematic. The company depended on a level of professional expertise not found in areas remote from the universities.[30] In 1962, the company still had many different products with short production series, each requiring the services of skilled employees. This made it difficult to move production plants without also transferring employees.

The request from the Ministry of Industry in 1962 followed the setting up in the previous year of the Regional Development Fund. The next few years saw the establishment of other funds such as the Reorganization Fund in 1963 and the Development Fund in 1965. Research Manager Holtermann understood that these developments represented an entirely new industrial policy:

> If the Labour Party's policy for the different areas corresponds with its chosen policy in terms of technological development, this implies that the left flank has lost in a struggle within the party, and that the Labour Party has decided to become a modern, socially liberal party in the future. Presumably, the near future will reveal whether this is the case.[31]

Conservative Holtermann was certainly not a member of the Labour Party, but he was familiar with its deliberations. He had participated in various

---

[30] NFR, 1, 69: PM by Bjørn Sinding-Larsen, February 23, 1962.
[31] NFR, 17, A, 3. skuff. Forskning.gen. II: "Dr. Holtermanns kommentarer og referat fra Konferanse om vitenskap og forskning 3. februar 1965, arrangert av DNA."

meetings held by the government and the Labour Party concerning industrial and technological policy. He was also a close friend of Finn Lied,
possibly the most important member of the Labour Party in regard to
research policies.[32] Holtermann offered an optimistic view of the new
technological policy:

> [It] seems to show clearly that the Labour Party *in this area* wants to promote a
> flexible, rational policy, aiming to modernize our country technologically, and
> with this purpose, is interested in achieving a better relationship with industry,
> and removing this area from the influence of politics.[33]

The new policy, which allowed small companies like Nyegaard to join
the established industrial elite, was a result of the fragmentation of government policy. The changes in policy had been poorly coordinated and
research policy was not integrated with industrial policy (Sejersted, 1993:
189–96). Norwegian Labour party governments since 1945 had also prioritized industrial developments in a narrow range of heavy industries—and
in shipping. The 1960s represented a broader approach that especially targeted research-based companies. The new policy owed much to European
considerations. It was initiated as a consequence of Norway's entrance into
the free-trade agreement of the European Free Trade Association (EFTA).
The French model of indicative planning seems to have been the main
inspiration. This is a type of joint planning in which representatives of
industry are obliged to support governmental policy. If industry acted in
compliance with state objectives, it could count on state assistance. This
could take the form of financial aid for industrial research, implemented in
the form of a dialogue, with industry responding to signals from the government (Sogner, 1994: ch. 4). In Norway, this system was built up through
the various funds mentioned above.

The new system brought massive governmental involvement in the development of a new Norwegian electronics industry.[34] It is doubtful that
any other Norwegian company followed events as closely as Nyegaard. The
company was excited about the new opportunities for partial financing of
its larger projects.[35] The possibility for forging new and productive interaction with the government was almost too good to be true. Nyegaard could

[32] Ibid.
[33] Ibid.
[34] Ibid.
[35] Yearly report, 1964.

do with some favorable conditions given that everything out in the export markets was not as rosy as had been projected.

"The world best contrast media" and problems with international marketing

Small firms in small nations routinely have problems breaking into international markets and Nyegaard was not an exception. After their initial and promising launches, Thrombotest and Isopaque did not sell particularly well. This eventually led to a deep rethinking about Isopaque, a product that was Nyegaard's own. This process, which was more about development than research, taught the company a great deal. Isopaque's sales in the beginning of the 1960s were disappointing and the company could see that the product was not as good as it had initially thought. Isopaque was sold in Scandinavia, with some small sales to licensees elsewhere. Turnover in 1966 was disappointing; slightly less than NOK 1.9 million, somewhat lower than that for Nyco Fruktsalt.

Thrombotest was slightly ahead, with sales of just over NOK 3 million in 1966 (Table 4.3). Yet, its sales on the international market were about the same as Globoid's domestic sales. Thrombotest sales nevertheless represented 11 percent of turnover in 1966, and the product was rather successful in Europe. A disadvantage was that a number of rival competitors had developed products such as the Quick test in the United States and the Poller tests in Great Britain. The Quick test was widely sold internationally. The competitors' products were sold at lower prices than Thrombotest. Nyegaard needed to convince the medical profession to switch over to a more expensive, standardized reagent. This was possible in countries that

Table 4.3 Operating revenues of product areas, 1959 and 1966 in million kroner; fixed prices: 1985 = 100 (SSB consumer price index)

	1959	1966
Pharmaceuticals	68	102
Reagents	1	15
Contrast agents	0	8
Total income	69	125

Source: Nycomed.

had a high standard of health services and no previously established tests, such as Norway, the rest of Scandinavia, and the Netherlands. In Great Britain and the United States, the task was not so easy.[36]

There was little Nyegaard & Co. could do with Thrombotest, but in Isopaque it had its own patented product that could be further developed. Isopaque was a tri-iodinated X-ray contrast agent (Grainger, 1982; de Haën, 2019). In other words, three atoms of iodine were bound to the benzene ring. X-ray contrast agents contain iodine because iodine stops the penetration of the X-ray beam, forming an image on X-ray film. In the 1960s, three tri-iodinated compounds dominated the market. These were metrizoate (trade name Isopaque), iothalamate (trade name Conray) from the US company Mallinckrodt, and diatrizoate (trade names Urografin, Renografin, and Hypaque) from Schering AG in Germany, Squibb in the United States, and Sterling Drug, respectively.

The most important contrast media companies were Schering AG, Mallinckrodt, and Sterling Drug. Nyegaard was a newcomer to the field, while Squibb was primarily occupied with marketing activities. Although Schering AG and Sterling Drug both sold diatrizoate, they were not cooperating with each other. Both companies had discovered diatrizoate separately at about the same time, in the first half of the 1950s. They became entangled in difficult law suits but eventually developed a complex market division. In the United States, Squibb sold Renografin on a license from Schering AG (de Haën, 2019; Amdam and Sogner, 1994).

Only small variations in the substances distinguished one contrast agent from the other. There was accordingly good reason for Nyegaard to think that metrizoate had some advantages over diatrizoate. Isopaque was water-soluble in heavier concentrations than the diatrizoate-based products, and this was advantageous in examinations requiring higher concentrations of iodine. Isopaque was also less viscous and therefore easier to inject.[37]

During these years, it was discovered that Hypaque (Sterling Drug) was different from Urografin (Schering AG) and Renografin (Squibb). All the products contained the same iodinated compound, diatrizoate, but as X-ray contrast agents were iodinated acids *which were dissolved* as salts, the choice of salt turned out to be important. Meglumine salt caused less pain to patients, and it was therefore preferred in examinations where this salt

---

[36] Interviews with Olav Bjørnson, February 11 and 25, 1991 and with Thor Andersen and Svein Nilsen, January 31, 1992; NFR, 20,1, reiserapp: Olav Bjørnson's travel to Sweden, January 7–8 and 12–13, 1959 and travel to Finland, January 9–10, 1959.

[37] NFR, 17, 1, A, Rkm. Isop.salter I: Holtermann to Watson (Frank B. Dehn & Co.), February 28, 1963.

media could be used.[38] Urografin and Renografin were based on meg-lumine salt, while Hypaque—and Isopaque—were, to their disadvantage, based on sodium salt. As a result, Hypaque lost market shares in the United States to Renografin.[39]

Nyegaard's researchers responded by trying to use meglumine in place of sodium salt.[40] This was successful but Isopaque had lost its advantage over these products in terms of viscosity. The next step for Nyegaard was to re-examine the entire salt issue and experiment with *salt admixtures*. Experiments with sodium, calcium, and potassium in physiological proportions were not successful, but in 1963 researchers obtained interesting results by experimenting with small doses of calcium and magnesium added to sodium-based Isopaque. Now there was a lower degree of toxicity than pure sodium salt. The company began the process of patenting these discoveries in February 1963, bringing the development of ionic contrast agents a step forward.[41] The next step was to develop the world's best contrast agent based on meglumine salt, and by adding small amounts of calcium to the meglumine salt-based Isopaque toxicity was reduced. The first version of a new Isopaque was put on the market in 1965.[42]

Experimenting with salts brought the small group of researchers at Nyegaard & Co. a step ahead of all other research teams in the world. Neither Mallinckrodt nor Schering AG had worked with salts in this way and Sterling Drug had just started. After Nyegaard's salt studies were concluded, it seemed that the X-ray contrast agents could be developed no further. Tri-iodinated contrast agents based on special salt admixtures resulted in very clear X-ray images, with relatively little discomfort to the patient. Maybe Nyegaard & Co. had the world's best contrast agent—by a fraction. This gave grounds for new export optimism. But did "the world's best contrast agent by a fraction" just represent research optimism?

---

[38] NFR, 17, 1A, Rkm. Isopaque. Klinisk II: Holtermann to Lyngsted Jepsen, February 20, 1962 and Holtermann to Ulf Blix, June 18, 1962; NFR, 17, 1A. Rkm. Isopaque. salter I: Holtermann to Watson (Frank B. Dehn & Co.), February 28, 1963.

[39] NOS: "Diagnostic Imaging in the 1980's—a Strategic Planning Document for SDI" by R. F. Albano and D. Shaw, Internal Sterling Drug report, *c*.1981.

[40] NFR, 17, 1A, Rkm. Isopaque. Klinisk II: Holtermann to Lyngsted Jensen, Ferbruary 20, 1962 and "Rapport av 12.6.62" by Per Amundsen.

[41] Ibid. NFR, 17, 1A, Rkm. Isopaque.salter I: Holtermann to Watson (Frank B. Dehn & Co.), February 28, 1963; NFR, 21, div.rkm: Holtermann to Bjørnson, October 2, 1963; interview with Holtermann, July 2, 1992; NFR, 17, 2A, SWII: Holtermann to Hoppe (SWRI), May 7, 1965.

[42] NFR, 17, 1A, Rkm. Isopaque. Klinisk II: Holtermann to Lyngsted Jensen, Ferbruary 20, 1962 and "Rapport av 12.6.62" by Per Amundsen; NFR, 17, 1A, Rkm. Isopaque.salter I: Holtermann to Watson (Frank B. Dehn & Co.), February 28, 1963; NFR, 21, div.rkm: Holtermann to Bjørnson, October 2, 1963; interview with Holtermann, July 2, 1992; NFR, 17, 2A, SWII: Holtermann to Hoppe (SWRI), May 7, 1965.

Divergent forces in a narrow space

During the first half of the 1960s, while the researchers were circling around Isopaque, the company studied a number of new areas: Especially important was the fact that the old liver project of the 1930s and 1950s was on its way back into the company and demanding space and resources. In order to coordinate research activities, Ulf Blix established a separate research committee in early 1964. He led this committee himself, and its other members were either in the company or closely associated with it: Head of Research, Hugo Holtermann and Director Olav Bjørnson from Nyegaard & Co. with Professor Søren G. Laland from the University of Oslo, and Sverre Blix from the National Hospital in Oslo.[43]

Ulf Blix and Per Laland, who held overall responsibility for research in different periods, were very different individuals. Laland was an enthusiastic and optimistic extrovert who eagerly participated in research activities himself. He was not short on self-confidence and his assumption was that he had the right to decide. Ulf Blix was a quiet, reflective, and facilitating kind of man who did not himself take part in research laboratory activities.[44] The new system introduced under Blix meant that the company gained a better overview of its own research activities. This was important because from 1963 until 1969, research spending amounted to 9–10 percent of turnover. Translated into people, that was not a lot for dealing with complex research issues: In the year 1966, 35 man-years were spent on research and development activities. Seven included engineers, four were university scientists, and seven were pharmacists. The services of external sources were also used for development work or applied research. The state-sponsored Central Institute for Industrial Research (SI) performed most of these assignments concentrated on testing compounds.[45]

Until 1965, the main research activities were divided into two categories: X-ray contrast agents and liver research, Per Laland's long-time passion. He continued his research during his retirement years, and in collaboration with Jens Dedichen and Professor Søren G. Laland, he returned to work on the discontinued liver project (L-Factor) that in 1962—Per Laland's first year as a pensioner—again became a part of Nyegaard's agenda. At that time, the liver research group once more thought it had

---

[43] NUB, 913, fk: meeting, January 28, 1964.
[44] A number of conversations with the person in question and others.
[45] NAA, 1015: "Omsetning og f-kostn. 1966–1980" by A. Arntzen, August 31, 1981; Heggim to Holtermann, August 13, 1966; "Personalstruktur i Nyco's F & U i 1966" by Holtermann, May 11, 1967.

discovered a previously unknown substance. "We had a substance which increased resistance and fought infections. We could detect it because of its fluorescence—it glowed—and we identified it because it was an enzyme inhibitor" (Dedichen, 1974: 105). "The substance was named "Urgocyton," a rewriting of "Cyturgon," which means "something that works with a cell." The liver project thus acquired renewed importance. This time, Nyegaard & Co. would cooperate with Glaxo (Dedichen, 1974: 106).

The research group also believed that it isolated the "Co-factor of Urgocyton," CoU. It thought that CoU was the active factor in Urgocyton. CoU, like Urgocyton, was identified by its blue fluorescence after irradiation by ultraviolet light. If this was a previously unknown substance with beneficial effects on an organism, important commercial opportunities were at hand (Dedichen, 1974).[46] As a scientific breakthrough, it would overshadow the results of research in contrast agents and would provide the finishing touch on a project that had been started years before the Second World War. Nyegaard & Co. invested heavily in CoU. In the fall of 1965, ten people worked on the project, as well as Søren Laland at the Biochemical Department of the University of Oslo.[47] The chemical structure of CoU was quickly identified and it could be produced synthetically.

The liver project challenged contrast media for scarce research resources. The project, which had the full attention of father and son Laland, had the attraction of building on Søren Laland's position at the University of Oslo. But the contrast media and the CoU projects both needed more resources to be successful, and the years between 1964 and spring 1967 were characterized by tensions and difficult decisions of prioritization. Management scaled down the contrast agents project, and by the end of 1966, Holtermann maintained that this had happened too suddenly; to rebuild would be like starting a new project. Only one person, Johan Haavaldsen, was still working on contrast agents.[48] Two of the people most active in contrast agents research, Kjell Undheim and Vegard Nordal, had discovered the chemical structure of CoU. Undheim, who later became a professor of chemistry, was hired in 1963 to work on X-ray contrast agents but was transferred to CoU research.[49]

---

[46] NUB, 913, fk: meeting, December 8, 1964; Søren Gustav Laland to Sogner, December 9, 1993.
[47] NFR, 17, 3A. Urgocyton: Holtermann to Ulf Blix, October 4, 1965.
[48] NUB, 913, fk: meeting, December 20, 1966; appendix to minutes from meeting, March 9, 1967: Holtermann to Blix, March 7, 1967.
[49] NFR, 17, 3A, Undh: Undheim to Holtermann, May 24, 1967/November 22, 1967.

By May 1965, there clearly was a conflict. Hugo Holtermann was in favor of continuing to focus on contrast agents. Member of the board of Nyegaard (where his father was minority shareholder), Professor Søren Laland preferred to concentrate resources on reagents and Urgocyton, maintaining that there were few opportunities for new advances in contrast agents. They were the main antagonists. Director Olav Bjørnson chose contrast agents and reagents.[50] He wanted sales and research to be seen in relation to one another. Nyegaard possessed broad competence in the fields of reagents as well as contrast agents. Isopaque had many unsolved problems; improving pharmaceutical formulations and ensuring uniform production quality would make the product better and therefore easier to sell. Focusing on Isopaque could increase profits and thereby cover the expense of earlier research activities.[51] Ulf Blix, possibly along with his brother Sverre, looked for a compromise, but in the years up to 1967 they increasingly prioritized the CoU project.

The disagreement between Laland and Holtermann reflected the divergent paths they had chosen in the 1940s. Søren Laland's doctorate was in biochemistry; Holtermann's was in organic chemistry. Heavy concentration on X-ray contrast agents in the years before 1965 had weakened the company's deep biochemical traditions. Laland's stance can therefore be seen as an attempt to revive the importance of biochemistry. Per Laland, his father, had worked on isolation techniques, while Søren was concerned with isolation, fermentation, and enzymes.[52] For a small company like Nyegaard, reagents were attractive because they were used in laboratories rather than in the human body; it was therefore easier to meet official approval requirements. The marketing channels already established could easily absorb new lines.[53] They had already found the person to assume the task of expanding reagent research: Bjørn Skålhegg, a former student of Laland, who had just left the Thrombosis Department at the National Hospital in May 1965. Skålhegg started working on reagents for Nyegaard & Co., trying to devise an enzyme method for determining steroid content in urine.[54]

Conflict between biochemistry and organic chemistry does not, of course, fully explain the situation. After all, Søren Laland's postgraduate

[50] NUB, 913, fk: meeting, May 25, 1965.
[51] NUB, 913, fk: meeting, May 25 and December 14, 1965.
[52] Interview with Søren Gustav Laland, August 11, 1992.
[53] NUB, 913, fk: meeting, May 25, 1965.
[54] NUB, 913, fk: meeting, May 25, 1965, June 7, and September 7, 1966.

studies were in the field of organic chemistry, and Holtermann's work with ACTH in the 1950s was primarily concerned with biochemistry. Yet, contrast media was the main focus at Nyegaard & Co. between 1957 and 1964 and for the first time the company worked on an area associated with organic chemistry. This explains Holtermann's point of view. He wanted to continue in the area that had already been established. Søren Laland's starting point was similar. He wanted to build on activities established before 1957, meaning biochemistry and liver research and the quest for a hitherto unknown substance with a potential therapeutic effect. By 1965, this project was progressing well and had almost completely taken over research activities.

There was a sense—formulated by Søren Laland and shared by many at the time—that maybe contrast media had to be seen as a mature field without much hope of further improvements. As would become even more apparent some years down the road, this was also a viewpoint at the time shared with the two major contrast media companies, German Schering AG and US Sterling Drug.[55] Holtermann was of another opinion, for reasons that had to do with his accomplishments and his perception of future possibilities based on his steadily increased insight into the field.

The proof of the pudding . . .

The years of internal tension were tough on the people involved, and in September 1966, Ulf Blix declared he had had enough. The time had come to "discuss the principle for prioritizing research resources."[56] Indecision from Blix may increasingly have been seen as part of the problem. In March 1967, Holtermann declared that it was "far easier to reduce a project to ineffectivity than to make the decision to discontinue it completely."[57]

Holtermann had been on the losing side for several years. He wanted to build on the experience gained from working with contrast agents. He had already expressed this opinion in the first research committee meeting early in 1964. The field of contrast agents was in a phase of rapid development, according to him, and if Nyegaard & Co. wanted to participate, it could not entertain the thought of reducing its tempo. Holtermann believed that

[55] Interview with Wolfgang Degen (Schering AG), May 11, 1993 and William Heike Jr (Sterling Drug), June 1 and 2, 1993.
[56] NUB, 913, fk: meeting, September 7, 1966.
[57] NUB, 913, fk: meeting, March 9, 1967.

there was a great deal to be gained and envisioned the company covering 10–20 percent of a world market of NOK 100 million.[58] In 1963, Nyegaard's total turnover had been slightly less than NOK 20 million, and for the time being, contrast agents were responsible for only NOK 600,000 of this figure.

Holtermann wanted to build on what had been learned while working with Isopaque, and his ideas in this area comprised an entire research program.[59] He advocated concentrating research into as few areas as possible, in order to get the best value for each krone of investment. This, he thought, was the only route to successful competition with large foreign corporations. In 1964, he could refer to more than five years of successful work with Isopaque when he stated that Nyegaard & Co. could be competitive. To the question of whether "a small research department [had] potential advantages that could compensate for the obvious handicap of being small,"[60] he concluded:

> It is not difficult to see what is needed, but it will require a great deal of effort in practice, as it demands highly organized and constant teamwork within nearly every sector of the company as well as in diverse external sectors. The potential advantage of a *small* research department lies in its flexibility and prospects for much broader, more thorough and faster communication internally and among the company's diverse sectors [. . .] all sectors being totally concentrated.[61]

Experience with Isopaque had already shown this to be the case. The research milieu that developed in connection with Isopaque was one factor. Another was the atmosphere created by the entire company working toward a common goal and by the fact that the company was able to establish an external network.[62] He argued that the company's research effort had to reach a certain threshold in order to succeed.[63] As he stated in 1966:

> If research resources are to be further divided into many areas, one must be aware that if an activity or focus in one area falls beneath a certain "lower limit", the investment will be so negligible that it will have to thought of as futile when

[58] NUB, 913, fk: meeting, January 28, 1964.

[59] NFR, 17, 3A. Forskning.generelt II: "Sammendrag av . . . Holtermanns orientering" by R. F. Engh, May 11, 1964.

[60] NFR, 17, 2B. Foredrag HH, November 27, 1967: note by Holtermann, April–May 1964 in connection with a talk to heads of research at the Norwegian Defence Research Establishment.

[61] Ibid.

[62] Interview with Holtermann, August 5 and 10 and December 13, 1991.

[63] NFR, 17, 3A. Forskning.generelt II: "Sammendrag av . . . Holtermanns" by R. F. Engh, May 11, 1964.

compared to the benefit one could expect by allowing research resources to be placed in their entirety into *one* sector, where activity of a certain magnitude could then be maintained.

Nyegaard & Co. could find itself relegated to a "mediocre position in three or four areas."[64]

His ideas had clearly been influenced by the new role attached to science that came with the Second World War. Tremendous investments were made in research during the war, and these resulted in important, tangible breakthroughs that provided the basis for a new attitude about the organization of research. A recipe for success through huge, collective research efforts had been discovered (Børresen, 1994). Merck in the United States was one of the first pharmaceutical companies to apply a big science-like policy, and Glaxo followed suit in the beginning of the 1960s. This was contested terrain, though, and, as mentioned before, Glaxo was a reluctant mover. When nuclear research was continued after the scientific breakthroughs during the war, a dispute opened up about the need for building the large European Council for Nuclear Research (CERN) with the world's largest particle accelerator. Those who had been performing research before the war thought they could come a long way by theoreticizing, while those who had participated in the extensive wartime research programs promoted the big science construction (Pestre and Krige, 1992).

Holtermann, a theoretician, had not participated in wartime research, and after the war he had studied with a prominent pre-war researcher. He was no believer in big science.[65] He described himself as a "bench chemist," a theoretician, one who aimed to think his way forward rather than engaging in large experiments. His theoretical orientation had been emphasized when his work was successfully being evaluated for a professorship. He was praised for his doctoral work at Oxford, when he had contributed to the completion of Sir Robert Robinson's extensive project, and for his interpretations of the specialized chemistry involved in Isopaque. As Professor Erdtman from Sweden noted: "His work in the industry has not only led to invaluable technical results, but also to unexpected and meaningful discoveries of general theoretical value."[66] He gave priority to "cautious and realistic evaluations" and promoted "project consciousness." In his words, "the most important single factor in choosing tasks is to have the willpower

[64] NUB, 913, fk: meeting, September 7, 1966.
[65] Interview with Hugo Holtermann, July 2, 1992.
[66] Opinion of Professor H. Erdtman (copy with the author).

to decide *not* to do something."[67] Holtermann, even though he came to find himself on opposing sides to Per Laland in resource allocation matters, had the utmost respect for Laland's organization building in the firm. He saw Laland as a pioneer in Norway, something which got confirmed in the mid-1960s when he had the chance to converse with counterparts in Norway's two largest chemical enterprises, Norsk Hydro and Borregaard.[68]

The arguments put forward by Holtermann in the internal struggle for access to resources underlined his seriousness and possibly strengthened the high esteem he already held as a researcher. That he also was the one who, in late 1965, discovered that the substance in the liver project, CoU, was not a biological substance but an "artifact," formed during the attempt to isolate the active principle in Urgocyton, probably increased the tension between him and Søren Laland.[69] Despite this shocking discovery, the project did not end. Compounds related to CoU were synthesized and tested. They were tried as cancer and cold remedies, as a hair lotion, and as an ointment for herpes sores. Some tests were carried out at Nyegaard but most were performed by Glaxo in England (Dedichen, 1974).[70] The aim was to find a disease that the substance could cure.

The fact that one project was selected in place of another in March 1967 does not seem to have resulted from a thorough debate. It rather reflected events that had taken place in the various project areas. While the CoU screenings following the artifact discovery brought few valid results (Dedichen, 1974),[71] developments with Isopaque were encouraging, placing Nyegaard's earlier research in a continually favorable light. By 1966, it was clear that Scandinavian radiologists considered the improved Isopaque a fully developed product, ranked among the best in the world. Contrast agent sales began to rise during 1966 and 1967, particularly in Sweden. In December 1966 and the spring of 1967, the US concern Sterling Drug negotiated with Nyegaard & Co. for the rights to market Isopaque in the United States.[72]

---

[67] NFR, 17, 3A. Forskning.generelt II: "Sammendrag av . . . Holtermanns orientering" by R. F. Engh, May 11, 1964.

[68] NFR, 17, 3A. Forskning generelt II: Copy of NTNF's minutes from "hearing" 8/1964 in NTNF's extended board meeting, May 25, 1964 and Holtermann's own minutes from the same.

[69] NFR, 17, 4, A. Urgocyton: Holtermann to the CoU staff meeting, November 30, 1965; interview with Holtermann, July 2, 1992.

[70] NUB, 913, fk: meeting, January 28 and December 8, 1964 and March 1, 1966.

[71] NFR, 17, 3, A, Urgocyton: Holtermann to Ulf Blix, July 5, 1968.

[72] "Rapport over konferanser med Sterling Winthrop" by Olav Bjørnson and Ulf Blix, May 23, 1967. Borrowed from Olav Bjørnson.

Holtermann had the support of Olav Bjørnson, the senior management figure. In April 1967, when the decisions were taken, he argued strongly for linking research and marketing. In order to continue its quest for export expansion and not end in stagnation, he wanted to prioritize both contrast media and reagents for research purposes:

> I believe that the company today is at a crossroads, where one road can help us become a Scandinavian pharmaceutical company of first-rate quality, and *thereby competitive* in the areas of our concentration, and where the other will lead us into stagnation, and consequently into a *difficult competitive situation.*[73]

Company strategy, he said, should not be linked to the older range of products directed toward the Norwegian market. Isopaque and Thrombotest should be given priority.

Ulf Blix's ultimate solution was similar to Bjørnson's suggestions and contained an element of compromise within a general victory for organic chemistry. The medical imaging line was built up again, and a new Biochemical Department was established under the leadership of Bjørn Skålhegg. The Urgocyton–CoU project was drastically reduced. Research activities at the biochemical department were centered primarily around reagents, a product line in which Nyegaard & Co. already had sales. Research in the field of reagents, among other things, would strengthen the company's external cooperation with Owren and Eldjarn.[74] The firm decided to separate research into two different departments and to assign a budget for each. In one sense, Holtermann was relegated as his responsibility ceased to be about biochemistry; in reality, he had had little to say about real priorities and obviously got something of a fresh start.

Nyegaard & Co. had chosen two diagnostic fields (although contrast media are classified as pharmaceuticals). The decision combined research and market considerations and further developed an area in which the company had both expertise and products with obvious sales potential. The 1967 decisions yielded a sense of harmony. Biochemistry returned in modern apparel but with a lower research status than contrast agents, the company's main area of competence. In the years that preceded the decision, from 1964 to 1967, consensus was conspicuous by its absence. The decision to continue research in the field of contrast agents had been far

---

[73] NTA: note April 4, 1967 by Olav Bjørnson.
[74] NFR, 17, 1, B, Testreagenser: "Rapport om . . . reagenser" by Odd Kåre Strandli et al., December 19, 1967.

from inevitable. The choice for contrast agents rather than Urgocyton–CoU ended a research project which had been in progress for nearly 40 years. The Laland group chose to continue its work outside of Nyegaard.

Conclusion

Contrast media and reagents became products for very different reasons. Nyegaard stumbled into contrast media, but there was no stumbling about the concentrated effort through various stages to create a significant export product. At the beginning of 1967, it looked like that may have been accomplished. What contrast media was not was a fruit of the Norwegian medical ecosystem. Obviously, Nyegaard & Co.'s efforts within contrast media benefitted from collaborations with Norwegian doctors and hospitals but not in a way that was really crucial for the effort. In this respect, the reagents field was entirely the opposite as the two product groups Nyegaaard sold were the results of research by two Norwegian doctors.

The 1967 decision to prioritize research in a new way marked an important turning point. In innovation studies, there is a concept called "absorptive capacity" (Cohen and Levinthal, 1990). Absorptive capacity is the ability of an organization to digest and make constructive use of outside developments. The knowledge that needs to be mastered in an evolving market place is an essential part of how corporations go about their own innovative projects. Until the 1950s, Nyegaard had the absorptive capacity of a generic producer operating purely in its home market. The evolution of the scientific content of new pharmaceutical drugs following the pharmaceutical revolution had been absorbed gradually. But in order to play an active part itself, to introduce new products that were to be tested, evaluated, and criticized by external experts based on detailed and accurate knowledge provided by the company was a wholly different challenge. Thrombotest, Seronorm, Isopaque were experiments down this road, and only Isopaque was the company's own contribution. The launching of the salt experiments with Isopaque and the digesting of the feed back from this, enabled Nyegaard to move up in the hierarchy of independently operational pharmaceutical companies.

Even if the kind of big science research agenda that came with the pharmaceutical industry in general and with Merck and Glaxo in particular was inspiring, Nyegaard and Holtermann applied a different logic. It was a "small is possible" approach, one that emphasized process, collaboration, and strict identification of relevant progress paths. Holtermann argued for attention to direction and clever use of scant resources. "Small is possible" was an attitude that also was being nurtured by the achievements of the Danish and Swedish companies, and "small is possible" may also be seen as a characteristic of the new and improved relationship with the Norwegian state. Gradually, the Directorate of Health adjusted its rigid price policies and thereby made funding for increased research a possibility. Simultaneously, Norway widened the scope of its industrial policy and emphasized the need to develop small and knowledge-based companies. With these two pieces added to an increased academic emphasis on research, the Norwegian system of innovation was rapidly changing for the better.

References

Amdam, R. P. and Sogner, K. 1994. *Rik på kontraster: Nyegaard & Co—en norsk farmasøytisk industribedrift 1874–1985*. Oslo: Ad notam Gyldendal.

Børresen, A. K. 1994. "Fire modeller for organisering av forskning og undervisning." *In*: Wicken, O. (ed.) *Elektronikk-entreprenørene. Studier av norsk Elektronikk-forskning og—industri etter 1945*. Oslo: AdNotam Gyldendal, pp. 125–151.

Cohen, W. and Levinthal, D. 1990. "Absorptive Capacity: A New Perspective on Learning and Innovation." *Administrative Science Quarterly*, 35, 128.

Dedichen, J. 1974. *Lege på flere måter: på spor av et nytt stoff*. Oslo: Cappelen.

Eldjarn, L. 1993. "Kvalitetskontroll og kvalitetshøyning ved norske klinisk-kjemiske laboratorier. Historikk og erfaringer." *In*: Palmer, H. (ed.) *Utviklingen av den kliniske kjemi i Norge*. Oslo: Norsk selskap for klinisk kjemi og klinisk fysiologi, pp. 184–195.

Grainger, R. G. 1982. "Intravascular Contrast Media—the Past, the Present and the Future. Mackenzie Davidson Memorial Lecture, April 1981." *British Journal of Radiology*, 55, 1–18.

de Haën, C. D. 2019. *X-Ray Contrast Agent Technology. A Revolutionary History*. Boca Raton, FL: CRC Press.

Hyldtoft, O. and Johansen, H. C. 2005. *Teknologiske forandringer i dansk industri, 1896–1972*. Odense: Syddansk universitetsforlag.

Jones, E. 2001. *The Business of Medicine. The Extraordinary History of Glaxo, a Baby Food Producer, which Became One of the World's Most Successful Pharmaceutical Companies*. London: Profile Books.

Næss, K. 1963. "Kan man stole på den farmasøytiske industri?" *Aftenposten*, September 24 and 25.

Nordby, T. 1989. *Karl Evang: en biografi*. Oslo: Aschehoug.

Norgren, L. 1989. *Kunskapsöverföring från universitet till företag: en studie av universitetsforskningens betydelse för de svenska läkemedelsföretagens produkt-lanseringar 1945–1984*. Stockholm: Allmänna förlaget.

Odelsting-Bill-No. 28. 1963–1964. *Om lov av legemidler og gifter m.v.* Oslo: Stortinget.

Odelsting-Bill-No. 59. 1961–1962. *Om lov av drift av apotek m.v.* Oslo: Stortinget.

Odelstinget. 1963–1964. *Odelsting Report XVIII*. Oslo: Stortinget.

Pestre, D. and Krige, J. 1992. "Some Thoughts on the Early History of CERN." *In*: Galison, P. and Hevly, B. (eds) *Big Science. The Growth of Large-Scale Research*. Stanford, CA: Stanford University Press, pp. 78–99.

Sejersted, F. 1993. *Demokratisk kapitalisme*. Oslo: Universitetsforlaget.

Sogner, K. 1994. *Fra plan til marked: staten og elektronikkindustrien på 1970-tallet*. Oslo: TMV-senteret.

Whitby, L. G. 1963. "Clinical Chemistry—Time for Investment." *The Lancet*, December 14, 2(7320): 1239–1243.

5

Breakthrough, 1967–1969

The pharmaceutical revolution had national, regional, and international characteristics. Many of the academic–business collaborations that drove innovation were national. Both the science in university institutions and the leading innovative pharmaceutical companies of the twentieth century were, however, international in scope. Less attention has been paid to the regional aspects of innovation, but they were particularly important in the case of Norway and of Nyegaard & Co., which experienced a significant breakthrough in 1969.

At that time, Nyegaard's research team succeeded in synthesizing what was to become the start of a new generation of contrast media. Not much more than two years had passed since the business had prioritized research into contrast media. This innovation would be known as a non-ionic product, but few in the company fully understood this event in those terms. The new molecules that the firm synthesized had surprising and benign chemical characteristics. Had chemists in the dominant contrast media businesses in the United States and Germany believed this avenue of chemical research would be technically possible, they would have tried it. In this instance, however, a national and regional effort opened up an entirely new and profitable line of pharmaceutical research and development. While the initial effort took place in Norway, Nyegaard was able to draw upon the ideas of the Swedish radiologist Torsten Almén as they explored contrast media (de Haën, 2019). The innovation was thus a Scandinavian accomplishment with strong national leadership, and while non-ionic contrast media may be ascribed to a Nordic medical ecosystem, it would soon find international markets.

Nyegaard & Co.'s research was the dynamic driving force in this process. The business built "the system" that developed constructive feedback and turned an idea into an innovative product. Too often, historians simply jump from new ideas in the medical sciences to new products and therapies; but they leave out the entrepreneurship that converts an idea into a novel and useful product. Leading the way in this instance was Nyegaard's head of research, Hugo Holtermann. He used the company's

Norway's Pharmaceutical Revolution. Knut Sogner, Oxford University Press.
© Knut Sogner (2022). DOI: 10.1093/oso/9780192869005.003.0005

acquired human resources in contrast media to create a significant niche product for an important medical process. He had carefully evaluated the contrast media business, and he did a thorough survey of the entire field, looking first at Norwegian, then at international, and then at Scandinavian resources. Holtermann found the medical community of neighbor Sweden to be a particularly interesting hunting ground because of its strong community of radiologists.

Developing a unique niche product

For several years, Holtermann had contemplated how best to go about such research. Stemming from both an academic education and an upbringing in a commercially oriented family, he wanted to bridge scientific excellence with technical and commercial realism. He formulated a three-pronged strategy to do so: create a new research team, connect research to relevant outside environments and experts, and lead research to niches that were much more interesting for small, home-market-oriented Norwegian companies than large international pharmaceutical corporations.

The changes started with a Holtermann memorandum from March 1967. In it, he said he was optimistic about Nyegaard's possibilities of successful innovation and defined an optimum minimum size for a research group to work on contrast agents:

> If the situation is such that we expect to remain in the field of contrast media, I am of the opinion that it is necessary to reconstruct and build further upon a group of expert authorities in chemical synthesis. This group should consist of 4–6 qualified chemists and the necessary number of assistants.[1]

Such a group was much larger than the firm's norm in the 1950s and early 1960s. The company could at that time probably not afford as many researchers for the whole company as Holtermann proposed for contrast media. This size, he maintained, was large enough for the task even though this was many fewer researchers than larger companies would employ. Continued research in this specialty was, he said, the company's best chance of scientific and commercial success. Drawing upon its long experience (1957–1967) in the field, the firm would benefit from putting almost

[1] NFR, 17, 4, A, Rapp: Holtermann to Ulf Blix, March 7, 1967.

all its eggs in one basket, following a single technological trajectory. Its size forced the company to stay with its historically rooted knowledge even though the business had heretofore been unwilling to focus that tightly on one type of science and technology. This was a hard pill to swallow for a company that had long hedged its bets by staying in shipping as well as pharmaceuticals.

By the end of March 1967, however, Ulf Blix had decided to prioritize contrast agent research as Holtermann advised. Holtermann partially re-established the Isopaque research group and brought in new researchers. He wanted to create a group capable of productive, internal brainstorming and discussion, all the while maintaining and developing personal contacts outside the company.[2] Holtermann's most important contact at that time was Chief Physician Per Amundsen at Oslo's Ullevål Hospital. He was also in close contact with Arne Lundervold and Svein-Inge Oftedal at the National Hospital.[3]

Bringing Swedish radiologists into the company's network had been a priority for a number of years, but it had been tough going. Olav Bjørn-son, too, had recognized this need for increased Swedish communication and warned the others in management in November 1963 that contacts with Swedish physicians were too limited. They did not show interest in Isopaque unless Nyegaard actively brought them in:

In many respects, the situation for ISOPAQUE in Sweden is quite critical. This applies to pharmacological tests as well as clinical activities, and to our chances of having this product used in different X-ray departments. It is absolutely necessary to place ISOPAQUE at the top of the list of priorities when it comes to its exploitation and further testing.[4]

Leading radiologists involved in testing and documenting salt experiments could position the company. Increased knowledge and awareness of Isopaque could open markets as well as interest from other leading radiologists. The 1964 symposium in Copenhagen gathered Scandinavia's leading experts in radiology. They heard thirteen different presentations

---

[2] NFR, 17, 4, A, Rapp: "Forskere-organisk kjemi," November 21, 1967 and Holtermann to Ulf Blix, March 7, 1967.

[3] NFR, 5, 2: "Metrizamid. Forskningsprosjektets historikk" by Leif G. Haugen, October 10, 1974 and NFR, 17, B, 2.sk, Foredrag HH: "Et forskningsprosjekt på Nyco" by Hugo Holtermann, November 19, 1974.

[4] NFR, 15, rapp.Sverige: "Ad: Reise/Gøteborg–20–21 November 1963," probably by Olav Bjørn-son.

on Isopaque and its competitors, and Nyegaard created a new awareness of X-ray contrast agents.[5] The firm, which thus connected with many of the world's foremost radiologists, saw the Copenhagen symposium as a means of developing the world's best contrast agent based on Isopaque.[6] But the Copenhagen experience was a tough experience with lots of rough critique from the esteemed radiologists. In a symposium in Sandefjord in Norway two years later, the renewed Isopaque was much better regarded by the same group.[7]

In generating interaction with physicians and radiologists, being a Scandinavian company was a definite advantage—at least once the Swedes were won over. Scandinavian radiologists, especially those from Sweden, were among the world's foremost in the 1950s and 1960s. After the war, radiologists from many countries, and particularly from America, flocked to Scandinavia and especially Sweden (Fischer, 1987). Swedish radiologists were extremely active on the international scene; Erik Lindgren and Torgny Greitz are recognized as among the founders of neuroradiology.[8] Perhaps the most famous Swede was Sven-Ivar Seldinger, who developed a catheter technique in 1953. This made it possible to direct the contrast agents directly into a vein and paved the way for selective angiography—and for Isopaque. This vibrant environment created a horizon of scientific exchange that contributed to Holtermann's optimistic attitude about the possibilities of moving technical frontiers in contrast media.

Swedish professors Olle Olsson and Ulf Rudhe offer an interesting explanation for the status of radiologists in Sweden. Gösta Forsell, the world's first professor of radiology in 1916, worked to establish radiology as an independent discipline. In most other countries, including the United States, radiologists were regarded as "assistants" to other physicians. Swedish radiologists like Olle Olsson, through *his* many assignments in international circles, worked to gain recognition for the Swedish model. By the 1950s and 1960s, Swedish radiology had expanded greatly. The radiology community connected with manufacturers of technical medical equipment such as Elema-Schönander and Svenska Philips. This was the Swedish research and

---

[5] NFR, 21, Div.rkm: minutes from Isopaque meeting in Nyco, November 16, 1964, Leif G. Haugen, November 19, 1964.
[6] Ibid.
[7] Interview with Olav Bjørnson, June 29, 1992.
[8] The two following paragraphs are based on five historical—as yet—unpublished lectures in Mälardalens röntgenklubb 1985–1989: by Ulf Rudhe, Ingmar Fernström, Tord Olin, Torgny Greitz, and Olle Olsson. They can be obtained from Nycomed AB in Stockholm, Sweden.

technology environment—with extensions into the other Scandinavian countries—that Hugo Holtermann sought to exploit.

In 1967, once contrast media research was back on track, Holtermann initiated contact with Swedish doctors. The communication was two-way, and the prominent pharmacologist Percy Lindgren at the Karolinska Institute supported this sort of academic–industrial collaboration. In November 1967, Lindgren summarized the significance of cooperation between physicians and Nyegaard:

> One must hope that this developmental work [. . .] will be a step toward better and less dangerous X-ray contrast media. In accordance with researchers in the field of contrast media, it is also my hope that the increased interest in active research in this area [. . .] from academic and clinical scientists will continue.[9]

Holtermann kept in touch with three radiologists in particular, Professor Torgny Greitz and two younger colleagues, Erik Boijsen and Sven Paulin. He invited Boijsen and Paulin to spend some time at Nyegaard & Co. Both later became professors, Paulin at Harvard University and Boijsen at Lund in Sweden. A fourth Swedish radiologist also came to be very important to the company: Torsten Almén.[10] But that was after Holtermann emphasized research on the myelographic field.

The company had to some extent dabbled in developing X-ray contrast agents for uses other than those covered by Isopaque, that is, the vascular system. When they decided to concentrate on contrast agents in 1967, Holtermann regarded these other arenas as possibly more important priorities than vascular treatment. They had started work on contrast agents for gall bladders in the early 1960s, and since 1966, Holtermann directed attention to agents for the spinal canal and fluid-filled brain cavities: the myelographic field.[11] The central nervous system other than the lower spinal canal could not be reached with contrast media, and the agents that were being used at the bottom of the spinal cord were neither perfectly safe nor particularly effective. The iodinated oils had after-effects because traces

[9] NFR, 17, 2, A, Isop.l.Sv: Lindgren to Holtermann, November 25, 1967.
[10] NFR, 17, 2, A, Isop.l.Sv: Boijsen to Holtermann, April 17, October 20 and 30, 1967; Holtermann to Boijsen, April 6, June 23 and October 27, 1967; Holtermann to Paulin, September 23 and 30 and October 16, 1968 and February 10, 1969; Paulin to Holtermann, October 14 and 18, 1968; March 8 and August 6, 1969; April 28 and July 6, 1970; April 26, 1971; Holtermann to Almén, December 18, 1967.
[11] NFR, 17, B, 2. skuff. Forskning Gen. III: Holtermann to Blix, April 30, 1968; 5, 12, Rkm. "Myelografiske . . . Noen summariske historiske data" by Leif G. Haugen, January 22, 1971.

of oil were left after the examination. The ionic compounds made for vascular use were sometimes tried, but these procedures were dangerous and prone to very allergic reactions if the contrast medium accidentally came to affect higher and very sensitive parts of the spinal canal.

Nyegaard's expertise in this area resulted from years of extensive external collaboration.[12] Holtermann had established contacts with the Belgian physician Richard Gonsette and the Norwegian physicians Per Amundsen, Arne Lundervold, and Sven-Inge Oftedal, as well as the Swedes and many others. Gonsette's work seems to have been especially important in learning about the effects of contrast agents on particularly sensitive areas of the central nervous system. The research department worked closely with him.[13]

In April 1968, Holtermann summarized the technical goals of this research:

> At the moment, it is our opinion [. . .] that we have a 50 percent chance, or more, of reaching our ambitious goal, that is, to develop a water-soluble agent for the entire area.[14]

Almén had not started working with the company this early. In April 1968, Holtermann gave another reason for this research, based on his assumption that Nyegaard could dominate the world market in this area:

> There is reason to believe that if we succeed in developing a preparation of this nature, it will be unique and therefore not exposed to much competition.[15]

Holtermann did not think that the larger foreign companies would be interested in research in myelographic contrast agents. Sterling Drug had confirmed Holtermann's opinion that there was a pressing need for a new product but that the market was far too limited to interest Sterling.[16] However, the French company Guerbet worked on a similar project and had

---

[12] NFR, 5, 2: "Metrizamid . . . historikk" by Leif G. Haugen, January 10, 1974 and NFR, 17, B, 2. sk. Foredrag HH: "Et forskn.prosjekt på Nyco" by Hugo Holtermann, November 19, 1974.

[13] NFR, 3, 49. Sandefj.-symp: note by "TG," September 24, 1966; NFR, 17, Gonsette: Dahlstrøm to Gonsette, April 28, 1967; Holtermann to Gonsette, January 12, June 26, and November 22, 1968; Salvesen to Gonsette, November 5, 1968, January 20 and May 20, 1969; NFR, 17. skuff. 4A.HH-UB: Holtermann to Ulf Blix, October 8, 1968.

[14] NFR, 17, B, 2. skuff. Forskning Gen. III: Holtermann to Ulf Blix, April 30, 1968.

[15] Ibid.

[16] NFR, 17, SWII: Hoppe to Holtermann, January 8, 1968.

developed the ionic compound Dimer-X on the basis of Mallinckrodt's vascular agent, Conray.[17] Guerbet had a connection with Mallinckrodt that typified the oligopolistic situation in the field of contrast agents. Just as Nyegaard & Co. was associated with Sterling, and Guerbet with Mallinckrodt, the Italian company Bracco had links with Squibb.[18] Three relatively small European companies involved in research in the field of contrast agents each had a much larger American partner that was not so deeply involved in contrast media research.

Holtermann carefully planned the research strategy. He had to articulate his thoughts quite explicitly given the difficulties he had experienced getting contrast media prioritized. His background encouraged confidence in the new effort. Holtermann had rubbed shoulders with the best organic chemists in the world while pursuing his doctorate at Oxford University; he obviously deserved confidence. Going forward, he built on extensive work over 10 years with the patentable but commercially not so significant contrast media Isopaque. Creating bonds and communication with the strong group of Swedish radiologists emphasized the academic seriousness of the undertaking. Yet, Holtermann and Nyegaard's main commercial aim in 1967 was still quite humble: To create something unique, primarily for the niche that was the myelographic market.

Teamwork across borders

As Nyegaard got underway, the firm already had contacts with the young Swedish radiologist Torsten Almén as he had sought professional cooperation with the company for many years. Almén, however, had struggled to get in touch with Nyegaard, quite possibly a symptom of how little esteem contrast media had in the company at that point. Almén's doctoral studies in radiology dealt with the effects of a radiological device. From 1962 to 1963, he became increasingly interested in the side effects (pain, burning sensations, and very rarely sudden death) of injecting established contrast agents into the bloodstream.[19] He had wanted for some time to address these problems together with a chemically knowledgeable pharmaceutical company.

[17] NKT, 606, FoU: PM by Holtermann, October 22, 1970.
[18] NFR, 15, div. II: minutes from meeting with Laboratoires André Guerbet at Nyco, May 2, 1974; NFR, 17, C1, staff meetings: "X-Ray Contrast Agents. Staff Meetings" No. 35/77, December 14, 1977.
[19] Interview with Torsten Almén, May 21, 1991.

Almén belonged to the active radiology environment in Sweden where researchers were focusing on existing X-ray contrast agents. He participated in some of the Swedish meetings Nyegaard & Co. organized for its salt-oriented research project around Isopaque (de Haën, 2019: 156–170). This environment exposed him to the current intellectual discussion about contrast media. But, as became apparent, he had creative ambitions for contributing more directly in developing new substances with fewer side effects. He read up on chemistry in order to be able to formulate new chemical ideas for new agents. Rare for a medical doctor, he was ready to put them into practice.[20]

Almén first contacted the major Swedish pharmaceutical company, Pharmacia. He was not granted a meeting. He chose Pharmacia because it sold an X-ray contrast agent. His logical next step was to contact Nyegaard & Co., which he did through its Swedish representative, Erco Läkemedel.[21] This turned out to be difficult and became a process creating distrust as Erco created a barrier between Nyegaard and Almén. Erco had represented Nyegaard & Co. since 1951 and had worked hard on Isopaque sales in Sweden and Denmark. Almén presented his ideas to Erco and its representative, Lars Fondberg, believing that he thereby communicated with Nyegaard.[22] Fondberg coordinated the important Isopaque research involving Swedish radiologists going on in Sweden at the time (de Haën, 2019: 156–170). However, Fondberg did not report the exchange with Almén to Norway; Nyegaard's impression at the time—and not knowing anything about Almén—was that *Erco* had started up its own research on contrast agents.

In January 1966, Lars Fondberg asked Hugo Holtermann some specific questions about the properties of Isopaque, with the goal of manufacturing "polymers" of that product. That would mean metrizoic molecules attached two and two (or more), thereby reducing the particle density by 50 percent or more. Holtermann replied that this was possible but that he thought a contrast agent of this kind would have a number of drawbacks.[23] Holtermann understood that such agents would have a lower *osmotic pressure* than traditional contrast agents like Isopaque and would therefore be less

[20] Ibid.

[21] NFR, 17, B, 1. skuff. Almén I: Almén to Holtermann, August 18, 1967; interview with Torsten Almén, May 21, 1991.

[22] NFR, 17, B, 1. skuff. Almén I: Almén to Holtermann, August 18, 1967; interview with Torsten Almén, May 21, 1991.

[23] NFR, 17, 4. skuff. UB fra HH: Holtermann to Blix, June 15, 1966.

harmful.[24] Osmotic pressure (or osmolality), is a result of particle density (the number of particles per unit volume) in liquids. When particle density is higher in the contrast agent than in the blood, blood vessels are temporarily damaged in areas containing a high concentration of contrast agent. Linking the contrast agent's molecules would reduce particle density. Ideally, contrast agents should have the same particle density (osmolality) as human blood (Almén, 1969).

Holtermann was not aware that Erco had heard Torsten Almén's theories about polymers being a solution to the osmolality problem; Almén did not know that Nyegaard & Co. was ignorant both of his meeting with Fondberg and his approach. The enterprise first became aware of Almén in June 1966, when Holtermann met both Lars Fondberg and Almén at a pharmaceutical convention. Holtermann was surprised that Almén wanted to talk to him. Fondberg, in the meantime, asked Holtermann to avoid discussing polymer contrast agents with Almén, and Holtermann honored Fondberg's request.[25] Therefore, Holtermann and Almén did not establish any meaningful contact. Holtermann summarized their first meeting:

> It was my distinct impression that Dr. Almén had not been warned by Fondberg about discussing his ideas with me, and that he in fact would have liked to go into them more thoroughly, and may have been quite surprised when I did not ask more detailed questions.[26]

Though Erco officially presented itself as a partner of Nyegaard, it kept information from the Norwegian firm. Nyegaard contacted Erco to hear more about its independent research, again without knowing about Almén. Despite numerous requests, Erco did not give any information about its own attempts to make polymeric contrast agents based on Isopaque.[27] Much time passed before Nyegaard realized that Torsten Almén also felt that Erco had deceived him.[28] But when Ulf Blix contacted Almén personally in September 1967, they quickly understood that they shared the same experience with Erco. Almén expressed his view of the situation forcefully:

> In February 1966 I presented to Lars Fondberg the idea of polymerizing the contrast agents by the method described in my doctoral thesis. Since then,

---

[24] NFR, 17, 4. skuff. UB fra HH: Holtermann to Blix, June 15, 1966.
[25] Ibid.
[26] Ibid.
[27] NFR, 20, 12.Polypaque: Bjørnson's note by January 7, 1970.
[28] NFR, 17, B, 1. skuff. Almén I: Blix to Almén, September 6, 1967.

the Polypaque project has been surrounded with a great deal of secrecy, even directed at me. Until now I have not received one single written report from Fondberg, or Erco, about Polypaque.[29]

Despite this, Almén had signed an agreement to give his patent rights to Erco as late as spring of 1967, under the impression that Nyegaard & Co. was also involved.[30]

In a recent book about the development of the contrast media business, Christoph de Haën, a former head of Nyegaard & Co.'s Italian competitor Bracco's Milano Research Center, has unearthed a deeper background of the Erco situation. He shows that Lars Fondberg probably acted out of his own understanding of the importance of lower osmolality and at the same time showing that Almén's ideas about osmolality also fed on input from the Swedish community of radiologists. Fondberg, as mentioned, was centrally placed within the Swedish contrast media community through his coordinating work for Nyegaard. de Haën's book also shows that Almén either has forgotten or suppressed this information about Fondberg. An alternative explanation is that Fondberg was already working with the polymer idea by January 1966, which comes through in his letter to Holtermann. Almén states that he did not inform Fondberg until February 1966, for what such imprecise information is worth. De Haën's implication, however, is more important: The polymer idea was not original, and Fondberg and Almén may have fed on the same inspirational source. The problem with this idea, which was why companies like Nyegaard did not act upon it, was that these substances with large polymer molecules would not work as contrast media.

Nyegaard and Almén finally established contact in the fall of 1967, but by then Torstein Almén was skeptical of the entire pharmaceutical industry. He now lived in the United States and tried to arrange meetings with some of the larger contrast agent companies. He met with Mallinckrodt, but they did not seem particularly interested. His experience with Erco had anyway taught him caution. Sterling Drug offered him a job in its biological division but without him having presented his ideas. The only company with extensive knowledge of Almén's ideas was still only Erco. In the spring of 1968, he at last had a portion of his chemical theories notarized in order to be able to prove that they were his own.[31]

[29] NFR, 17, B, 1. skuff. Almén I: Almén to Blix, September 8, 1967.
[30] Ibid.
[31] Interview with Torsten Almén, May 21, 1991.

Then, Nyegaard & Co. took the decisive initiative to establish contact with Almén. Holtermann met him in a New York hotel room on February 2, 1968. When Holtermann left New York City, he was convinced that Almén would not cooperate with his outfit.[32] Almén was of another opinion and soon sent a message that he wanted to collaborate with a Scandinavian company. This, "as well as the dynamic impression I was given of the contrast agent research at Nyegaard & Co by Dr. Hugo Holtermann, is the main reason that I did not sign Sterling Drug's proposal."[33] Once more, the regional as well as the personal professional relationships were important.

By May 1968, Nyegaard had integrated Torsten Almén into its research team. From this time on, Almén cooperated through meetings and correspondence. The business now had established a link with a radiologist who had ideas—and a strong interest—in new contrast agents. Almén was an easy-going person who, to the horror of Holtermann's group, addressed Holtermann as "you, Hugo" rather than as "Dr. Holtermann." This event turned out very well as Holtermann's colleagues (going back 15 years) now shook hands with him and from then on addressed him as Hugo.

A non-ionic X-ray contrast agent

In retrospect, Torsten Almén has been given a lot of credit for Nyegaard & Co.'s breakthrough. He also rose to a very important position in the world of radiology. His contribution to Nyegaard's breakthrough was undoubtedly important, and he is named as one of three persons on the patent that the firm filed for its first product of the new generation. His academic position as a visionary scientist shaping the contrast media field with the new generation is well earned (Haën, 2019). But his actual role in the path breaking chemical breakthrough is slightly unclear, and that is partly because of the story he has been telling himself.

Torsten Almén had for a long time promoted contrast media with lower osmolality. Making contrast agents with lower osmolality had been both his and Fondberg's goal. Osmolality was a result of particle density, which two factors regulated (Almén, 1969). The first of these was the original particle density in the contrast agent solution, and this is what Almén sought to change by linking the iodine-containing molecules together.

---

[32] NFR, 20, 1: travel report USA January–February 1968, February 20, 1968 by Holtermann.
[33] NFR, 17, B, 1. skuff. Almén I: Almén to Holtermann, February 28, 1968.

However, the problem that held back the chemically knowledgeable companies from going down this road was that the final solution—with its larger molecules—would be very viscous and therefore difficult to inject. A finished X-ray contrast agent contains up to about 75 percent of the basic substance in solution and is barely soluble with normal-sized molecules.

However, the number of the particles doubled when the iodinated molecules were dissolved in water. To dissolve the iodinated molecules in water, base is added to form a salt, splitting the molecule in positive and negative ions, doubling the number of particles in the solution. Almén has claimed he suggested making contrast agents which were not salts (non-ionic); these would not split into electrically charged particles and would therefore have lower particle density than traditional contrast media. By so doing, he hoped to reduce particle density (osmolality) without an undue increase in viscosity. Nyegaard & Co.'s researchers actually accomplished this, and the new generation of contrast media got their name—non-ionic—as a reference to their non-electric properties and low osmolality. But it must be pointed out that it is unclear—and improbable—that Almén can be said to have proposed this path to a non-ionic solution in a clear and directive way.

The chemist Christoph de Haën, too, is doubtful about the directive given by Almén. He does acknowledge Almén's attempt at formulating new contrast media but suggests that Almén in his later recollections exaggerates the precision of his own vision at the time. As evidence of his vision, Almén has provided the aforementioned affidavit notarially confirmed in Florida in March 1968. Almén made this affidavit to protect his intellectual property after his troubled relationship with Lars Fondberg. Says de Haën:

> Completely on its own the single page from the affidavit reveals neither the intention to abolish ionicity [ionic] nor that to achieve elevated water solubility mediated by numerous hydroxyl groups. Yet in historical papers Almén has always described his affidavit as doing just that, and documented it with the mentioned page, supplemented by emphasizing marks. [. . .] Only the missing nine pages of the affidavit could clarify the issue
>
> (de Haën, 2019: 181).

De Haën goes on to show that the ideas about hydroxyl groups as promoting water solubility was well known at the time and cites a Hugo Holtermann publication from 1961 as one of the examples. Here, Holtermann also mentions that hydroxyl groups may give lower toxicity. These insights must be seen as part of the justification for his arguing why Nyegaard & Co. in the mid-1960s should continue research into contrast media.

The research group at Nyegaard was not really convinced that Almén's broad proposal of several types of molecules could be implemented. Holtermann had little confidence in its success, but he was willing to try. Nyegaard's research group, for its own reasons, only tried out one of Almén's crude suggestions: the non-ionic iodinated molecules had to be hydroxyl compounds.[34] Nyegaard's researchers had already worked with iodinated substances containing hydroxyl groups, based on observations made by the head of the biological department, Sigbjørn Salvesen. Hydroxyl groups facilitated water solubility, and Salvesen and Nyegaard's research group thought that they also reduced toxicity *in the subarchoid area* but not the vascular one. This would enable use of contrast agents in the spinal canal and in cerebral fluid.[35] When applied to Almén's ideas for new contrast agents, this line of research met with success.

Nyegaard & Co. synthesized the world's first water-soluble, non-ionic, tri-iodinated substances in November 1968. After only a few months, it became clear that many of the other substances were also promising.[36] One might suggest Nyegaard & Co.'s researchers sooner or later would have tried this way out by their own inclinations, but they succeeded by doing it as a response to Almén's input. Consequently, in the patent later filed by Nyegaard & Co., Almén, along with two Nyegaard researchers, Haavaldsen and Nordahl, were named as inventors. Doing it with Almén also meant that the interpretive consequences of the invention for medical purposes and vascular use were well taken care of. Following Almén took the company down a path that conflicted with what its researchers and chemists in general thought possible.[37] They believed that substances containing such a high iodine content had to be salts in order to achieve solubility in high concentrations. Comments Almén received in late April 1969 from a consultant about an article he had submitted to the *Journal of Theoretical Biology* in August 1968 illustrate this:

---

[34] Interview with Hugo Holtermann, August 11, 1993.
[35] NFR, 17, B, 2. skuff. Forskning Gen. II: Holtermann to Ulf Blix, April 30, 1968. With the author: Holtermann to Sogner, October 29, 1993.
[36] NFR, 5, 12: "Røntgenkontrast. Myelografiske prosjekt. Noen summariske historiske data" by Leif G. Haugen, January 22, 1971; 17, B, 1. skuff. Almén I: Holtermann to Almén, November 11, 1968.
[37] NFR, 5, 2: "Metrizamid Forskningsprosjektets historikk" by Leif G. Haugen, October 10, 1974.

The general principle of Dr. Almén's proposal is probably sound. The imple-
mentation of it is probably impractical. He seems to be unaware that the ionic
nature of the iodinated compounds is an essential property for their solubility
in water—so part of his proposal, i.e. using non-ionic hydrophilic compounds,
may be invalid.[38]

The *Journal* and the company's researchers were wrong and collaboration
with Torsten Almén had brought Nyegaard a giant stride forward. Together they invented what came to be called non-ionic contrast media.
Together they had created a new and positive research "atmosphere."[39]
They united Almén's optimistic visions with Nyegaard & Co's laboriously
developed chemical knowledge, and it must be emphasized that the company's researchers had clear ideas of their own that blended well with one
of Almén's. Almén was an optimist, a much more relaxed and direct person than the serious, somewhat reticent and deep-thinking Holtermann.
Holtermann had spent four years in German prisons and concentration
camps after being caught as a courier by the German occupation power
in the fall of 1941, an experience which, combined with his intellectual demeanor, made him appear rather unapproachable. Almén helped
to establish—also for Holtermann—a more easy-going atmosphere that
encouraged experimentation, even with radical ideas.

When Almén and Nyegaard put their heads together in 1968 and
1969, there was a meeting of minds between an individual and a research group. It may be a moot point whether one or the other could
have developed a non-ionic contrast agent alone. The important fact is
that they succeeded together—over 80 different substances were synthesized. In November 1969, after biological and pharmacological testing,
Nyegaard declared Compound 16 (also called "Sweet Sixteen") the best
substance.

Less than six months passed between Almén's first meeting with the
research group and the development of the first non-ionic compound. It
took another six months before they produced Compound 16 and a few
additional months of testing before they chose it as the best non-ionic
compound. In an astonishingly short time—from June 1968 to November
1969—a collaboration was established and ideas from the team and from

[38] After Almén: NFR, 17, B, 1. skuff. dr. T. Almén I: Almén to Holtermann, May 3, 1969.
[39] Used by Leif G. Haugen: NFR, 5, 2: "Metrizamid. Forskningsprosjektets historikk" by Leif G.
Haugen, November 10, 1974. Supported by Holtermann in interview, July 2, 1992.

Almén translated into a substance, called metrizamide, which ultimately became the basis of the product known as Amipaque.[40]

Constructing a product

This startling and rapid success must be attributed to the long-term efforts of both sides. Almén, as a physician, had studied the effects of contrast agents on the human body for many years, and he had searched for alternative chemical solutions. He may also be said to represent distillated wisdom from the Swedish radiologist community. He had a definite goal as regards the properties he wanted in contrast agents and was not bound by chemical conventions. On the other hand, he worked with what may have been the world's leading chemistry team in this field. Research at Nyegaard & Co. had been achieving good results ever since the 1950s, and its re-established and refocused research team had been constantly working toward new solutions. Those solutions directed the creation of the new product along lines suggested by Almén's visions.

The knowledge that Nyegaard had gained from research into contrast agents for the spinal canal (specifically that hydroxyl groups reduced toxicity) helped to bring the invention to another level of importance. Holtermann and Nyegaard had pursued myelographic use, and in the end that was the product niche initially chosen. It would be misleading to focus exclusively on the non-ionic aspects of the invention. That was Almén's vision (or one of them) and that was for a vascular purpose. Nyegaard's emphasis on creating a substance with low chemotoxicity—relevant for myelographic use—at a later date also came to reduce side effects for vascular use—quite apart from the effect of low osmolality (de Haën, 2019). Chemotoxicity is a measure of the toxic influence of the actual structure of the molecule.[41] This is not to diminish Almén's contribution but to underline the particular contribution of Nyegaard.

Metrizamide (Amipaque) was not only—or even primarily—successful as a myelographic medium because it was non-ionic and had low osmolality. Low osmolality was a concept that concerned the blood, not necessarily the liquid in the spinal canal and around the brain. Following Holtermann's lead, Nyegaard had searched for a molecule with low

[40] NKT, 606, FoU: "Røntgenkontrastmiddelforskningen. Status ultimo okt. 1970" by Holtermann, October 22, 1970.
[41] Interview with Almén, May 21, 1991.

chemotoxicity and achieved just that. And this low chemotoxicity—and not the fact that it was non-ionic with low osmolality compared with blood—made the new substance suitable for myelographic purposes (de Haën, 2019: 218f). The low toxicity also proved to be extremely important when the non-ionic principle a few years later was used in vascular contrast media. The two non-ionic products—from Nyegaard and Bracco, respectively—that succeeded in the long term in the vascular segment were the two products with the lowest chemo toxicity (de Haën, 2019: 226 and 281f). Their low chemotoxicity was a very important part of their constitution and their international success as non-ionic contrast media.

Torsten Almén originally intended new contrast agents with low osmolality to be used in vascular examinations.[42] Holtermann had chosen to go for the myelographic market, obviously with the consent from Ulf Blix.[43] Both he and Almén completely understood that these new molecules could also open up possibilities in the vascular area. Holtermann had, however, directed the research to achieve a product for myelographic use and he saw no reason to change that course: He was uncertain about how the new invention would be met in the vascular market. He believed the product—regardless of choice of markets—needed to be far superior to the existing contrast agents used, and if the product like the one Nyegaard & Co. was developing had to have a higher price because it was expensive to produce and came with higher viscosity, then the challenge in the market for vascular media could be huge. Such a marketing effort would be very uncertain and also costly; it would take much more time than going for the myelographic market. For that market, he was pretty certain that the new invention—if everything went well—would have a chance of international market penetration.

Holtermann cites lack of resources as the reason why the synthesis that Italian Bracco later accomplished was not fully covered by Nyegaard patents; Holtermann said they had just one man on the job.[44] The choice to make an amide (metrizamide—see later, and in later products different choices were made) was based on the myelographic choice. The chosen amide had the disadvantage of having to be freeze-dried and that made it very expensive to produce. The rationale was that if the project was successful, the finished product would command prices that were so much higher

[42] Interview with Almén, May 21, 1991.
[43] With the author: Holtermann to Sogner, October 29, 1993.
[44] Interview with Hugo Holtermann, October 7, 1992.

than prices for the existing myelographic contrast media that production costs of the kind foreseen would be negligible.[45]

Amipaque was "completely superior to the other potential water-soluble agents and those on the market,"[46] Holtermann summed up in 1970. He knew exactly what they had achieved. While Guerbet's Dimer-X could only be used in the lower portion of the spinal canal, metrizamide (Amipaque) gradually showed that it fulfilled the goal of being applicable for the *entire* spinal canal.[47]

The molecule that constituted Amipaque was very expensive to produce on an industrial scale, and the process of deciding to go for that molecule took some time.[48] Development work on Amipaque would have been stopped, though, had not Holtermann, through countless comprehensive interviews, gained insight into the price that Amipaque as a myelographic agent could command. In principle, there were two ways to determine its value. The first was to work from previously established price levels for myelographic contrast agents, which the marketing department at Nyegaard & Co. did in 1969. The second method was to treat Amipaque as an entirely new concept, one that literally opened up new rooms in the body for X-ray examinations. Holtermann chose this approach. He estimated in 1970 that the new product as a myelographic agent could command a price at least five times higher than the original estimate: "The neurological experts whom we have consulted maintain that price is of minor importance."[49]

Amipaque satisfied Nyegaard's objective of developing an exclusive product. Isopaque had proven that a small Norwegian company had to achieve more than just developing a product that could be patented. Years of experience with Isopaque taught the company that it had to develop a unique, niche product. Unlike Isopaque, Amipaque was not competing against Sterling Drug's Hypaque, nor was it in competition with Urografin, Renografin, or Conray. Choosing Amipaque as a myelographic agent was an attempt to establish a totally new international concept: the first contrast

---

[45] With the author: Holtermann to Sogner, November 14, 1993.
[46] NKT, 606, FoU: PM by Holtermann, October 22, 1970.
[47] Ibid.
[48] Amipaque is based on the glucose amide of metrizoate (Isopaque). Thus, Amipaque's generic designation, metrizamide: "metriz" from the first two syllables in Isopaque's generic name and "amide" identifying Amipaque as a glucose amide. That Amipaque could be based on Isopaque was fortunate. The Nyegaard team tested all of the familiar contrast agents (Urografin/Hypaque, Conray, and Isopaque) to determine the properties of their glucose amides, and Isopaque was chosen as the definitive winner. Interview with Hugo Holtermann, July 2, 1992.
[49] NKT, 606, FoU: PM by Holtermann, October 22, 1970.

agent for use in the entire spinal canal. In effect, Nyegaard created its own product area.

The business had long been active in the field of contrast agents, and the breakthrough of Amipaque must be seen in this perspective. A reciprocal and coordinated mutual understanding between the company and the outside, between the company and the medical environment, had already been established. The Amipaque breakthrough in 1969 was thus the fruit of two independent processes: Nyegaard's research within the field of contrast agents and an extensive medical effort in radiology in the Nordic countries.

This effort blew open the constraints on the company's research. For all practical purposes, the company had done it alone until then. Characteristically, the two Norwegian medical doctors who previously were genuinely important to Nyegaard & Co., Paul Owren and Lorentz Eldjarn, were never involved in *research collaboration* with the company. They came to the company with virtually finished products, seeking help for marketing purposes. Both kept their rights to the primary production stage, and both founded limited companies for production. Nyegaard & Co.'s collaboration with doctors like Jens Dedichen and biochemists like Søren Laland cannot be compared to the substantial Nordic and transnational environment the company became part of in the field of X-ray contrast media.

For Holtermann, collaborating with Torsten Almén was a new and thoroughly gratifying experience. Christoph de Haën points out that when Amipaque was about to be launched, Holtermann made an effort to highlight Torsten Almén's contribution. Holtermann gives a lot of credit to Almén's ideas and the way they contributed to its success. "So much reference to Almén in view of an input that in originality was modest indeed raises the question of motive," says de Haën (de Haën, 2019: 183). He does not think Almén represented a revelation for Nyegaard's researchers. He rather thinks Holtermann in Almén sought an outsider to promote the new concept (whatever that was) in the medical world, and that he also needed an ally in terms of legitimizing contrast media research for internal reasons. At this point in time (in 1973), the fortune of non-ionic contrast media was completely unknown, and the place of contrast media research within Nyegaard could not be guaranteed given other possible research avenues.

De Haën makes important points. In 1973, Hugo Holtermann had every reason to fear that research on contrast media was not guaranteed for the future. By giving in to his will in 1967, research director Ulf Blix had made what was for him a difficult decision that entailed prioritizing scarce resources to the contrast media field. A lot of effort had been put into

Amipaque, which was still in 1973 an unproven commercial entity. There was no guarantee that a setback of sorts would not be very damaging to future research in contrast media.

De Haën also notes how Almén has been "widely considered to be the only father of the new technology. He himself did not a little to foster this image" (de Haën, 2019: 213). De Haën would rather place Almén as one of several fathers and mentions Holtermann, other Nyegaard researchers, and researchers from Cilag Chemie and Bracco. In reacting to some of de Haën's criticisms against his role as the invention's father, Almén reiterated that he thought so himself: "The concept of nonionic contrast media arose in my brain as a consequence of an intellectual analysis trying to combine low osmolality and low viscosity in watersoluble contrast media."[50]

It is very probable that Torsten Almén believes what he is stating. That does not mean he is right. The idea about non-ionic contrast media as a solution to the osmolality challenge was not original, as shown by de Haën and his example from Cilag Chemie's efforts in the early 1960s (de Haën, 2019). Amipaque was the start of a new generation of contrast media that became known as non-ionic. Their defining characteristic is their low osmolality. Low osmolality is an advantage for vascular contrast agents, not myelographic ones. Torsten Almén became the global champion of vascular contrast media with low osmolality. He also nurtured relationships with Nyegaard & Co. for decades after his contribution to Amipaque. But the advantage of the new generation of non-ionic contrast agents was also their low chemotoxicity, something that was achieved not by a general principle but by testing individual molecules and their toxic properties. The search for low chemotoxicity was championed by Nyegaard & Co. and Holtermann for the purpose of finding a superior myelographic agent. Low toxicity as a consequence of individually tested substances is not the stuff of grand visions for the future, but it was both the motivation behind the research project that led to the non-ionic principle and the commercial aspiration that fueled the continued exploration of what the initial molecules of 1969 were good for in practice. Achieving low chemotoxicity was no less important for the post-Amipaque generation of non-ionic contrast media. They, too, had to qualify themselves for their chemo toxic properties even though they were non-ionic and had low osmolality.

In retrospect, Hugo Holtermann acted very much in a Schumpeterian spirit. Without his efforts to set the stage for invention and innovation,

---

[50] RA, Nycomed, 2nd part. E-0009.0001: Almén to Sogner, February 12, 1995.

the breakthrough with non-ionic contrast media would not have happened. Torsten Almén was neither an entrepreneur nor a chemist. Almén mattered because he had good ideas; as a person he mattered too. He helped create a lighter and more optimistic attitude among Nyegaard's researchers in general and for Holtermann in particular. Holtermann and Nyegaard's researchers used, and added to, a growing body of knowledge developed by neuroradiologists and neurosurgeons in Sweden, Norway, and other countries. Holtermann and his team had learnt from many years of communication with these outside experts and were preoccupied with emphasizing research that should fulfil myelographic needs of low toxicity in medical practice.

Conclusion

To some extent, the success of the 1969 invention was the result of a Scandinavian system of innovation for contrast media. The success most certainly fits the interactive perspective of this system's approach as collaboration and learning between companies and doctors over time paved the ground for the success. The tight involvement in the final stages of the process of the Swedish radiologist Torsten Almén underlines the system perspective.

Yet, this was not a system that Nyegaard & Co. simply inherited. Nyegaard had created a business system from the early 1960s in order to recreate Isopaque as an exportable product. When "a system" was in place, courtesy of the company's efforts to create a working external network, Holtermann could argue for the exploitation of this network or system, which he did. Nyegaard created and exploited the network and thereby succeeded.

Ever since the 1940s, Nyegaard & Co. had been eager to become an innovative pharmaceutical company. One of the many bumps in the road along the way was a product of its unclear vision of how to accomplish this goal. Inspired to do research by the big companies Merck and Glaxo, and to do research with Merck and Glaxo, a shift in focus in the 1960s to emphasize building on its own competence in contrast media changed its research fortunes.

Changes in organizational set-up more generally were a necessary precondition to Nyegaard's quest. The new top leadership involved large segments of the staff in the extensive work to launch and qualify original products in the highly regulated pharmaceutical field. The whole company had ears, interpreted, learned, and became qualified to address issues of relevance to the contrast media field. This created legitimacy for Holtermann's ambitions. As head of research, and with a firm grasp of the technical issues involved, he could spearhead a collective process that could fulfill technical, financial, and organizational goals at the same time. The company had to change its organizational principles in order to make what proved to be a correct decision. In the first part of the 1960s, during the launch of Isopaque, this emphasis was unproblematic. But in the face of opposition from the liver researchers, Holtermann's views won through after only three years. He argued along the same lines as economist Edith Penrose. The company should exploit its research base; it should use the deep and specialized knowledge—its resources—assembled over more than 10 years.

The invention of the new generation of contrast media has come to be known as non-ionic, and that name has been associated with the Swedish radiologist Torsten Almén, who claims to have been the visionary behind the concept. He most certainly was behind such an emphasis, and his quest for new contrast media with fewer side effects cannot be questioned. But to make and sell non-ionic contrast media was not in itself a successful for-mulae, and the meticulous chemical understanding that led Holtermann and Nyegaard to search for molecules with low chemotoxicity that could be used as myelographic media was more important as a driver of innova-tion. The confidence stemming from mastering the chemistry of contrast media was clearly behind Holtermann's deliberate drive to make contrast media the one research priority of the company, an effort that was opposed and must therefore have been difficult for him. In pursuing the contrast media field as research arena, Holtermann to a great degree acted alone and "broke free" from the constraints of the company, joined forces with Nordic and international radiologists, and thereby created a wholly new technological platform that subsequently proved successful.

The tools with which "an international system" was created, or networks forged, were scientific investigations. Aiming to understand the biological and chemical properties involved, the firm had to create a new context. It was not there in the form of a Norwegian innovation system that could carry the intellectual challenge posed by the company but through the ac-tions of Holtermann and Nyegaard. Norwegian academic contacts were supplemented with Danish and especially Swedish links. Thus, the success-ful breakthrough of 1969 was a consequence of an innovation system, and it is an important confirmation that the old model of academic–business relationship in the pioneering countries that inspired Nyegaard & Co. to pursue being innovative in the first place functioned. This was not a national system, nor purely a national academic–business collaboration. And the contribution of the academic input was vital but was still secondary to the entrepreneurial effort of the corporation, Holtermann, and its research team. This was a national, a regional, and ultimately an international phenomenon.

References

Almén, T. 1969. "Contrast Agent Design. Some Aspects on the Synthesis of Water Soluble Contrast Agents of Low Osmolality." *Journal of Theoretical Biology*, 24(2): 216–226.

Fischer, H. W. 1987. "Historical Aspects of Contrast Media Development." *In*: Felix, R. et al. (ed.) *Contrast Media from the Past to the Future*. Stuttgart: Georg Thieme Verlag, pp. 3–18.

de Haën, C. 2019. *X-Ray Contrast Agent Technology. A Revolutionary History*. Boca Raton, FL: CRC Press.

6
The Rise of the Knowledge-Based Companies

The early 1970s was not an opportune time for a small Scandinavian firm to be cracking into the global market for pharmaceuticals. The new and much tighter regulatory approach of the United States following the Thalidomide tragedy spread to Europe and elsewhere. Demands to get a new drug registered increased. The possible liabilities that could follow from serious side effects impacted Swedish Astra in its home market, where it was the representative for Thalidomide. The innocence of modern chemistry was gone, and Danish Novo experienced heavy criticism when the news broke that workers in a British factory producing enzymes were sickened. Two years later, the Food and Drug Administration (FDA) ruled that there was nothing wrong with the product, a huge success for Novo (Richter-Friis, 1991: 225–230). But in the meantime, a Ralph Nader-influenced campaign against enzymes in washing powder shaved off 80 percent of the value of Novo's enzyme sales.

In addition to hostile regulators, small firms had to face an international marketing system that was still in somewhat of an embryonic phase. Some companies, like Merck (which had become Merck, Sharp and Dohme in 1953 when the research house merged with a marketing house) had since gradually developed an international organization (Galambos, 1991). But not all national markets were easily conquered, as the difficulties getting a foothold in the huge German market proved for the US corporation. Glaxo, which lacked a US sales organization until 1977, lagged behind Merck in going international (Jones, 2001). These and other innovative companies used licensees and representatives instead of promoting their own organization in their foreign markets. As Novo's experience in the United States illustrated, there were substantial risks involved in investing abroad.

Yet the new and stricter regulations had one possible upside. Selling drugs—in particular innovative and potent drugs—was increasingly done in tandem with information-creating clinical trials. In order to get a new pharmaceutical registered, a firm had to supply additional information

Norway's Pharmaceutical Revolution. Knut Sogner, Oxford University Press.
© Knut Sogner (2022). DOI: 10.1093/oso/9780192869005.003.0006

over and above the traditional chemical properties and general effects on the body. The general effects and the toxicological characteristics of the drug needed to be based on large, well-documented clinical trials with strict controls on methodology. Production practices, too, had to comply to strict norms. The effectiveness of sales forces functioning in this demanding environment world was likely to increase as the same company sold and did clinical studies of the products. The hassle of clinical trials could thus be turned into sales arguments. Companies collaborated with trial-performing doctors who also either were or became customers. Often, these were doctors with high standing within their profession, and they impacted what other doctors prescribed. Nyegaard & Co. took advantage of this situation as it sought to establish its new product, Amipaque, on the world market.

The challenge

Nyegaard's initial challenge was daunting. The size of an ideal sales and clinical research organization grew from the mid-1960s on. Two or three substances produced at low unit cost and sold through a small number of established sales organizations dominated major vascular contrast media markets like the United States, Japan, and West Germany. Isopaque had not broken into these markets, being too similar to established products sold by much larger companies. Nyegaard had neither the finances nor the administrative resources to launch a large-scale marketing program.

With Amipaque, however, the firm had a product based on new chemical and pharmacological principles and was able to focus its marketing on the niche myelographic market. The company started this task with two categories of marketing channels in place. The first one dealt with a broad range of pharmaceutical products designated primarily for the domestic market. These included older products such as Globoid, Nyco Fruktsalt, a growing number of products licensed from Glaxo,[1] and Isopaque, which had continued to log Scandinavian sales. The second involved the sale of reagents on the international market. Nyegaard had succeeded reasonably well in Japan and Western Europe. Hospitals bought both Isopaque and the reagents.

---

[1] NFR, 15, Glaxo: many new contracts were signed after the Betnovat agreement in 1968.

Nyegaard had built this export organization gradually. It developed an organization for the reagents from 1959 onward and renewed the organization for Isopaque in the late 1960s. Glaxo never managed to build up substantial sales of Isopaque in Britain, its home market. Consequently, Nyegaard had built its own sales organization for the United Kingdom and Ireland.[2] It also created its own contrast media organization for Sweden and Denmark. As mentioned earlier in chapters 4 and 5, Erco represented Nyegaard in these two important markets and played an important role in establishing a network of radiologists, to the Norwegian firm's benefit. When, in the fall of 1967, Dutch Organon purchased Erco, however, a deep conflict emerged. Nyegaard feared Organon would take advantage of the inside knowledge of contrast media Erco had acquired from Nyegaard. After learning about this purchase through a third party in September 1967, Nyegaard cancelled its contract with Erco and simultaneously established its own subsidiaries in Sweden and Denmark. These soon became successful.

So too did the clinical trials with Amipaque through its own organization for Norway, Sweden, Denmark, and the British Isles. From 1970 to 1974, Nyegaard & Co. ran a comprehensive testing program, which in particular benefitted greatly from the experience of Swedish and Norwegian physicians. When, in April 1972, Amipaque progressed to the stage where it could be tested as a myelographic medium in human beings, Richard Gonsette in Belgium, Per Amundsen at Ullevål Hospital in Oslo, Arne Engeset at Oslo's National Hospital, and Professor Torgny Greitz of the Karolinska Institute in Stockholm supervised the first hospital tests.[3]

Amipaque proved to be an excellent myelographic X-ray contrast agent. By 1975, it had been tested on between 4,000 and 4,500 patients at 41 clinics in 9 countries, mainly in Norway, Sweden, and England. Nyegaard applied for registration in Norway and Sweden in February and March 1974, respectively; by November and December of the same year, first Sweden and then Norway registered Amipaque.[4] Registration followed quickly and the company also collaborated intensely with a group of prominent

[2] Interview with Svein Nilsen and Thor Andersen, January 31, 1993.
[3] NFR, 5, 2: "Metrizamid . . . historikk" by Leif G. Haugen, October 10, 1974; NKT, T, 580, Koord.kom: Holtermann to Rosenberg (SWRI), March 28, 1973, appendix to minutes of meeting, May 7, 1973.
[4] NFR, 5, 2: "Metrizamid . . . hist." by Leif G. Haugen, October 10, 1974; NKT, T, 580, Koord.kom: Holtermann to Rosenberg (SWRI), March 28, 1973, appendix to minutes of meeting, May 7, 1973 and meeting, April 1, 1974; ". . . kl.utpr. Amipaque" by L. Hol, Kamilla Dahlstrøm, and T. Renaa, April 22, 1975.

physicians in Scandinavia and internationally. In many ways, the Scandi-navian ecosystem of radiology and contrast media business played a central role in bringing this new product into use.

Moving from Scandinavia to the global market was still an enormous challenge. The two major contrast agents companies, Sterling Drug and Schering AG, were multinational enterprises, up to 100 times the size of Nyegaard & Co.[5] The Japanese market illustrated the challenge that faced Amipaque. After the United States, Japan was the world's largest market, with a population of more than 100 million. Schering AG's subsidiary, Nihon Schering, dominated in respect of contrast agents. While Nyegaard had 250 employees in the mid-1970s, Nihon Schering alone had more than 900, distributed among its headquarters in Osaka and 32 other offices in Japan.[6] Japanese radiologists had great confidence in *this* company.

Although the dominant players were far more powerful than Nyegaard, no single company had a global presence. Four contenders featured on "the world market," which, for pharmaceuticals, to a great degree was constituted by the four largest national markets, the United States, Japan, Germany, and Great Britain. Schering AG, with its formidable research fa-cilities, dominated the German and Japanese markets. It had subsidiaries in most of the western world, with the important exception of the United States. The US corporations Sterling Drug, Squibb, and Mallinckrodt dom-inated the US market. Squibb, a licensee of diatrizoate, had no important research activity in this field and only limited sales outside the United States. Sterling Drug had a global network of subsidiaries but did not sell in Japan or West Germany. Mallinckrodt was a major competitor in Japan and West Germany too through strong representatives (Dai-ichi in Japan, Byk-Gulden in West Germany). Mallinckrodt also worked with the French company Guerbet, which had just developed Dimer-X, a myelographic-directed product which would compete with Amipaque.

Nyegaard could not see a way to create its own marketing organization in countries like the United States and Japan. Furthermore, as the market for contrast agents was already well organized, it could be fatal to work with distributors who were not already well known. In Japan, the company Eisai

---

[5] Both enterprises had at some points of time in the period 1970–1980 more than 20,000 employees. Nyco had between 200 and 250 from 1970 to 1975: NFR, 15, Schering AG 1964–1981: ". . . Information about Schering . . ." approx. 1979–1980; NFR, 15, Sterling 1969–78: "Sterling Drug INC," PM by Olaf Bjørnson, April 1969.

[6] NFR, 15, Schering AG, 1964–1981: "Momenter fra møte hos Schering AG Berling" by Bjørn Holst, August 22, 1977.

marketed Nyegaard's coagulation reagents, but there were many uncertainties about the best way forward. In Europe, the company had Scandinavian
subsidiaries and a distribution network, but there were substantial uncertainties about Germany, France, and Southern Europe. The Swiss company
Cilag Chemie represented Nyegaard in the vast West German market, but
the arrangement had not been a success. Schering AG, with 60 percent
of the market in the mid-1970s and Byk-Gulden, with 30 percent, dominated Germany.[7] These companies had comprehensive links with German
radiologists, which in Schering AG's case dated back to the 1920s. In the
United States, Nyegaard had a promising dialogue with the contrast agent
company Sterling Drug.

In the spring of 1969, two nearly simultaneous incidents paved the way
for closer collaboration with Sterling Drug. First was the Amipaque innovation. Simultaneously, and officially unrelated, Sterling Drug applied to
register Isopaque for the US market.[8] Nyegaard realized then that Sterling
Drug might well be a successful partner in the marketing of Amipaque in
the world's largest market, the United States.

A channel leading to the world

Sterling Drug had a strong marketing network for X-ray contrast agents
in the United States and was represented in many other countries. Sterling
Drug also had broad technological insight into this field through its own
research and would probably be in a good position to gain FDA approval of
Amipaque and to communicate the importance of the new non-ionic concept to radiologists. The relationship with Sterling had developed gradually
since 1962, and since that first meeting Nyegaard had nurtured Sterling in
much the same way as Glaxo: as a partner who could help in its long-term
ambitions to become an independent, innovative pharmaceutical house.
Nyegaard originally contacted Sterling Drug to acquire production rights
to make Isopaque by the cheapest method. Prior to this request, Nyegaard
approached Schering AG, but due to the patent situation between Schering
AG and Sterling Drug, Schering could not grant Nyegaard this right. Nyegaard declined Schering AG's offer of selling relevant finished substance in
bulk from its production site in Germany instead, something it was willing

[7] Pr. 1977: NRBP, Amipaque, Schering AG 1977: Holst to Bjerke Paulssen and Svein Nilsen, March
8, 1977.
[8] NFR, 20, 20, II, SW 1970–1973: Thor Andersen to Cooke, October 13, 1970.

to do in return for extensive marketing rights to Isopaque in the United States and Germany, among other countries. Nyegaard wanted to maintain control of production and rather decided to approach Sterling Drug.[9]

In the course of two meetings, Nils and Ulf Blix and Olav Bjørnson achieved their goal.[10] In return, Sterling Drug was given the sole rights for (the original) Isopaque in the United States and non-exclusive rights in Canada and large areas of South America.[11] The agreement represented more than a straightforward exchange of rights. Sterling Drug thereby achieved control of a potentially competitive product in Isopaque. Given the state of play within the X-ray contrast media business, where Sterling and Schering had more or less divided the world market between them, Sterling's position was improved (de Haën, 2019: 140f). Just how much of a threat Isopaque actually represented in the hands of Schering AG is open to interpretation. Quite possibly, Schering AG questioned the viability of marketing the product in the United States. Anyway, the agreement between Sterling and Nyegaard protected Sterling's position on the US market.[12]

In retrospect, Nyegaard's managers were naïve. Did they believe that since the patent rights for Isopaque would last longer than they did for Hypaque and Renografin, Sterling Drug had an obvious interest in selling Isopaque in the United States? They must have hoped so. They acquired something—production rights on a product for which they had no international marketing organization to speak of—in exchange for marketing rights for a continent. But Sterling Drug was not only a partner in an asymmetric exchange. Nyegaard could also use the new contact as a means to understanding what was actually going on in the international contrast media business. As the relationship between Sterling Drug and Schering AG had shown after the court cases about diatrizoate were settled, the world's two leading contrast media companies communicated about business matters on a high level. For a small, and in this context poor company, forging

---

[9] NFR, 20, 20, Sverige-Tyskland, Schering 1958–1962: "Konferanse med Schering AG, Berlin den 11.juli 1961" by Olav Bjørnson; board meetings June 19 and October 18, 1961 and November 12, 1962.

[10] NFR, 20, 20, I W./SD: Nils Blix to Winthrop Products, March 26, 1962. Olav Bjørnson to Knut Sogner, August 7, 1992.

[11] NFR, 20, 20, I W./SD: Bjørnson to Winthrop Products, April 14, 1962; Moore to Bjørnson, May 11, 1962; Nils Blix to Winthrop Products, May 22, 1962; Wylie to Bjørnson, May 31, 1962 and June 13, 1962; Bjørnson to Wylie, June 18, 1962; Ulf Blix to Wylie, July 14, 1962; copy of Sterling PM "ISOPAQUE Patent Situation" by T. L. Johnson, April 9, 1963.

[12] NFR, 20, 20, I W./SD: copy of Sterling PM "ISOPAQUE Patent Situation" by T. L. Johnson, April 9, 1963.

alliances with these two companies possibly seemed like a much better option than competing with them.

This partnership strengthened greatly afterward. In 1965, Sterling gained the rights to use Nyegaard's patents for salt admixtures.[13] Simultaneously, the two companies renegotiated their association into a single comprehensive contract, and this included the provision that the two would cooperate if one of them were to develop a new contrast agent. In 1967, Sterling Drug decided to take advantage of its rights to market the improved Isopaque in the United States.[14] They discussed research collaboration in 1968 and 1969.[15] At the time, Sterling Drug did not do contrast agent research, something Nyegaard saw as an advantage for future contact between the companies—although not necessarily for contrast media research.[16]

Sterling Drug could market Amipaque on the huge US market. In October 1970, Nyegaard & Co. indeed aimed toward "a product with such superior characteristics that it will conquer at least 70 percent of the market, including the market in America."[17] In April 1969, Olav Bjørnson underlined his firm's hopes:

> From 1962 to 1969—many years have passed. But a satisfactory and consolidated alliance has been achieved, and many personal contacts have been established. A contract is a framework, a set of guidelines—but constructive cooperation is dependent upon personal contact and constant follow-up during virtually all of its phases. If we can do this, we have reason to look forward to satisfactory and very important results.[18]

Nyegaard's leaders needed to understand the inner workings of its new counterpart. What Sterling thought or did might differ from what its negotiator said. In 1971, Olav Bjørnson worried that Nyegaard's contacts at Sterling, although in high positions, might not have the final say when it came to selling Isopaque in the United States.[19] He was proved right, but this did not become apparent until many years later. When a Nyegaard employee visited Sterling Drug in the fall of 1971, Bjørnson was very precise

---

[13] Papers from Olav Bjørnson (with the author): "Rapport over konferanser med S-W over perioden 19.–28.4.67 av 23.5.67."

[14] Board meeting, October 19, 1965, January 18 and March 15, 1966; NFR, 15, Sterling 1969–1978: "Sterling Drug Inc.," PM by Olav Bjørnson, April 1969.

[15] NFR, 15, Sterling 1969–1978: "Sterling Drug Inc.," PM by Olav Bjørnson, April 1969; NFR, 15, f-samarbeide SW: Holtermann to Ulf Blix, February 20, 1969.

[16] Interview with Ulf Blix, November 24, 1992.

[17] NKT, 606, FoU: PM by Holtermann, October 22, 1970.

[18] NFR, 15, Sterling 1969–1978: "Sterling Drug Inc.," PM by Olav Bjørnson, April 1969.

[19] NFR, 20, 20, II, SW 1970–1973: Bjørnson to Dahlstrøm, September 3, 1971.

about what the individual should learn: "The more information you can get about the hierarchy, and the more contacts, the better it will be."[20] In the early summer of 1972, when Nyegaard first told Sterling about Amipaque, the Norwegian company had laid the proper groundwork and knew a great deal about the key personnel in Sterling Drug's organization.[21]

Nyegaard evaluated Sterling continuously. Nils Blix reminded Olav Bjørnson in May 1973 that: "From time to time, letters arrive with 'small jolts' about Sterling Winthrop's marketing methods in different areas—as recently as today, from Johnson & Johnson in Brazil. There is probably no reason to assume that they are any better in other contract areas."[22] Johnson & Johnson wanted to sell Isopaque in Brazil and informed Nyegaard that Sterling Drug made no effort to sell Isopaque, despite official statements to the contrary. In fact, Sterling sold its own product, Hypaque. Johnson & Johnson said: "There has been no commercial activity with respect to ISOPAQUE in the Brazilian market."[23]

Nyegaard did not see such cases as impediments to an agreement for selling Amipaque. The company had long been aware that Sterling's international organization was not performing well enough on its behalf.[24] Sterling Drug's organization in the United States was, however, the attraction, and Nyegaard had close and trusting relationships with key employees there. In June 1972, Olav Bjørnson talked to one of them, who admitted that Sterling tried to keep Isopaque off the market. Bjørnson emphasized this openness as positive rather than focusing on the underlying problem.[25]

In the spring of 1973, Nyegaard signed contract options with Sterling Drug for the sale of Amipaque in the United States, South America, Central America, Canada, France, Italy, the Philippines, Australia, and South Africa, among other countries.[26] The thorough and complex knowledge Nyegaard had about Sterling's organization was essential to the finalization of these arrangements. Nyegaard placed its trust in Sterling's US organization. Marketing Amipaque as a myelographic medium made the choices of finding representatives easier. Amipaque was a niche product that did not compete with Hypaque. Mallinckrodt had its own product coming

---

[20] Ibid.

[21] NFR, 20, 20, II, SW 1970–1973: Bjørnson to Rosenberg, June 30, 1972 and Bjørnson to William Heike Jr, June 30, 1972.

[22] NFR, 20, 20, II, SW 1970–1973: Nils Blix to Olav Bjørnson, May 7, 1973.

[23] NFR, 20, 20, II, SW 1970–1973: Johnson & Johnson (Brasil) to Nyegaard & Co., April 30, 1973.

[24] NFR, 22, 29: "Isopaque i USA og i deres internasjonale områder" by Kamilla Dahlstrøm, September 27, 1971.

[25] NUB: ". . . reise til USA juni 1972" by Olav Bjørnson, June 19, 1972.

[26] NKT, T, 580, Koord.kom: minutes of meeting, April 3, 1973.

along. Squibb could have been an option, but Squibb was Schering AG's partner. Collaboration with a known entity, where there existed personal relationships between key people, was as much assurance as Nyegaard could get.

A feared partner

Nyegaard & Co. did not rush into establishing a complete marketing network. It contacted Sterling Drug when Amipaque entered clinical testing in the spring of 1972. By the end of 1973, only the partners for marketing in the areas covered by the Sterling contract and Nyegaard's own European export channels were chosen.[27] No arrangements had been made for West Germany and Japan, the largest markets after the United States.

Amipaque's first difficulty surfaced unexpectedly in Japan. Sterling Drug had previously helped to arrange a contact with the company Torii, which marketed Isopaque in Japan. Torii had previous experience with myelographic agents from its sales of a US iodinated oil, Pantopaque. Since Amipaque had been received elsewhere as a fantastic new product, Torii's negative opinion in September 1974 came as a surprise.[28]

Torii saw no need for an exclusively myelographic agent like Amipaque and concluded that selling it would not be profitable. Since the Japanese government required Japanese documentation, the registration process alone would take four or five years and require huge organizational and financial resources. In addition, Torii did not believe Amipaque could achieve the same price level it seemed to be able to enjoy in Europe. Torii thought that prices for the existing myelographic agents would determine Amipaque's price. When Nyegaard asked its distributor of reagents, Eisai, to market Amipaque in Japan, the answer was the same (although it was a source of internal disagreement). As soon became apparent, neither of the Japanese companies correctly read the market.[29]

In June 1974, Schering AG approached Nyegaard & Co. about selling its new product. Nyegaard was hesitant. It feared Schering's tremendous

[27] NKT, T, 580, Koordinasjonskomitéen: Bjørnson to Metrizamidkomitéen v/Preparatsjef Odd Fr. Ekfelt, November 22, 1973.

[28] NFR, 15, Torii: Bjørnson to Tsuji, September 24, 1974; Bjørnson to Tsuji, November 27, 1974; Akazawa to Bjørnson, May 13, 1975; NFR, 22, 82: "Rapport fra besøk i Tokyo" by Carl Christian Gilhuus Moe, March 8–14, 1975.

[29] NFR, 22, 82: "Rapport fra besøk i Tokyo" by Carl Christian Gilhuus Moe, March 8–14, 1975; NFR, 15, Torii: Akazawa to Bjørnson, May 13, 1975; ". . . reise til Japan og Hong Kong" by Carl Christian Gilhuus Moe and Svein Nilsen, May 28–June 13, 1976.

influence on the market; it had virtually swept Isopaque and the distributor Cilag Chemie out of West Germany. Nyegaard would have preferred Byk-Gulden as its Amipaque distributor in West Germany; however, Byk-Gulden sold the competing product Dimer-X.[30] Schering AG also wanted sales rights in many other markets, as well as further technological collaboration. Nyegaard first agreed to give Schering AG's exclusive rights for West Germany, similar to Sterling Drug's contract in the United States. Nyegaard delivered the substance in glass vials, and Schering launched Amipaque in Germany as early as May 1976. The registration proved quick and efficient with the German authorities, thanks to Nyegaard's thorough preparatory work. Schering AG expressed admiration for the way in which the documentation had been amassed in such a short time by Nyegaard.[31] Schering AG subsequently also got the task of selling Amipaque in Japan. Nihon Schering became Nyegaard's Japanese representative. It had nationwide coverage, in a country second only to West Germany for Schering's sales of X-ray contrast agents.[32] Unfortunately, Japanese authorities required additional national testing and delayed Amipaque's registration until 1980.[33] Nevertheless, forging these marketing relations under uncertainty was one of the greatest challenges Nyegaard's top management faced in the beginning of the 1970s, and its completion reflected the increased confidence in Amipaque's uniqueness and its increased chances of real commitment from foreign representatives.

A collective approach

Although the changes in the beginning of the 1960s put Nyegaard on a path to change, the deeper and more profound cultural changes had commenced with the salt experiments of Isopaque and continued throughout the process of launching Ampiaque. A rather hierarchical company increasingly emerged as a collectivized and flexible organization depending on a highly educated staff. The Norwegian pharmaceutical industry owed its hierarchical structure in part to its national role as part of the supply

[30] Interview with Svein Nilsen, January 20, 1993 and Ulf Blix, November 30, 1993.
[31] Borrowed from Kamilla Dahlstrøm: minutes from meeting with Schering AG, December 11, 1974; NFR, 15, Schering AG. kont: Bjørnson to Schering AG, December 20, 1974; minutes from meeting Nyco–Schering, January 30, 1975; NRBP, Amipaque, Schering AG 1977: "Besøk hos Schering AG, Berlin 28. April 1976" by L. Hol.
[32] NFR, 15, Schering AG. kontr: meeting, Nyco–Schering, January 17, 1977; NFR, 15, Schering AG. 1964–1981: "Momenter fra møte hos Schering AG Berling" by Bjørn Holst, August 22, 1977.
[33] NFR, 15, Schering AG.kontratsforh./utkast: meeting, Nyco–Schering, January 17, 1977.

system. It emerged in tight communication with the authorities. Sverre Blix additionally shaped a financially steered company which aligned well with the hierarchical approach. Blix built Nyegaard as a paternalistic company too. He brought in competent co-workers on all levels and initiated pension plans, health services, and sports activities. In effect, he built a closed company. He gave employees little information about administrative policy. Nyegaard was small enough to allow a general overview of company activities, and the fact that employees did not have precise details of the previous month's sales was no cause for concern. Some changes came gradually, while others, such as the company's concentration on Thrombotest and Isopaque, came more abruptly and methodically.

The pressure from more innovative pharmaceutical companies to better control their export doubly and suddenly challenged Nyegaard in 1967. Organon's takeover of Erco, as discussed earlier, represented a tremendous challenge. Nyegaard did not know what to do, and setting up its own export organization was a high-risk matter for such a small and inexperienced organization. At about the same time, Schering Corporation, Nyegaard's most important licensor, demanded better sales efforts and laid claim to a larger percentage of the profit. Nyegaard had no desire to comply with these new demands even though Schering's products were important to the company. Manufacturing Schering Corporation products helped to secure Nyegaard & Co.'s financial foundation. In 1967, its marketing department invested nearly 75 percent of its time on Schering products, sales of which increased to about 10 percent of total operating revenues.[34] Nevertheless, the company declined to comply with Schering's demand for a new contractual agreement and let it expire. The company held a firm line and later learned that Schering Corporation would have been prepared to compromise if Nyegaard had shown greater willingness to negotiate.[35]

Determined to remain independent at any cost, the firm banked on having the best contacts in the Norwegian market. It worked to consolidate this position by expanding cooperation with Glaxo. When the Schering contract expired on January 1, 1969, Nyegaard lost many good products, although for the most important one, Celestoderm, an identical Glaxo product called Betnovat proved an excellent replacement.[36] The sales of

---

[34] Minutes of board meeting, March 22, 1968.
[35] As told by Thor Andersen, November 23, 1993.
[36] NFR, 15, Schering: Nils Blix to all employees, November 4, 1968.

Betnovat indicated that Norwegian physicians had confidence in their home-grown business and its products.[37]

The problems with Erco and Schering Corporation were dramatic at the time.[38] Both cases triggered hectic meeting activity and unusually extensive discussions at the board meetings.[39] That both events happened suddenly and simultaneously increased the danger in the situation. If both of them were to go wrong, the consequences for Nyegaard & Co. would be disastrous. The drama reflected a Scandinavian restructuring. The market was changing, and in Norway "patented medicines, imported as finished products, have taken over a large portion of the market."[40] The share of domestically produced medicines sold in Norway, by value, decreased from 45 percent in 1959 to 31 percent in 1969.[41] Both Nyegaard and Erco felt pressured, but they reacted differently. Erco lost many contracts with large, foreign companies in the 10 years up to 1967.[42] By selling out to Organon, Erco surrendered as an independent company. Its answer to the new situation was to prioritize Organon and become its sales arm. Nyegaard's position reflected its leaders' resolve to remain active and independent. It maintained a strong position in the Norwegian market by taking a firm stand against Schering and deepening its relationship with Glaxo. Simultaneously, it established marketing organizations in Sweden and Denmark.

In the process, Nyegaard changed. The major and invisible response to the outside challenges was organizational development in the direction of collective responsibility by allowing competent staff freer and more responsible opportunities for influence. Nils Blix had already moved in this direction as early as 1961. He delegated responsibility with considerable skill. Economist Odd Heggim, who joined the staff in the mid-1960s, appreciated being trusted and listened to. Blix encouraged independent thinking.[43] Personnel Manager Rolf Horn emphasized that Nils Blix was genuinely concerned about informing all employees about company activities.[44] He initiated "information evenings" in 1961, a forum which met

---

[37] As told by Rolf Bjerke Paulssen, August 24, 1993.
[38] Interview with Thor Andersen, September 21, 1992, Bjørn Sinding-Larsen, December 10, 1991, and Odd Heggim, August 12, 1992.
[39] Board meetings, September 20, November 6 and 29, 1967 and March 22, 1968.
[40] HD, AkH7, Q58, 1964–1968: Nomi (Lister) to Industridepartementet, December 12, 1966.
[41] Dagbladet, February 2, 1971.
[42] NADM, Erco, 218: "Voldgiftsdom" by Supreme Court lawyers Brunsvig, Dæhlin, and Løken, March 31, 1970.
[43] Interview with Odd Heggim, August 12, 1992.
[44] Interview with Rolf Horn, November 30, 1992.

every two or three years.[45] Although sporadic, the meetings represented an important innovation for a privately owned joint-stock company that had not hitherto shared much information.

In early 1967, this new policy of openness became more pronounced. At the information meeting in February, members of top management presented details about company finances, and revenue. They asked for confidentiality. Nils Blix also outlined an export strategy that accepted the loss of Norwegian market share to be replaced by increased exports. Management also announced that the new Employee Committee, a result of an agreement between the Norwegian Federation of Trade Unions (LO) and the Norwegian Employers' Confederation (NAF), would have a special profile at Nyegaard & Co. By regulation, the Committee was to have five representatives from administration and five from the employees, but Nyegaard's management gave up one of its allotted places so that each of the company's six employee categories could be represented. This emphasized the management's determination to consider input from the entire company.[46] Two years later, Nils Blix very clearly stated the same objectives and challenges:

> In the first place, we have become very aware of the necessity to be on constant guard against situations that can put us in a position of being dominated by foreign companies. Secondly, re-gathering our forces can be wise after so many consecutive years of progress. This makes it necessary to evaluate our objectives and our strategies carefully.[47]

Nils Blix maintained that although Nyegaard had stagnated on the Norwegian market, there was still hope: "We can be proud of our steadily increasing exports, which may become in the future a 'to be or not to be' situation for us."[48] The speech represented a new form of communication with employees in general and middle management in particular. By 1969, top management organized larger annual meetings to inform participants about the company's financial status and to invite contributions to

---

[45] N., Pers.avd, Pdir, Info-aftener fra 1964: meetings, June 28, 1961, October 7, 1964, February 28, 1967, February 18, 1969, and February 2, 1971.
[46] N, Pers.avd, Pdir, Info-aftener fra 1964: meeting, February 28, 1967.
[47] N, Pers.avd, Pdir, Info-aftener fra 1964: meeting, February 18, 1969.
[48] Ibid.

Table 6.1 Operating revenues of product areas,
1966 and 1970 in million kroner; fixed prices:
1985=100 (SSB consumer price index)

	1966	1970
Pharmaceuticals	102	76
Reagents	15	23
Contrast agents	8	19
Total income	125	118

Source: Nycomed.

discussions about the future. These exchanges influenced the daily work in the company.[49]

Nils and Ulf Blix had more or less grown up inside and with the company. They knew their employees through many years of collaboration and felt secure enough to show them a new element of trust. And change worked. Losing Schering's products did result in lower pharmaceutical sales (see Table 6.1) on the domestic market. 1969 was expected to be a catastrophic year because of the loss of those products,[50] but the financial results turned out to be excellent. The company adjusted successfully to the new situation both at home and abroad. From 1966 to 1970, operating revenues in fixed prices were almost stagnant, but export revenue increased from 20 to 32 percent of turnover. Reagents and contrast media (with the advantages of the salt admixtures) consequently had a similar increase in sales. The Netherlands also became a decent market for contrast media in these years.[51] Both Paul Owren and Lorentz Eldjarn continued to develop new reagents to be sold through established international marketing channels.[52]

The new collective leadership style came at a time when the company faced challenges which were met by top management in closer cooperation with employees. It increasingly leaned on ideas from middle and lower management and from external sources in an entirely new way. And along the way, quite possibly, it looked harder for ways to improve the fortunes

[49] Interview with Odd Kåre Strandli, October 2, 1992; Hugo Holtermann and Leif G. Haugen, July 14, 1993; NFR, 15, O: "Referat fra Elingaard-møte," May 24–28, 1970.
[50] Board meeting, December 20, 1968.
[51] NFR, 20, 20, Pharmachemie: "Isopaque-situasjonen i Holland" by Kamilla Dahlstrøm; NFR, 20, 20, Belgia: "Rapport fra konferanse med Delforge" by Olav Bjørnson, February 7 and 8, 1969.
[52] NFR, 22, 65: "Sales of Thrombotest" by Thor Andersen, May 6, 1970; NFR, 22, 9: "div. oversikter," 1970.

of the company and to have something of value to say. Nyegaard & Co. had come to resemble a large family[53]—for good and bad.

The formation of an ethical profile

Going wholeheartedly into new pharmaceuticals demanded much more of the whole organization than before. Dealing with original drugs meant dealing with entities that always—and especially at the beginning of their life—needed to be deeply and thoroughly understood for their chemical properties and their effect in the body. They had to be critically investigated from several angles. People working with pharmaceuticals needed to take a responsible attitude and help understand and define the products. That meant complying with an ethical code. Nyegaard developed a new awareness for such ethical responsibility during the 1960s.

The new focus on ethical codes emerged as a consequence of the Thalidomide tragedy. When a substance could be developed, tested, and approved by an official regulatory agency without its serious side effects being discovered, there was good reason to re-evaluate current practice. The scandal led to criticism of the industry in general. A second source of the criticism of the day was the age-old skepticism about combining financial profit and medicinal products. The pharmaceutical industry's large profits provoked unease, as did incidents of medicines not approved in industrial countries being sold in countries with low living standards.

Nyegaard & Co.'s regular contact with physicians made it aware of the industry's negative image. Olav Bjørnson assumed responsibility for developing the company's ethical profile, and the two aforementioned symposiums about Isopaque in 1964 and 1966 proved important learning experiences not only for actual research but also for ethical considerations. The Swedish radiologists demanded published documentation of the improvements made on the product, written by independent experts.[54] When critique of Isopaque came in the first international symposium in Denmark in 1964, Olav Bjørnson described how instructive this was: "We do *not* have the world's best contrast agent; this is the

---

[53] Thor Andersen on several occasions.
[54] NFR, 21, div.rkm: report, February 11, 1963 (Assoc. Prof. Andrén, Malmø); Olav Bjørnson in interview, February 11, 1991.

cold and hard conclusion that we should reach from the symposium."[55] However, many of the participants admired the fact that Nyegaard had not tried to conceal the results of its Isopaque evaluations.[56] This attitude worked to the enterprise's advantage in its later contacts with Scandinavian radiologists.[57] At the next symposium, in Sandefjord in 1966, the impression of Isopaque was much improved.[58] The meeting was a great success, confirmed both by the product and new-found trust relations.

One tactic for gaining the confidence of physicians was to ask leading members of the medical profession to publish articles and to speak about the company's pharmaceutical products. The results of Nyegaard's conferences on Isopaque in 1961, 1964. and 1966 were all published. *Farmakoterapi*, Nyegaard's journal, published the first conference papers, and the findings from 1964 and 1966 appeared as supplement to the independent professional journal *Acta Radiologica Diagnosis* (Acta Radiologica, 1967). In 1967, Nyegaard & Co. established a clinical department to coordinate work on Norwegian and foreign clinical tests and to ensure that the documentation was published.

Nyegaard consciously developed a stringent ethical attitude regarding pharmaceutical documentation. Olav Bjørnson wrote to Norwegian newspapers, reminding the public of the importance of the pharmaceutical industry and the dangers of not having an ethical standpoint. Like officialdom and physicians, industry had to assume responsibility for its own actions:

> Has the new pharmaceutical product withstood the complexities of purity tests, toxicological and pharmacodynamic testing that prove their harmlessness in effective doses? Have all the tests that are considered necessary been made, and are their results interpreted in compliance with scientific principles and reported fully and truthfully? This responsibility must be assumed by the industry, which should discuss it with the health authorities in order to ensure that it is carried out correctly.

> Bjørnson (1968)

---

[55] NFR, 20, 1, reiser, England: Bjørnson to Nils Blix, November 19, 1964.

[56] Ibid.

[57] NFR, 21, div.ang.rkm: report, May 20, 1963 by Kamilla Dahlstrøm (from Sweden); report, May 20, 1963 by same (from Denmark); report, February 11, 1963 (Assoc. Prof. Andrén, Malmø); report, October 22, 1965 (Dr Lindaker and Dr Hansen, RH); NFR, 20, 21, rkm, Konf.1963/74: minutes from "Radiologkonsulentmøtet," September 10, 1965; minutes from meetings in Stockholm January 2–25, 1965; interview with Kamilla Dahlstrøm and Kari Sveen, August 29, 1992.

[58] Personal communication Olav Bjørnson, December 15, 1993.

These key lessons from the Thalidomide scandal stood out: gaining sufficient knowledge of a specific medication was extremely complicated and the problem could not be solved within a single scientific discipline or by a single institution. Understanding pharmaceuticals necessitated collaboration across disciplines and between institutions. Basic ethical requirements for *reporting the truth* had to be established, standards which industry should observe.

Bjørnson in part responded to signals from the medical profession. Government practice also moved in the same direction. Very quickly after the Thalidomide situation, the United States adopted stricter pharmaceutical regulations. The 1962 Drug Amendments established a control authority for all clinical testing in the nation. The drugs needed not only to be safe but also effective, and they had to be be produced under specific standards and subject to federal inspection. The US control agency, the FDA, was allocated additional staff and given broader interventional authority (Temin, 1980: 120–126).

The stringency of the new regulations was due in part to the fact that the Thalidomide case had been the subject of Senate hearings. Senator Estes Kefauver strongly criticized the industry for profiteering and for selling products that it should have known to be ineffective even as the serious side effects of Thalidomide were becoming public knowledge. The United States was one of the few countries that had not approved Thalidomide for clinical use. But the United States did not have suitable legislation for the testing of unapproved pharmaceuticals, and a number of children were born with deformities caused by Thalidomide. The Kefauver hearings had been losing their momentum just as the side effects of this drug became public. The hearings gained a new importance, and the resulting legislation dealt with far more than the testing of pharmaceutical products (Temin, 1980).

The United States' stringent legislation influenced developments in the European Free Trade Association (EFTA) countries. A group of companies organized as the Pharmaceutical Industries Association of EFTA (PIA) also helped develop stricter legislation for pharmaceutical production. The association believed it important to establish one, and only one, international set of laws. If legislation were to be tied to supranational inspection routines, duplication of plant inspections could be avoided. This would be both practical and economical and would prevent industrial espionage. By linking inspection to standardized production rules, the industry would meet the requirements of the most demanding nations.[59] In 1968, four years before EFTA, PIA adopted its own standards for good manufacturing procedures (Bjørnson, 1974: 42).

EFTA passed conventions on mutual inspection and uniform production procedures in 1971 and 1972. Norway thus committed to follow Basic Standards of Good Manufacturing Practices (GMP) regulations, and to support a mutual inspection system for companies that produced pharmaceutical products. Inspection of British production by British authorities was also valid for Norwegian authorities if the products were to be registered in Norway. The GMP system called for changes in production systems and made a number of stipulations about production facilities, equipment, hygiene, documentation, procedures, organization structure, and quality control.[60] PIA's direct role within EFTA was evidently influential in the European coordination of the new, stricter requirements triggered by the Thalidomide tragedy.

Industry reacted immediately to the Thalidomide affair, aiming in principle to set its own affairs in order, to win essential public confidence. Olav Bjørnson started from this situation. He brought an ethical dimension to the quality control process as a way of handling the criticism levelled at pharmaceuticals. His objective was an ethical code for industry that would parallel the professional ethics of physicians and pharmacists. Bjørnson also played a key role in international circles. He believed that industry had a definite responsibility for its actions and that elements in European industry were not complying with this ethical code. After attending a major seminar in 1969, Bjørnson related his thoughts to management at Nyegaard. He summarized the criticism of the pharmaceutical industry and gave his opinion about what had gone wrong:

> It seems that the industry's marketing methods are being spoiled by a number of practices, such as careless information about product applicability in an attempt to promote sales. This was documented by some of the members of the panel as well as from the floor, concerning a few—certainly not insignificant—pharmaceutical companies on the Continent. On this last point, I believe that the pharmaceutical industry still has a good deal to learn.[61]

---

[59] NAFI, 741, PIA, Prot. 1966–1972: "Summary . . . Plenary Meeting of PIA," June 7, 1966, p. 15.
[60] NFR, 17, B, 2. skuff. Industri: "Perspektivanalyse for norsk farmasøytisk industri," October 1974.
[61] NFR, 15, Rapporter, Sveits: Intern, "Rapport fra Symposium on the impact of Drug Legislation on the Drug Industry," Rüschlikon, by Olav Bjørnson, August 28–29, 1969.

Bjørnson worked to improve the entire pharmaceutical industry, was the president of PIA for some time, and in this capacity continued to make the industry's responsibility an issue.[62]

In the course of the 1960s, Nyegaard developed a clear ethical profile. This was a consequence of the pressure the entire industry was under and may also have been inspired by the professional ethical position that physicians and pharmacists for a long time had sought and experienced. Nyegaard's actions also reflected the scientific perspective that had characterized major sections of the company since the end of the Second World War. The company's operations developed in close association with disciplines such as pharmacy, medicine, and chemistry. For this reason, the company could better recognize when science needed the support of an ethical code.

Norwegian regulation principles eroded

Contrary to what seems logical, Nyegaard's ethical profile was not really a consequence of its embeddedness in the Norwegian innovation system. That is not to say that the firm's ethical profile did not resonate with its Norwegian surroundings. It did. But the Norwegian innovation system— the regulatory arm of it—did not develop these new standards in quite the same stringent way as other countries. Nyegaard's ethical attitude reflected its international and scientific orientation.

Support for a clear ethical focus was, of course, widespread in Norway in the aftermath of the Thalidomide scandal. Measures taken after that tragedy were far more stringent in the United States than in Norway because the FDA was a more influential agency than the Proprietary Medicines Board. The Norwegian regulatory scope exceeded that of the United States by a huge margin and in theory could control the use of drugs through a number of measures. In the United States, the distribution of pharmaceuticals was not controlled the way it was in Norway, so the FDA function as a scientific and ethical gatekeeper was of fundamental importance to the US pharmaceutical market. Nevertheless, changes gradually appeared in Norway and Sweden. Both countries required more exacting documentation for new pharmaceutical products.[63] However, Norway

---

[62] NAFI, 741, PIA, Prot. 1966–1972: "Summary . . . PIA," March 2, 1970, p. 7; borrowed from Olav Bjørnson: "Welcome address during the banquet" at joint GIIP/PIA meeting, October 5 and 6, 1972.
[63] Interview with Kamilla Dahlstrøm and Kari Sveen, August 29, 1992.

found the change from control by professionals to extensive scientifically motivated procedures difficult.

The professional approach remained at the core of the Norwegian regulations, as became abundantly clear when the Director General of Health in 1964 opposed the idea of an appeals forum for decisions made in the Proprietary Medicines Board. Karl Evang summarized the situation based on professional judgment:

> When one finds it absolutely necessary to disagree with an appeals institution that could review both the formal and professional aspects of a case, it is due primarily to the fact [. . .] that in a country like ours, it is not practical to establish a professional (medical) agency that has greater professional authority than that which the Director General of Health and his special board of experts represent. If this were possible, it would in fact imply that the Health Director had neglected his duty to obtain the most competent professional counsel.[64]

This professional authority gave the Director General of Health strict control and also implicitly accorded individual physicians strong influence on areas not subject to official regulation. Evang's argument was explicitly set in a national context, and other countries handled approval procedures in different ways. By 1964, Sweden had determined that each product to be clinically tested had to be reported to the State Pharmaceutical Laboratory for initial approval. Sweden was close on the heels of the new US system. The objective was to protect patients (Liljestrand and Norlander, 1970: 1204), an aim certainly motivated by the Thalidomide case. Norway lagged behind (Skobba, 1970: 6–9). In 1971, Professor Knut Næss at Oslo University's Department of Pharmacotherapy harshly criticized the Norwegian government's omissions in regard to issues such as side effects and clinical testing of new medications:

> The principle has been to allow for a free interplay of forces, with direct contact between companies and physicians, without any single agency knowing about, or having a record of past events. In addition, the tests have not been subjected to any form of control, even though they have dealt with testing products that were not yet registered, i.e. that had not yet been evaluated and approved by any national agency
>
> (Næss, 1971: 1961f).

---

[64] HD, H7, Q10 1964–1968: note by Evang, May 13, 1964.

In February 1977, under the auspices of the Norwegian Medicines Control Authority, preliminary governmental evaluation of clinical testing
was established.[65] The Investigative New Drug Applications Law which
covered testing on human beings was not passed, however, until 1981
(Odelsting-Bill-No. 71, 1980–1981). The Norwegian system had long been
based on a high degree of trust in the country's individual physicians.
They had, slowly, opened up to roles for pharmacists in regulatory positions, but seemingly as a group, led by Evang, they rather focused on
the possible inadequacies of the industry than their own shortcomings.
An illustrative example appeared in the aftermath of the Swedish nationalization effort around 1970. Sweden had—unlike Norway—already
introduced much stricter regulation on clinical trials. When the Swedish
Social Democrats arranged for the Swedish state to take over the pharmaceutical company Kabi (as well as all pharmacies), the Norwegian Labour
Party reacted quickly and wanted to evaluate if Norway too should have
greater public control over medicinal supply. A special committee was set
up that included such prominent members as former minister of Social
Affairs Gudmund Harlem and future Director General of Health Torbjørn
Mork. They saw the situation pretty much the same way as the Swedish
Social Democrats: "The committee also thinks that one should evaluate
government take-over of one or more pharmaceutical firms, and complete
nationalization of the pharmacies."[66] The committee was expressly concerned about expansion of foreign industry on the Norwegian market. The
authorities, they feared, were losing control of the market.[67]

The Labour Party initiative was a response to the international situation
and was characterized by massive criticism of the industry's ethical standards. However, it seems to have been more a reflection of the original
Kefauver hearings than the Thalidomide issue; its criticism aimed more
toward the profits and motives of private industry than toward scientific
fallibility. The answer to scientific fallibility would not necessarily be more
governmental control or more public administration but new procedures
that would control the element of human failure more efficiently, regardless
of the form of ownership.

Industry, nevertheless, felt the pressure. In a debate at the Association
of Industrial Pharmacists in the spring of 1971, Torbjørn Mork met strong

[65] Hd, N140, 1976–1983: SLK (Halse) to H-direktøren, December 4, 1978.

[66] NFR, 17, C2: "Produksjon, omsetning og kontroll av legemidler" by Edvardsen, Gudmund
Harlem, Torbjørn Mork, Nordbø og Skobba.

[67] *Dagbladet*, February 2, 1971.

opposition. In the Oslo newspaper *Dagbladet*, Nyegaard's Olav Bjørnson defended the industry in two feature articles.[68] Bjørnson described the ethical role the industry had taken and said that the pharmaceutical companies in European Economic Community (EEC) and EFTA countries contributed to the standardization of national regulations that applied to Norway too.[69] Although the Norwegian Need Clause and price controls conflicted with the stipulated principles, Norway insisted on keeping both because of its national health policy.

Norway's insistence on retaining its own national procedures was awkward when international agreements increasingly took more consideration of health than Norwegian ones. As the Head Pharmacist in the Directorate of Health, Bjørn Jøldal, pointed out in 1971, pharmaceutical control in Norway was inconsistent:

> We often maintain that the Proprietary Medicines Board is among the most rigid in the world, but this "rigidity" applies mainly to the Need Clause and a general restraint in terms of registering parallel products. In terms of quality control of products that are already on the market, for example, much has been left undone.[70]

Close attention was paid internationally to quality control follow-up from the early 1960s. As the World Health Organization noted, it was "a difficult or even impossible task for a government control laboratory to examine and analyze every batch of every pharmaceutical preparation in the world" (WHO, 1962). Nor could follow-up quality control discover every characteristic of a product, such as its stability over time. A clearly defined set of production regulations was thus essential to establish. Industry within EFTA had been working on such rules, but they came as a shock to the pharmacies, Norwegian industry's long-time competitors.

EFTA's regulations caused a problem for the governmental control system in Norway. The pharmacies could not comply with the new production requirements. Each pharmacy had the traditional right to produce all of its own pharmacy-manufactured medications. But production gradually became centralized after the mid-1950s, as some pharmacies began to specialize and sell their products to others. In the 1960s, nearly all such

[68] NFR, 17, B, 2. skuff. Foredrag HH: minutes from meeting, April 22, 1971; *Dagbladet*'s chronicles, January 20 and February 24, 1971.
[69] NFR, 17, B, 2. skuff. Farm.Industri: "Organisasjonsmessig internasjonalt samarbeid ..." by unknown author, March 15, 1966.
[70] Hd, Ak, F, 301: Bjørn Jøldal to Helsedirektøren, January 6, 1971.

production was centered in five specific pharmacies.[71] But as Pharmacy Inspector Gunnar Hopp stated in 1970, pharmacies were far from being able to satisfy the new requirements for production:

> Inspection of the present production pharmacies has left me with the professional knowledge that none of the facilities are of a satisfactory professional level. [. . .] I could go so far as to say that when evaluated on the basis of present production conditions at the present pharmacy facilities, certain expressed wishes to increase production bear witness to a lack of responsibility in terms of the quality of the products being offered, and a general lack of understanding the gravity of the situation.[72]

This provided the impetus for the decision of the Norwegian Association of Proprietor Pharmacists to establish its own manufacturing facilities, NAF-Laboratoriene A/S, in April 1970. The Directorate of Health wanted the same regulations for pharmacies and industry. When NAF suggested that industry would have an easier time than pharmacies, it was contradicted: "Jøldal replied [. . .] that when it came to Norwegian industry, there is the same inspection control as for pharmacies [. . .] Pharmaceutical production should meet the same requirements, wherever it takes place."[73] The pharmacists' production facility at Elverum started operating in 1975 and gradually took over production for the individual pharmacies.[74] With this, extensive production activity in both large and small pharmacies ceased.

No one could foresee what the final outcome of these new regulatory developments would be, and industry went through years of uncertainty. The establishment of a production facility for pharmacies, especially at a time when the Labour Party was considering nationalizing pharmacies and taking over one or more industrial companies, led industry to fear that Norway would end up with a system similar to Sweden's. Norges Medisinindustriforening (NOMI), the industry's professional organization, and the successor to No-Fa-Ki, asked Supreme Court attorney Jens Bugge to prepare a written report on the issue of nationalization.[75]

---

[71] Hd, Legemiddelavd . . . 454.41: proposition of March 8, 1985 about production at Norwegian pharmacies (by working group).
[72] Hd, H7, J3a pr.apotek 1970–1972: note to H-dir., January 14, 1970.
[73] Hd, H7, J3a pr.apotek 1970–1972: minutes of meeting between H-dir., NAF, L-apotekene and Pr.nemda for L-apotekene, June 10, 1970.
[74] Hd, Legemiddelavd . . . 454.41: proposition of March 8, 1985 about production of Norwegian pharmacies (by working group).
[75] Interview with Rolf Bjerke Paulssen, October 9, 1992. Borrowed from Bjerke Paulssen: "En vurdering av statsinngrep mot den farmasøytiske industri i Norge" by Jens Bugge, October 1973.

In the long run, developments in Norway finally worked to industry's advantage. Nothing came of the nationalization threat. Norwegian politics proved strikingly powerless. The change immediately after 1970 did not so much affect industry as it did the position long held by physicians and pharmacies. The absence of more rigid controls prior to the 1970s can well be explained by the strength of these professions in Norway. Their professional standards and ethics permeated the state apparatus of Norway, which gave them a blind eye to their shortcomings when pharmaceutics evolved as an intricate field built on a broad scientific basis.

Change came through pressure from outside sources. Information about ethical practice—rooted in the challenge of scientific complexity—and obligatory legislation for increased safety in the use of pharmaceuticals came from abroad. Sweden took patient safety very seriously in the testing of medications, and EFTA set safety requirements for production which Norwegian pharmacies found impossible to follow. Norwegian industry, however, could meet the EFTA requirements. Through the PIA, the Norwegian industry was instrumental in making demands for new legislation. Its viewpoint reflected its deep commitment to science.

The Norwegian system of pharmaceutical regulation was internationalized in about 1970, and at the same time the strong position held by physicians and pharmacies was exposed. Their domain seemed too secure in the light of the need to tighten requirements for patient safety. Their entrenched position also reflected the basic national orientation of the Norwegian state apparatus. From the early 1970s, however, the regulatory system was increasingly supported by a new logic: most of the pharmaceutical restrictions established earlier in the century were meant to regulate *industry*, but now the focus was on *safety*. The system shifted from certifying the practitioners, and the framework in which they operated (physicians, pharmacies, industrial companies, product types, and the number and types of specialty products), to certifying the products (clinical testing and production standards). Before 1970, regulating industry seemed to be regarded as synonymous with taking safety precautions. After 1970, safety precautions involved more than industrial regulation; physicians and pharmacies also had to keep in step.

Nyegaard & Co. on the offensive

Nyegaard emerged from the 1960s as an increasingly self-confident organization. Armed with a new chemical substance that might cause havoc on the contrast media market, the firm set out to become export-oriented and thoroughly committed to selling original pharmaceuticals. The new and purposely created organizational openness reflected and supported these processes in the spirit of "small is possible."

For a small company, Amipaque represented a huge financial challenge. Nevertheless, it was to be launched within a framework that included additional finance for other research projects. Nyegaard had become a company with an enhanced technological focus, and in 1974, when financially strained, the discussion involving items for cutbacks included magazines, book purchases, night watchmen, and cleaning services, not technology.[76] In the inflationary period of the early 1970s, fixed Norwegian product prices and rapidly increasing prices for raw materials and inputs became a problem again.[77] As is evident in Table 6.2, operating profits between 1969 and 1974 had not kept up with the company's need for capital. No major investments were made between 1970 and 1972. If the operating results had been better, one could have expected the company's own resources to have covered the investment requirements for the development of Amipaque. Shareholders' equity as a percentage of the total assets of nearly 30 percent was good in terms of Norwegian industry but small relative to the international pharmaceutical industry. The company had hidden reserves in the form of write-offs, but these were of little help in financing the forthcoming expansion. The figures for 1973 illustrate this. Building a new chemical plant in Lindesnes in Southern Norway in 1973 reduced shareholders' equity by as much as 7 percentage points. The company would soon need operating capital.

The main cause of weak financial results was not increased costs but huge expenditures on research and development, as is shown in Table 6.3. In 1968 and 1969, the breakthrough years, total research and development (R&D) investments amounted to about 10 percent of turnover. From 1970, the company aimed to keep R&D investments steady at about 10 percent, on top of its investments in the development of Amipaque, which were held at 4 percent of turnover. These levels were lowered only once—in the difficult year of 1974. If total investments in R&D had not exceeded 10 percent from 1970 onward, the equity ratio in 1974 would have been far more favorable. A measure of the amount invested in R&D can be seen

[76] NFR, 15, O: "Organisasjon- og policykonferanser jan/feb.1974" by Rolf Horn.
[77] Yearly report, 1974.

Table 6.2 Key figures in the accounts, 1967–1974; operating revenues (OR) in million kroner; fixed prices: 1985 = 100 (SSB consumer price index, net operating profit (NOP), and income before taxes (IBT) in percent of OR); solidity (SOL) in percent of assets

Error! Bookmark not defined.	OR Year	NOP Million	IBT Percent	SOL Kroner
1967	119	8	10	25
1968	128	6	8	26
1969	123	13	10	29
1970	121	7	6	30
1971	131	6	4	30
1972	134	10	7	29
1973	130	4	3	22
1974	137	3	5	23

Note: Royalties included.
Source: Nycomed.

Table 6.3 R&D costs in percentage of operating revenue, 1968–1976

	Total of these R&D costs	R&D costs Amipaque
1968	9.9	–
1969	10.6	–
1970	12.8	4.0
1971	13.7	4.5
1972	13.5	3.9
1973	14.3	4.2
1974	12.9	5.5
1975	13.7	4.4
1976	12.7	2.7

Source: Nycomed.

by comparing annual profit and R&D costs. In 1969, these amounts were equal; by 1974, R&D costs were 13 times greater than profit.

The decision to maintain such an ambitious level of research and development had an explanation: the company had come more on to the offensive, and the government was now its partner. Nyegaard took full advantage of the government programs supporting research. To some extent, government financial schemes offset the risk in launching Amipaque. The company was able to borrow NOK 1.1 million from the government's Industrial Fund in 1969 and 1971. This amounted to about 11 percent of

Amipaque's total development costs between 1970 and 1974. If Nyegaard & Co. had no success with Amipaque, these loans would be forgiven.

The government both gave support and eliminated some financial risk. During the years up to 1974, Nyegaard borrowed another NOK 1.8 million on favorable terms by establishing a production plant for contrast agents in Lindesnes, one of the Regional Development Fund's designated areas. In addition, the company received NOK 900,000 in direct support.[78] Nyegaard & Co. had no guarantee for a full return on its investment in Lindesnes if the project were to fail, but the Regional Development Fund had contributed enough to cover about 10 percent of its cost. Additional grants were given for the relocation and training of new personnel. Loans were in the form of mortgages with favorable terms. The annual interest rate was 6 percent, with no down payment required in the first two years. Added together, these loans and grants comprised about 40 percent of the necessary capital for the Lindesnes project. The government covered about a further 30 percent through a loan by the Norwegian Bank for Industry. The government also compensated for research risks by subsidizing certain projects outside of contrast media.[79] For the first time, the government directly became an important participant in the development of Nyegaard as a result of the major changes in government industrial policy in the 1960s. The level of support made it safer—and easier—to take the offensive.

By keeping high R&D investment levels, exclusive of Amipaque, Nyegaard spread its risk. Protective measures were taken in case Amipaque should, for one reason or another, fail. Yet the company's large R&D investment involved substantial uncertainty. Most of its financial resources were being used to develop new products. Nyegaard set this new technology course by being very much a "family business." The owners knew their company. They had a complete overview of the financial situation and of the aggressive strategy they chose. A strategy of this nature could not have evolved without the owners' deep involvement. Between 1970 and 1974, Nils, Ulf, and Sverre Jr followed in the footsteps of their father, Sverre Blix, but they pursued matters differently. The Norwegian government was not a contributing partner in the 1940s in the way it would be 30 years later. Sverre Blix had created a financially oriented Nyegaard & Co., but his sons

---

[78] Nycomed: DUF to Nyco, June 11, 1974; NADM, økonomi, 22: accounts for I/S Ramslandsvågen, 1973 and 1974; accounts for Nyegaard & Co., 1973 and 1974; NADM, økonomi, 83: Nyegaard & Co. to Oslo Ligningskontor, March 29, 1974.

[79] Ibid.; Nycomed: "Støtte fra NTNF til FoU-prosjekter," March 23, 1984; "Utviklingskontrakter . . ." note by AA, March 22, 1984.

redirected the company to focus on technological innovation. Sverre Blix created a hierarchical company, while his sons opened the company up and supported internal dynamism. The business had become a family company in the sense that management and the organization acquired a collective character.

Conclusion

The vision of the new Nyegaard & Co. of the early 1970s was fully grounded in a scientific reality. Developing its own product that was original and very promising created needs for testing and documentation according to new and strict global standards for safety control. The old Nyegaard & Co. had pursued scientific objectives too, but in a more restrained, controlled, and hopeful way. The challenge of marketing a new chemical entity in a world of increasing skepticism about new chemical entities demanded the attention of the whole organization.

Creating an innovative company—one that was prepared to market a new chemical entity—demanded the attention of certain kinds of outside actors. Nyegaard's management understood that dealing with original drugs as proprietor or licensee meant complying with international scientifically rooted ideals. Being a Norwegian pharmaceutical company within a Norwegian medical and pharmaceutical environment was not enough. The company needed to develop its own standards based on good international values. The guiding principle of regulation was no longer the age-old Norwegian idea that the crucial matter was *who* was responsible; the new idea focused on *the way* things were done and that was heavily influenced by scientific developments. Even good men and women could not oversee the full consequences of their scientific results. Strict regulatory standards were called for. Nyegaard now aimed at becoming a scientifically based company just like Glaxo and Merck, Sharp and Dhome.

To achieve this, the business radically transformed the strict and financially oriented hierarchical company into a more collective and internally communicating organization. The collectivization of the leadership paralleled more general societal developments in the period, including a trend toward general decentralization and increased worker-participation. It also reflected a deep-seated internal factor: the ambition to become an independent and innovative pharmaceutical company. This ambition took precedence over other ambitions such as financial security or stable power structures. The many demands—in research, laboratory testing, clinical trials, communication with independent doctors and foreign and much larger corporations—demanded a broad intellectual effort on the part of a number of individuals as well as an internal climate conducive to informational exchange. The company integrated organizationally.

Internal collaboration was supplemented by external collaboration. Contacts with Norwegian doctors were a minor part of the company's outreach to doctors generally. There was no extensive collaboration between Nyegaard and other Norwegian companies. There was no national, collective capitalism, to borrow a concept by William Lazonick (Lazonick, 1991). The Norwegian state, through its financial assistance, did help in the process of innovation, taking some of the uncertainty and risk away. Yet the actual process of going forward was more international than national, and the concept of collective capitalism—*without* national frontiers—seems appropriate to the process at hand. There was extensive collaboration between Nyegaard, Scandinavian doctors, and foreign contrast media companies; this made the process *international*. Success—should it come—would not be a result of any national specific advantage giving condition but would come through a process involving transnational collaboration driven by a small, research-oriented, and increasingly scientifically inclined Norwegian company.

References

Bjørnson, O. 1968. "Den farmasøytiske industris ansvar I modern samfann." *Aftenposten*, August 30.

Bjørnson, O. 1974. *Nyegaard & Co 100 år*. Oslo, private publication.

Galambos, L. 1991. "Values." *In*: Sturchio, J. L. (ed.) *Values & Visions: A Merck Century*. Rahway, NJ: Merck, Sharp and Dohme, pp. 5–156.

de Haën, C. D. 2019. *X-Ray Contrast Agent Technology. A Revolutionary History*. Boca Raton, FL: CRC Press.

Jones, E. 2001. *The Business of Medicine. The Extraordinary History of Glaxo, a Baby Food Producer, which Became One of the World's Most Successful Pharmaceutical Companies*. London: Profile Books.

Lazonick, W. 1991. *Business Organization and the Myth of the Market Economy*. Cambridge: Cambridge University Press.

Liljestrand, Å. and Norlander, M. 1970. "Klinisk prövning av nya läkemedel." *Nordisk Medisin*, 84.

Næss, K. 1971. "Registrering og klinisk utprøving av legemidler." *Tidsskrift for Den norske Lægeforening*, 91(27): 1961–1962.

Acta Radiologica, 6 (270): 7–243.

Odelsting-Bill-No. 71. 1980–1981. *Om lov om endring i lov av 20. juni 1964 nr. 5 om legemidler og gifter*. Oslo: Stortinget.

Richter-Friis, H. 1991. *Livet på Novo*. Copenhagen: Gyldendal.

Skobba, Tor Johs. 1970. "Registrering av bivirkninger/komplikasjoner ved medikamentell terapi." *Tidsskrift for Den norske Lægeforening*, 90(1): 6–9.

Temin, P. 1980. *Taking your medicine: drug regulation in the United States*, Cambridge, Mass, Harvard University Press.

WHO (World Health Organization) 1962. The Quality Control of Pharmaceutical Preparations. *WHO's Technical Report Series*. Geneva: WHO.

7
The Profits and Problems of Success

Amipaque was an almost instant commercial success in all of its markets. It quickly propelled Norway and Nyegaard into a new role in the emerging Scandinavian pharmaceutical complex. They finally joined the other Scandinavian countries as original providers of important pharmaceuticals. The 1970s was a coming of age of the research-based Scandinavian pharmaceutical exporter, a development characterized by flourishing academic–business relationships within Scandinavia. Novo was particularly successful by deepening its commitment to insulin (Sindbæk, 2019). In Norway, a number of academic efforts launched new research projects, some of which were picked up by Nyegaard, which was broadening its research and development (R&D) effort. This was thus an important turning point for the national innovation systems of all three Scandinavian countries, each of which provided new platforms for their pharmaceutical companies.

Yet, all of those companies found the alluring internationalization in the second part of the 1970s challenging. There were new demands for clinical trials and new types of quality controls, a development that contributed to a dramatic shake-out of smaller and medium-sized companies in the US pharmaceutical industry, and the same situation obviously existed elsewhere (Lacy Glenn Thomas, 1996). Astra, Pharmacia, Novo, Nordisk—the most important Scandinavian companies—had comparatively robust organizations prepared to meet these challenges. Building on their past successes, they could use established knowledge and networks to their benefit. Nyegaard, which was experiencing increased commercial success as each year went by, had just begun building its knowledge base and networks in contrast media at the international level. Right from the beginning of the sale of Amipaque, management wanted to know what the next step would be. It was launched as a myelographic medium, but the product and the chemical principles could be used as a vascular one and reach much bigger markets. Because it was a new principle, non-ionic contrast media, it attracted a number of competitors wanting to cash in on the

Norway's Pharmaceutical Revolution. Knut Sogner, Oxford University Press.
© Knut Sogner (2022). DOI: 10.1093/oso/9780192869005.003.0007

new technology. It was not obvious how Nyegaard should respond to this competitive setting.

The Amipaque breakthrough created a wholly new global market for contrast media, a market that posed technological as well as commercial challenges. The Blix brothers, owners as well as managers, had succeeded in their role more as facilitators than as visionaries, having nurtured and steered an organization that they, to a large degree, had inherited. Now they had in their control an extremely valuable product and business, succeeding after the success was by no means a certainty.

A global niche success

At first, however, all the news was good: the international markets welcomed Amipaque from the very beginning. Nyegaard succeeded with the new concept and its new price level, everything essentially going as planned. The company quickly accomplished its long-term goal of joining the ranks of the world's science-based business innovators.

There were impressive financial returns. The firm did a decent job in its own markets, and Sterling and Schering AG's launches through their well-oiled and extensive marketing systems performed excellently. Amipaque had a privileged entrance into a world market characterized by oligopolistic competition. During the five-year period from 1969 to 1974 before the impact of Amipaque, turnover was virtually stable; between 1974 and 1979, Nyegaard's total sales almost doubled, as is shown in Table 7.1. Sales of pharmaceuticals in Norway and of reagents in Japan and West Germany increased substantially, alongside the great increase in contrast agent sales.[1]

Table 7.1 Operating revenues in product areas, 1974 and 1979 in million kroner; fixed prices: 1985 = 100 (SSB consumer price index)

	1974	1979
Pharmaceuticals	73	82
Reagents	35	52
Contrast agents	25	99
Total income	133	233

Source: Nycomed.

[1] NFR, 24, Kronestat: "Kronestatistikk 12. periode 1976."

Table 7.2 Key figures in the accounts, 1974–1979; operating revenues (OR) in million kroner; fixed prices: 1985 = 100 (SSB consumer price index, net operating profit (NOP), and income before taxes (IBT) in percent of OR); solidity (SOL) in percent

	OR	NOP	IBT	SOL
Year	**Million percent kroner**			
1974	137	3	5	23
1975	147	5	4	17
1976	156	5	5	14
1977	167	9	11	15
1978	194	15	14	19
1979	249	25	21	24

Note: Royalties included.
Source: Nycomed.

As is shown in Table 7.2, profits also rose. Income before taxes reaching NOK 30 million in 1979. This was 21 percent of turnover, as opposed to 5 percent just three years previously. This was the Amipaque effect. Despite total assets having risen from NOK 60 million in 1977 to NOK 109 million in 1979, the equity ratio increased by 9 percentage points in the same period. In 1980, the equity ratio of 29 percent of assets was at the same level as when Amipaque was about to be launched in 1972. The new contrast media enabled the business to keep its strength, while also growing.

In 1979, a year of remarkable financial success, Amipaque was responsible for one-third of the company's sales and most of the profit. These results largely reflected Amipaque's success in the United States. The US market provided about 40 percent (NOK 18.8 million) of the company's income from Amipaque. In the second largest market, West Germany, Amipaque's sales produced NOK 5.6 million.[2] Until Amipaque was marketed in these countries, Nyegaard did not have substantial sales of contrast agents there.

Schering AG's efforts in West Germany immediately made an impact. Even by early 1977, Amipaque's sales in West Germany were considered very good. By November 1976, 75 percent of university hospitals used Amipaque. Schering AG estimated that it had a market share of 60 percent in February 1977. Byk-Gulden quietly withdrew Dimer-X, the competing product and also a newcomer on the market. Once hospitals endorsed Amipaque, no great effort was made to restore Dimer-X to

---

[2] NAA: Regnskapsmappe, 1979.

its former position. Schering AG foresaw a gradually expanding market for myelographic media as knowledge of Amipaque's positive properties spread. Schering's people expected general reservations about myelography to evaporate.[3]

Once Amipaque proved its success as a myelographic medium, Nyegaard worked toward gaining approval for its use as a vascular (blood flow) agent.[4] Torsten Almén performed some early vascular tests at Malmö General Hospital in early 1975, which proved quite sensational: "Angiographies of extremities like these are often extremely painful, and the fact that the tests were virtually painless with Amipaque for these patients has made a strong impression on the physicians at the hospital."[5] Painless procedures provided for both patient comfort and better pictures because patients kept still. This report on the status of Amipaque pointed out three new applications: areas of painful diagnostic imaging, examination of small children, and examination of especially weak patients.

Amipaque's vascular phase began in July 1977, when Director Rolf Bjerke Paulssen decided to take the initiative.[6] The company had debated the wisdom of using such an expensive contrast agent in vascular examinations, but the fact that Amipaque entailed less pain dispelled the skepticism.[7] A marketing model established by Thor Andersen to analyze the vascular market proved that even in selective segments, the need for vascular examinations was extensive—three to seven times larger than for myelography. Nyegaard aimed for a portion of this market, and by 1978–1979 was marketing Amipaque as a contrast medium for special vascular examinations.[8]

Amipaque quickly had a huge impact that was conceptual as well as commercial. Sterling Drug acknowledged this: "Prior to Amipaque, the contrast agents market was basically flat. The advent of the non-ionic contrast agent Amipaque has opened a new era for contrast enhancement."[9] Amipaque not only sold well in the United States, but it also created a far

[3] NRBP, Amipaque, Schering AG, 1977: "Møte hos Schering AG–Berlin," November 8, 1976 and Holst to Bjerke Paulssen and Nilsen, March 8, 1977.
[4] NKT, T, 580, Koord: "Statusrapport over klinisk utprøvning med Amipaque" by L. Hol, Kamilla Dahlstrøm and T. Renaa, April 22, 1975.
[5] Ibid.
[6] NFR, 15, Paulssen: Rolf Bjerke Paulssen to several, July 5, 1977.
[7] Interview with Rolf Bjerke Paulssen, February 5, 1993.
[8] NFR, 15, O: "Amipaque. Fremdrift-markedsstrategi" by Rolf Bjerke Paulssen, June 20, 1978; NTA, "Red Book": "Amipaque—sales potential in the vascular field" by Thor Andersen; interview with Thor Andersen, September 21, 1992 and Rolf Bjerke Paulssen, February 5, 1993.
[9] NOS: ". . . imaging in the 1980's—a strategic planning document prepared for SDI" by Albano and Shaw, *c.*1981.

Table 7.3 The US market for contrast agents, 1978–1980
in USD million (current prices)

	1978	1979	1980
Non myelogr.	80	88	88
Pantopaque	4	3	5
Amipaque	4	16	26
Total	88	107	119

Source: NOS. "Diagnostic Imaging in the 1980s—a strategic planning document prepared for SDI,"
by Albano and Shaw, ca. 1981.

larger market for myelography. As is shown in Table 7.3, it changed the entire US market, with 1980 sales comprising 22 percent of all contrast media sales in the United States. This technological and medical breakthrough supported the high price level that had been determined by Nyegaard and Sterling.

What next? In retrospect, the launch of Amipaque looked easy. Once the initial decisions had been taken about going for the myelographic niche, and a number of good decisions and good, solid work on clinical testing and scaling up for production had been done, along with contracts with marketing organizations signed, success followed. But Amipaque was expensive to produce, and Italian Bracco had developed a new and possibly challenging substance. Competition loomed and it was not the only problem that followed the successful breakthrough.

The difficulties of technological leadership

The most pressing goal was to find a non-ionic contrast medium for general vascular use that could be delivered ready for use and was less expensive than Amipaque to produce.[10] The company had the technical qualifications for this task and was able to cooperate with Sterling Drug and Schering AG as it pushed forward with non-ionic contrast media research.

The Norwegian firm had, in fact, been struggling to solve this problem since 1976 when (on April 1) a researcher discovered some crystals in a solution. The following day, it was clear that this disaster was no April Fool's prank by Mother Nature. The solution had been shaken mechanically overnight, and what had once been a transparent liquid now looked

[10] NKT, 606: "Rkm-forskningen. Status . . ." by Hugo Holtermann, October 22, 1970.

like milk.[11] This transparent solution, named C-29, was supposed to become the successor to Amipaque. The company had actually worked with it for three years before it suddenly turned into a useless milky substance. What had happened was quite simple. C-29 had been dissolved in water on countless occasions without any problem, but in April 1976, it spontaneously crystallized. New and unknown substances such as C-29 had unknown solubility in different media like water. The formation of the grains of crystal required for crystallization can take years, and on April 1, 1976 this occurred with C-29, a development that placed its future as a contrast agent under a dark cloud.

In retrospect, the event was not surprising. Non-ionic molecules with a high iodine content should not be sufficiently soluble in water. Two months after the tragedy, news came that the Italian company Bracco had applied for patent rights on a compound that might threaten Nyegaard's position as the world's only supplier of a non-ionic contrast agent. The production process for Bracco's substance would probably be much cheaper than Amipaque's, possibly enabling Bracco not only to outsell Amipaque but also to conquer the vascular contrast agents market that so far belonged to Isopaque, Hypaque, Urografin, and Conray. In August, news came that French Guerbet had produced a new contrast agent, an ionic substance that would be a step forward compared to traditional ionic contrast agents. Bracco and Guerbet's new compounds threatened Nyegaard's position.[12]

The Norwegian company's most basic problem was one of resources. Although investing 13–15 percent of turnover in research, less than half of the research budget funded work on contrast agents. This did not increase during the first half of the 1970s. The research group working on C-29 when it crystallized was the same group that had created Amipaque; it now had the added burden of troubleshooting production activities in addition to synthesizing new substances. Holtermann regularly complained in 1975 and 1976 that Amipaque took too much time from basic research.[13] He worked himself to exhaustion, and by the end of 1974 he wanted to step down as head of research and work on less demanding tasks. At the end

[11] NKT, unummerert.staff meetings: "Minutes from Chemists' Meeting," April 6, 1976.
[12] NFR, 17, C, 1, staff meetings: "Report from the VI Congress of the European Society of Neuroradiology" by Sigbjørn Salvesen, September 23, 1976; meeting, September 29 and 30, 1976; "Notes from 2nd Congress of the European Cardio-Vascular Radiology," Golman to Leif G. Haugen, June 2, 1977.
[13] NFR, 15., A-råd: meeting, August 8, 1975 and January 26, 1976; NFR, 17, C, 1, staff meetings: "Metrizamide, Centrifugation grade," meeting, August 27, 1976.

of 1976, he took up a regular research position.[14] Leif G. Haugen, who had been with the company since 1955, took over Holtermann's previous obligations. Technical Director Ulf Blix began to participate more actively in research discussions.

They faced major challenges. C-29 was not the first contrast agent candidate that had crystallized and shown insufficient solubility. In January 1974, an impressive substance was dropped because of its toxicological properties. Later in 1974, it crystallized.[15] Nevertheless, C-29 was the first promising candidate. In mid-March 1976, the Nyegaard researchers thought that C-29 fulfilled the goal of developing a non-ionic contrast agent for vascular use that could tolerate autoclaving. No researcher could present a better alternative, and work on product development was due to start.[16] Two weeks later, C-29 crystallized, creating the shock wave which ushered in a difficult period for the company.

Between March 1976 and the end of 1978, research was in a dilemma. The properties of substance 545 had been declared as good as those of C-29, but chemically 545 was very similar to the crystallized substance: "The compound should be kept as a substitute for [C-29] if this failed, although it was probable that 545 would fail on the same parameter," it summed up early in 1976.[17] Would substance 545 crystallize too? No one was sure.[18]

545's geometric structure—its isomeric composition—caused concern. Chemically identical molecules can have different geometry, possibly resulting in differing physical or chemical properties. Substance 545's geometry was complicated, which could be an advantage in that a complicated geometry might resist crystallization. However, to determine how the different geometric forms were distributed when 545 was being produced was difficult. Researchers feared that health authorities would refuse to approve 545 because of uncertainties about how the different structures would influence the substance's effect.[19]

So they shelved substance 545 and work was resumed on the geometrically simpler C-29. Tests were made to determine whether some of the groups with geometrically similar molecules crystallized.[20] Efforts to save the C-29 project continued for more than a year after the first time it

---

[14] Interview with Holtermann, June 23, 1993.
[15] Interview with Leif G. Haugen, February 2, 1993.
[16] NFR, 17, C, 1, staff meetings: meeting, March 11, 1976 and March 25 and 26, 1976.
[17] NKT, unummerert, staff meetings: staff meeting, January 22, 1976.
[18] NFR, 17, C, 1, staff meetings: staff meeting, October 14, 1976.
[19] Interview with Hugo Holtermann and Leif G. Haugen, July 14, 1993.
[20] Ibid.

crystallized. May 1977 marked the definitive end. The project had lost its viability; C-29 was crystallized once and for all.[21]

The company's research team began synthesizing new substances. It followed the trail that Bracco had chosen, in that it dealt with simple molecular structures. It synthesized several substances, and a number of them looked promising. Then, one after another, they crystallized. In two meetings held in February and March of 1978, it was debated whether the search for non-ionic contrast agents should be discontinued.[22] The team sought inspiration from Professor Nils A. Sørensen at the Norwegian Institute of Technology (NTH), asking for information about NTH's research in the chemistry of glucose. Sørensen replied that derivatives of ether seldom crystallized. Taking this advice, the team began to recover.[23] By the end of 1978, it had produced a promising substance, later named Iopentol.

The company had by then already decided to market substance 545 in cooperation with Sterling Drug. In the fall of 1977, Ulf Blix recognized that his research group was too small and that it would have to find a partner. A few months later, Sterling Drug agreed to start marketing substance 545.[24] Sterling did not see substance 545 as a problem. It saw the isomeric problem from a different perspective. In retrospect, Nyegaard's research group did not know enough about foreign regulatory practices. Being in Norway, its researchers were far away from the registration authorities. They read the formal guidelines from the US Food and Drug Administration (FDA) and had experience in documenting the isomeric structure of Isopaque and Amipaque. But that background apparently was insufficient to interpret the situation with substance 545. By this time, Nyegaard was performing better at creating new substances than at interpreting the registration procedures in the United States.[25]

[21] NKT, unummerert, staff meetings: meeting, April 29 and June 17, 1976; NFR, 17, C, 1, staff meetings: meeting, August 10 and November 18, 1976 and May 26, 1977; interview with Leif G. Haugen, February 2, 1993.

[22] NFR, 17, C, 1, staff meetings.: meeting, March 24 and April 21, 1977, February 9 and March 6, 1978.

[23] Interview with Hugo Holtermann and Leif G. Haugen, July 14, 1993; NFR, 17, C, 1, staff meetings: meeting January 26, February 9 and 13, March 2, April 20 and 27, 1978; "Report of a meeting between Professor N. A. Sørensen . . . and Dr. H. Holtermann and Dr. M. Kelly . . .," Kelly to Haugen, March 30, 1978; NKT, 629, staff meetings: meeting, June 16, 1978.

[24] NFR, 17, C, 1, staff meetings: "Notes from 2nd Congress of the European Cardio-Vascular Radiology," Klaes Golman to Leif G. Haugen, June 2, 1977; meeting, June 1, August 4, September 8, November 3 and 25, 1977; NFR, 15, D-møte: meeting, January 28, 1977; NFR, 15, Sterling 1969–1978: Ulf Blix to Bjerke Paulssen, August 1, 1977; NFR, 15, Schering AG 1964–1981: Ulf Blix to Degen (Schering AG), October 7, 1977; NKT, 629, staff meetings: meeting, November 30 and December 1, 1978.

[25] Interview with Hugo Holtermann and Leif G. Haugen, July 1993.

Nyegaard named substance 545 Iohexol, a generic substance that later would be marketed under the trade name Omnipaque. It would become a huge commercial success. Iopentol was the generic name of the other substance, later marketed as Imagopaque. Nyegaard's research group could by this time reflect on its position as the leading achiever of contrast media research in the world. Its base was narrow, as shown by Sterling's constructive intervention, but its knowledge was deep.[26] These were the world's leading researchers in X-ray contrast media. By this time, Schering AG, Sterling Drug, Mallinckrodt, Guerbet, and Bracco too were experimenting with contrast agents.[27] But the Norwegian firm led the field for 20 years, with regular breakthroughs: Isopaque, and all of its improvements; the first-generation non-ionic contrast agent, Amipaque; second-generation Omnipaque and Imagopaque; and "third-generation" Visipaque (Iodixanol, synthesized in 1980), which appeared on the market only in the 1990s.

The technological developments of the 1970s put the company's postwar history in a new, progressive perspective. As landmark discoveries followed in quick succession, a core group of company employees could look back on more than 30 years of employment; in fact, they were then on the brink of retirement. Hugo Holtermann (hired in 1946) was still a key person. He was the business's most highly trained researcher and the one who had steered the company into the contrast media field. He, among others, was on the Visipaque patent. Engineer Knut Wille (hired in 1947) was also part of the Visipaque patent, a fact all the more remarkable in that he had worked on production issues rather than research for most of his career with the company.

Another impressive performance was that of 63-year-old pharmacist Fridtjov Rakli (hired in 1940), whose work led to a new patent in 1976. Rakli led the Pharmaceutical Development Department and patented an autoclaving technique, a sterilization method for Iohexol. Rakli's patented method consisted of using a special buffer for autoclaving, the amino compound TRIS. Without this, the iodine ions would have been liberated. This patent turned out to be significant as it covered an important stage in the production of non-ionic contrast agents.

---

[26] NFR, 17, C, 1, staff meetings 1978–1981: meeting, June 21, 1979: the work with dimers; interview with Leif G. Haugen, February 2, 1993.

[27] NFR, 17, C, 1, staff meetings 1978–1981: "Internal report from Contrast Material Symposium May 26–29, 1979, Colorado Springs," Klaes Golman to Sigbjørn Salvesen, June 13, 1979.

The new situation created by the breakthrough of Amipaque explains how employees with such long histories could be so productive near the end of their careers. Amipaque created a new and well-defined path with new opportunities, and the firm's technical personnel were experienced and fully competent to seize these opportunities. After the war years, Nyegaard built up multi-level competence in research, development, and production in this special field. The developments of the 1970s clearly illustrate this. They also quite possibly show the limitations of this competence and explain why Sterling Drug was brought in. Another way forward that Ulf Blix proved reluctant to adopt was to appoint one or more chemists at the theoretical level of Holtermann. He rather prioritized building research projects in biochemistry, obviously hedging for failure in contrast media research—but also making failure in contrast media more likely.

Approaching the market with partners

The contact between Nyegaard and Sterling in the fall of 1977 concerning substance 545 became a turning point for the Norwegian company. This marked the beginning of extensive cooperation with Sterling Drug in particular but also subsequently with Schering AG. Close teamwork with these two firms provided alliances in meeting the competition from Bracco and Guerbet. Had there been no concern about timing and had the plan been clear and straightforward without all the crystallizations, Nyegaard may have stood a better chance of going it alone.

Ulf Blix played an important part in deepening the alliances with Sterling and Schering. Ulf Blix had to work hard to maintain a good relationship with Sterling Drug. Sterling's lackadaisical marketing efforts for Isopaque have been mentioned previously, but this was a never-ending story that reappeared when Blix brought Sterling into the 545 situation. Isopaque was registered for use in the United States and Japan in the mid-1970s, and Sterling Drug ordered a great deal of Isopaque substance in bulk. Hardly any of this was sold. Ulf Blix came into possession of a memorandum which instructed Sterling's marketing force to sell Hypaque instead of Isopaque, but he kept this information to himself.[28] After 1978, Nyegaard bought

---

[28] Interview with Ulf Blix, March 9, 1993; NUB: "Isopaque," undated (c.1975) and unsigned document from Sterling Winthrop.

back 30 tons at an advantageous price and then sold it in other markets.[29] But Isopaque did not get a foothold in the vast markets of Japan and the United States. It was not easy to be a junior national partner in a thoroughly international industry.

Schering AG had done an excellent job promoting Amipaque, and Schering needed Nyegaard's collaboration in order to access non-ionic technology in the short term. The leading global firm in terms of contrast media competence had fallen behind, and the Norwegian alliance represented a reasonable path forward.[30] But these relationships soon became very complex.[31] Schering's determined effort to not be left behind in the vascular non-ionic game meant that it ended up by representing Bracco in Japan and France and Nyegaard in West Germany.[32] Loosing Schering in Japan was a challenge for Nyegaard, but through a contact arranged by Sterling Drug Daiichi agreed to market Omnipaque in Japan.[33] Steering through these complexities meant that Wolfgang Degen of Schering AG and Ulf Blix developed deep personal trust.[34]

The race to reach the markets first obviously was very important for the complicated choices made. The choices to go with Sterling and Schering to promote Omnipaque were finally made at the end of 1978, and the competition with Bracco was at the heart of the process. In Bracco's corner were Squibb and eventually Schering AG. Both groups feared a third combination, Guerbet and Mallinckrodt, who had the ionic substance Hexabrix.[35] The Bracco group led in the race to come fastest to the market, and Bracco had strong partners, not least because Squibb had become such a forceful seller in the US market. By 1980, Squibb's share of the US vascular contrast media market was 55 percent; Mallinckrodt had 25 percent, with Sterling Drug's steadily diminishing share at 20 percent.

[29] NRBP, SW-Isopaque 1974–1979: Odd Heggim to Ulf Blix, June 29, 1978; Strandli to Ulf Blix, July 6, 1978; Heike to Ulf Blix, August 1, 1978; Ulf Blix to Heike, October 6, 1978; Heike to Ulf Blix, November 20, 1978 and November 13, 1979.
[30] Interview with Wolfgang Degen, May 11, 1993.
[31] NFR, 17, C, 1, staff meetings: "X-Ray Contrast Agents. Staff Meetings" No. 32/77, November 3, 1977.
[32] Interview with Wolfgang Degen, May 11, 1993; NKT, 629, staff meetings: "Discussion with Dr. Speck, Schering AG," Sigbjørn Salvesen to Leif G. Haugen, March 10, 1979.
[33] Interview with Odd Kåre Strandli, May 25, 1993 and William Heike Jr, June 2, 1993.
[34] Interview with Wolfgang Degen, May 11, 1993.
[35] NRBP, Iohexol 1979–1980: internal Sterling Winthrop Research Institute (SWRI), memo by F. J. Rosenberg, January 11, 1979 (copy).

Schering and Sterling, however, gave Nyegaard strong support in launching Omnipaque, a collective effort that moved forward faster than expected. By January 1980, it could be tested on healthy human volunteers. Close teamwork between the three firms continued throughout the process.[36] Kamilla Dahlstrøm (hired in 1958), the head of Nyegaard's Clinical Department, coordinated the project. This was the first time the Norwegian business had performed clinical tests with an eye toward the entire international market. This involved following the extensive control systems of the US FDA and required far more paperwork than usual for European radiologists.[37]

The three companies enlisted the services of contact networks in their respective countries, and the work of each company thus acquired a national character.[38] Not surprisingly given the prior experience with elder brother and pioneering product Amipaque, Omnipaque proved to be a safe and highly versatile non-ionic contrast medium. In May 1982, Omnipaque was approved in Norway, and many European approvals followed within the next 18 months. In most cases, Bracco's product preceded Omnipaque, but in the United States, the products came onto the market almost simultaneously after being approved in December 1985.[39] Nyegaard & Co. had maneuvered quite expertly in a situation that was by no means easy.

Global production

Producing Omnipaque for the world market was now big business, something completely alien to what small-country generic specialist Nyegaard had been involved in before. Compared with other pharmaceuticals, making contrast media is also a particularly voluminous production in tonnage as the amount of substance that goes into each dosage is relatively large. Making contrast media is also a two-stage process consisting of making the chemical substance and then making the finished liquid product.

---

[36] NKT, 629, staff meetings: meeting, January 18, 1978; NFR, 15, D-rådet: meeting, December 14, 1978, August 31, 1979 and January 4, 1980; NFR, 15, Paulssen: "Notater fra telefonsamtale by R.B. Paulssen," December 22, 1978 and Paulssen to Ulf Blix, June 5, 1979.

[37] NRBP, Iohexol, Forskning/fremdrift 1980–1981: "Statusrapport ... iohexol" by Kamilla Dahlstrøm, April 1981.

[38] *Acta Radiologica* supplementum 362 (1980) and 366 (1983) expresses this.

[39] NTA, Red Book: "Registration status Omnipaque" by E. Vellan, January 27, 1986; "Introd. dates—new products," note by KSa, January 16, 1987.

Production of Isopaque had been built up gradually over a 20-year period, and it was already quite considerable by the time Sterling Drug started purchasing it. Nyegaard continuously worked to improve the production process and brought in the Swedish company Bofors AB as a vital subcontractor for chemical substances.[40] Yet quantity was not the only, or even the real, difficulty when it came to the production of Amipaque. It was complicated and costly to produce; its production line looked more like an overgrown laboratory than an industrial process.[41]

Nyegaard built on its own knowledge of industrial-scale chemical synthesis when setting up production of Omnipaque. Cooperation continued with Bofors and a new subcontracting agreement was signed with the large Norwegian chemical company Borregaard.[42] The key figure in developmental work at Nyegaard was Knut Tjønneland (hired in 1947), a man who had long thought of chemical syntheses as large-scale industrial processes.[43] The challenge with Omnipaque was that time was running out, but again collaboration with Schering AG and Sterling Drug proved constructive.[44] Toward the end of 1980, however, Schering AG withdrew from the process development, possibly because the company by then felt sure it had developed its own non-ionic substance. This resulted in Schering AG purchasing the substance in bulk from Nyegaard rather than producing it itself.[45]

Production involved two different processes: A modern plant for primary production of chemicals at Lindesnes and a modern plant for secondary pharmaceutical production with a requisite sterilization department in Oslo were constructed. Both plants were new. The Lindesnes operation had been ready to produce Isopaque in 1974, and over the years it went through four expansions and modernizations for Isopaque and later Amipaque.[46] Nyegaard's organization of production were not good enough for Sterling Drug, though. Between 1979 and the fall of 1980, the new plants were completely reorganized according to Sterling Drug's

---

[40] NKT, 580, Programidéer: "Memo over oppgaver og . . . høsten 1967" by Knut Tjønneland, 1967.

[41] Interview with Odd Kåre Strandli, February 5, 1993.

[42] NKT, 620: Tjønneland to Trond Jacobsen and Odd Kåre Strandli, June 10, 1980.

[43] NKT, 534: "Noen refleksjoner," April 1, 1963 and "Tanker omkring langtidsplanlegging," c.1965, both by Tjønneland.

[44] NKT, 629, reiserapp: minutes from meeting between Schering AG, Sterling Drug, and Nyco, September 10–12, 1979 and October 1 and 2, 1980.

[45] NFR, 15, Sterling 1979–1980: "Hovedpunkter fra samtaler med Sterling . . ." by Jan Erik Mikkelborg, October 15–22, 1980; Ulf Blix to Trout, November 5, 1980; NKT, 629, reiser: Sterling–WRI minutes, February 24, 1981.

[46] NOS: undated note over investments at Lindesnes.

instructions. Nyegaard's production complied with the European Good Manufacturing Practice (GMP) regulations, not the more stringent US requirements according to Sterling. The FDA had inspected and approved the plants as recently as November 1979, but Sterling, which pointed out areas for improvement, wanted its supplier to maintain faultless production facilities.[47]

Nyegaard yielded reluctantly to this superior production system.[48] Sterling's interpretation of the strict US regulations for production processes was complied with. Although most countries had developed exacting production standards, the US FDA required written standard operating procedures (SOPs) which could not be altered without FDA approval. A company's quality assurance procedure was not only to have a control function, but it also assumed a total responsibility for ensuring the existence of adequate systems and compliance with the SOPs (Ballance et al., 1992: 147). The requirements were so rigid that it had to be proven that the production process was always uniform. All stages were to be inspected and documented. Duplication of each step in each production batch had to be possible, and two signatures were required on all documentation papers.[49]

Nyegaard reorganized its nearly new production department in the summer of 1980. All of the facilities were adapted to SOP demands. In particular, major changes were made in the sterilization department.[50] By the mid-1980s, the firm had acquired substantial competence in production matters in Oslo and Lindesnes. It had expanded its staff and made frequent visits to Sterling Drug's factories in the United States and England.[51] Having a US partner benefited Nyegaard. As a small Norwegian pharmaceutical company, it had hitherto found it very difficult to compete on a global market with enormously complicated regulations. Cooperation with other, stronger companies proved a solution, something that could not have been achieved without the contrast media inventions motivating the whole collaborative venture. By the late 1970s, Nyegaard was an important participant in an international X-ray contrast media milieu.

[47] NFR, 15, SLK: Bjerke Paulssen to SLK, March 25, 1980 and Bjerke Paulsen to foreign agents, March 20, 1980; NFR, 15, Sterling 1979–1980: Elliot to Ulf Blix, November 19, 1979; copy by Regan to Elliot, July 11, 1980.
[48] Interview with Odd Kåre Strandli, February 5, 1993.
[49] Interview with Øivind Nyegaard, Nils Oma, Ole Chr. Whist, and Asbjørn Wiggen, February 23, 1993.
[50] Interview with Odd Kåre Strandli, February 5, 1993 and Nils Oma, Ferbruary 12, 1993.
[51] Interview with Odd Kåre Strandli, February 5, 1993 and Odd Heggim, August 12, 1992.

A culture of innovation

Although the Norwegian enterprise was in many ways fast becoming a specialized contrast media company, its leaders aspired to innovate more generally. Innovation could be a tool to hedge against failure in the contrast media business. In the course of the 1970s, they launched several new and ambitious projects in biochemical research. The projects originated outside the company, and Nyegaard assumed the role of coordinator between Norwegian researchers and foreign pharmaceutical companies. The 1970s, paradoxically because of Nyegaard's internationally rooted contrast media success, was the breakthrough decade of academic–business relationships in Norway.

The firm employed an enterprising and creative new head of biochemical research, Bjørn Skålhegg. A former student of Søren Laland at the Institute of Biochemistry at the University of Oslo, he would be joined by other former students of Laland. The two that started at the turn of the year 1970–1971 would fill many important positions. Carl Christian Gilhuus-Moe initially worked with reagents, while Øivind Grimmer, whose thesis formed the basis of an upcoming metaphase retardant project,[52] worked both with this and in the field of allergens.

Skålhegg initiated immunology research in Nyegaard in 1970, building on two external projects that opened up the possibility to use Rosalyn Yalow and Solomon Berson's development of a new technique for radioimmunoassay (RIA) in 1960 and its subsequent development.[53] One of these projects was the reagent Antithrombin III, a test for one of the coagulation factors of blood. Nyegaard developed testing methods in collaboration with two Norwegian physicians.[54] Though sales prospects were substantial, the product had little commercial success. The second was the "Allergen project," an attempt to improve diagnosis and treatment of allergies.

Spurred by the Norwegian Professor Kjell Aas, who criticized Nyegaard's old line of allergen extracts, the firm started a new project purifying allergens.[55] Allergens are active substances found in an allergic source. An allergen extract can be used for diagnostic as well as therapeutic purposes. By pricking a patient's skin with an allergen extract, it can be determined whether or not the individual is allergic. By injecting it into the skin in

---

[52] Interview with Søren G. Laland, December 8, 1993.
[53] NFR, 17, 1B, Testreagenser 3: Bjørn Skålhegg to Ulf Blix, September 1, 1970.
[54] NFR, 17, 1B, Testreagenser 3: Skålhegg to Blix, September 1, 1970.
[55] NFR, 2, 56: minutes from meeting, July 3, 1969 between Nyco, Aas, and Helsedirektoratet.

a highly diluted solution, the patient gradually develops resistance to the substance; eventually, the patient builds up an increased tolerance to the allergens, and they can be injected in larger doses. This treatment is called hyposensitization.[56] The project received a government development grant for the period 1970–1973 in recognition of the need and the uncertainty of the commercial possibilities.[57] Each purified allergen required an entire research project; creating a portfolio of allergens was a comprehensive task.[58]

Thus, formal cooperation with Swedish Pharmacia began in August 1977 and continued into the 1980s. Pharmacia would market Nyegaard's purified allergen extracts in all markets excluding Norway, paying royalties. Nyegaard's technology and trade name (Spectralgen) would be used. Nyegaard & Co. would be responsible for production for sales in Norway as well as 10 percent of Pharmacia's sales in other areas. By this agreement, Kjell Aas, Nyegaard & Co., and Pharmacia planned to conquer the world market through purified allergens.[59] Through collaboration on immunological techniques with university researchers from Uppsala, Pharmacia had developed several new diagnostic tests in the 1970s (Silverstein, 1989: 346f). Pharmacia's innovative techniques, RIST and RAST, made it possible to test for allergies in the laboratory (Norgren, 1989: 58–66). Previously, it had been necessary to perform tests directly on the patient's skin.[60]

The metaphase retardant project was an even more ambitious scientific undertaking. Metaphase is a stage in human cell division, and Nyegaard had a group of substances which delayed metaphase and thus cell division. Administered in combination with chemotherapy in the treatment of cancer, healthy cells seemed to become more resistant. The use of metaphase retardants thus allowed an increase in chemotherapy dosage. Søren G. Laland from Oslo University's Department of Biochemistry had worked with these substances since the 1960s, with support from the Royal Norwegian

[56] Interview with Øivind Grimmer, February 16, 1993.
[57] NAA: "Utviklingskontrakter . . ." note, March 22, 1984 by AA; HD, AkH7, Q100, Nyco 1973: Evang and Mellbye to I-dep, January 23, 1970; NFR, 2, 56: minutes from meeting, July 3, 1969 between Nyco, Aas, and Helsedirektoratet.
[58] NFR, 15, Pharmacia 1971–1979: minutes from meeting, Nyco, January 17, 1974.
[59] NFR, 15, Pharmacia 1971–1979: meeting, Nyco and Pharmacia, March 29, May 4 and June 8, 1977; "Samarbetsavtal," August 3, 1977 and "Avtale . . . vedr. Allergenekstraktprodukter," September 1, 1977.
[60] NFR, 15, Pharmacia 1971–1979: Aas to Roth, December 19, 1972; Aas to Natvig, September 13, 1972; Roth to Aas, January 11, 1973; Ulf Blix to Virding, May 22, 1973; Bjørnson to Sjøberg, December 20, 1973; Bjørnson to Virding, July 11, 1973.

Council for Scientific and Industrial Research (NTNF). Kjell Undheim, from the Department of Chemistry, synthesized many substances similar to the original metaphase retardant; Reidar Oftebro at the Norwegian Radium Hospital tested them.[61] In 1976, Nyegaard & Co. entered into an alliance with Glaxo, which also synthesized many substances, and this partnership continued into the 1980s.[62] The project was discontinued in 1986 for lack of conclusive results.[63]

The last and truly extraordinary project dealt with small protein chains, *peptides*, and originated from a group of doctors at the National Hospital. The project posed a bold theory about the biochemical functions of the body which had been the basis for Roger Guillemin and Andrew Schally earning a Nobel Prize in 1977 with Rosalyn Yalow. Her technique of RIA supported the work of the two other laureates (Silverstein, 1989: 346f). The peptide project had a good deal in common with Nyegaard's former ACTH project. ACTH is a peptide hormone secreted from the pituitary gland, stimulating production of many other substances that affect the body. In the 1970s, medical specialist Olav Trygstad, later in collaboration with Assistant Medical Director Karl Ludvig Reichelt and Professor Martin Seip examined the idea that other peptide hormones existed.[64]

The concept behind the project was that people with extreme metabolic or psychic disturbances released peptides in urine and that these peptides could be isolated and used in the diagnosis and treatment of such illnesses. By isolating anorexia peptides, schizophrenia peptides, peptides for manic depressive disorders, and for extreme cases of exhaustion and alcoholism, a world of new products opened up. The anorexia peptide technique meant not only that anorexia could possibly be diagnosed but also that overweight persons might be treated with an appetite-regulating peptide.[65] No one could refuse support when Reichelt, Seip, and Trygstad contacted Nyegaard, or when the firm in turn applied for a government research and development contract. As the Ministry of Health commented to the Department of Industry, "If one were to achieve positive results [...] this

---

[61] Interview with Søren G. Laland, August 16, 1992 and Øivind Grimmer, February 16, 1993.
[62] NFR, 15, D-rådet: meeting, February 13, June 18, July 30, and September 9, 1976; February 2 and July 6, 1979; February 28, 1980; April 30 and May 15, 1981.
[63] Interview with Tore Skotland, April 6, 2020.
[64] HD, H7, Q100, Nyco 1980–1983: "Utredning . . ." by Olav Trygstad, March 16, 1977; Nyegaard to Sos-dep., October 13, 1977.
[65] Ibid.

would be a revolutionary medical discovery and at the same time represent important opportunities for industrial utilization."[66] Nyegaard also saw the enormous potential but remained extremely cautious in view of the timescale and risks involved in the project.[67] With that in mind, it brought Pharmacia in as a partner.

New biochemical projects carried Nyegaard's innovative ambitions further. The research projects were not only a response to market requirements. Scientist outside the company also pushed them. They were all cooperative enterprises. The government gave support through the Research Council and through its R&D contracts. Norwegian hospitals and the University of Oslo payed salaries. Pharmacia and Glaxo shared the risk with Nyegaard, which contributed only a share of the investment, and was the technological coordinator. Other actors and organizations helped cover the costs. Nyegaard had discovered a way to continue its concentration on ambitious research objectives, to stay in control of them, and to distribute its risk among different projects and entities. The aim was to develop potential alternatives—or additions—to contrast agents while exploiting and strengthening the Norwegian system of innovation.

With hindsight, it is apparent that this broader research effort to some extent undermined the firm's position in contrast media. There were grounds for putting more resources into the contrast media research in the 1970s than was done. Dealing with Amipaque as well as with its possible successors were huge efforts, and the processes that eventually Sterling and Schering contributed to could perhaps have been avoided. The whole history of contrast media research back to the 1960s is that of a "thin line" of effort from a small group of people, at times in direct opposition in a fight for resources for research from biochemistry. Ulf Blix must have wanted it this way as a reluctant supporter of contrast media research. Which is not to say that he was not behind the commercial activities with contrast media. From the mid-1970s, he was replacing Holtermann as the architect of major decisions, in many ways building on Holtermann's platform. But he remained reluctant to increase the investment in R&D and to hire new and outstanding chemists who could extend what had been created. Balancing biochemistry and contrast media research reflected an uncertainty about the company's whole situation that came to a critical moment in 1980.

---

[66] HD, AKH7, Q100, Nyco 1980–1983: H-dir. to I-dep, October 18, 1977.
[67] HD, AKH7, Q100, Nyco AS 1980–1983: Nyegaard to Sos.-dep, October 13, 1977.

Global suppliers of technology or a Nordic marketing channel?

While Nyegaard was positioning itself to become a worldwide supplier of contrast agents, at the same time exploiting the Norwegian medical ecosystem for biochemistry, the company also acted as a marketing channel in Norway as Glaxo's licensee. Glaxo aspired to make more out of its commercial possibilities in foreign markets, though. As the 1970s turned to the 1980s, Glaxo put pressure on Nyegaard to conform to its wishes. Glaxo wanted to buy Nyegaard and the Blix brothers were willing to consider that idea.

Nyegaard valued its relationship with Glaxo. In 1979, sales of Glaxo's products comprised NOK 15 million or 11 percent of Nyegaard's total, and rapidly increasing, sales. However, Amipaque's sudden rise to importance came with an unhealthy dose of uncertainty, and in Norway Nyegaard depended on the products it sold for Glaxo. In prescription drugs, the most important category, Glaxo products constituted 64 percent of Nyegaard's 1979 Norwegian sales.[68] Glaxo could be a good fit for the research portfolio outside of contrast media, and the two companies already collaborated in one of them. Glaxo was a powerhouse in biochemistry, Ulf Blix's very own scientific field.

Glaxo wanted to purchase Nyegaard in order to acquire its own sales company for the Nordic countries. If Nyegaard refused to sell, its licenses from Glaxo would be taken away. Secret negotiations about ownership had been going on since 1973, and in 1976 the two companies signed a letter of intent.[69] This did not bring immediate results, however, since the Blix family did not want to act hastily.

It considered selling partly because of the younger generation. The family had joined Nyegaard in 1921 through Sverre Blix, and his three sons also joined the company. These three now had eight children, and the grandchildren's position in and around the company now remained unclear. A second factor influencing the family was its uncertain situation. There was no guarantee that Nyegaard could continue to be run in the relatively conservative and methodical way it had been managed.[70] The rapid growth

---

[68] NFR, 15, div I.Glaxo-opphør: Nyegaard sales in January 1979.
[69] NFR, 15, Glaxo.dr: Girolami to Nils Blix, December 17, 1973; David Smart to Bjørnson, February 5, 1974; Bjørnson to David Smart, February 14, 1974; Austin Bide to Nils Blix, March 21, 1974; agreement of March 8–11, 1976.
[70] Interview with Ulf Blix, March 9, 1993.

of the company made entirely new demands on its capital and organizational resources. In 1976, the Blix brothers considered a floatation on the stock exchange until it became clear that this would not yield enough new capital. Nor would this step bring in fresh managerial competence. The best solution seemed to be to search for an industrial partner who could strengthen and develop the company both financially and in terms of human resources.[71]

Glaxo was an obvious candidate and was already interested. In 1980, the issue came to a head, and Glaxo presented a gloomy picture of what Nyegaard could expect if the Blix brothers refused the offer:

> You are, of course, enjoying excellent results at the moment but they are in large measure due to the outstanding success of one product. This may or may not be sustainable but there must be a risk in it. We could guarantee the future viability of the company.[72]

Glaxo wanted to distribute Nyegaard's products on the international market and establish the organization as a Nordic production center. The alternative was that Glaxo would market its own products in Norway and throughout the Nordic area.[73]

Glaxo's arguments made sense also because of the special political climate in Norway at the time. Partly because of the huge Norwegian oil reserves, Norway practiced a very strong counter-cyclical policy until 1978 to fight the world economic crises of the 1970s. This drove up costs for Norwegian industry and hit the pharmaceutical industry's profitability. For Nyegaard, this did not matter in the short term because of the huge earnings from Amipaque. But if these earnings fell away, Nyegaard could very well be in a situation that was financially worse than before the sales of Amipaque took off.

The Blix family listened carefully to Glaxo. They were concerned about the future of small and medium-sized pharmaceutical companies but did not think that the situation in Norway allowed a sale: "It is almost ironical that our current period of excellent results will make these arguments even more difficult to present," Ulf Blix wrote to Glaxo in 1980.[74] The family consulted Kåre Willoch, leader of Norway's Conservative Party, about a sale to

[71] NUB: Odd Heggim to Nils and Ulf Blix, January 6, 1976; unsigned PM, October 30, 1978; Nils Blix to Ulf Blix, Bjerke Paulssen, and Heggim, November 1, 1978.
[72] NFR, 15, Glaxo.drøftelser: Douglas Back to Ulf Blix, June 10, 1980.
[73] NFR, 15, Glaxo. drøftelser: Douglas Back to Ulf Blix, June 10, 1980.
[74] NFR, 15, Glaxo. drøftelser: Ulf Blix to Douglas Back, July 1, 1980.

a foreign company. Willoch replied that he could virtually rule out Glaxo receiving a concession even if the conservatives were to win the 1981 election. Nyegaard had earned a high profile in Norway as a research-based company, and the general feeling was that the company was a national resource.[75] This was one side of the story.

On the other side, Glaxo's commercial interests and Nyegaard's strong technological orientation clashed. Glaxo primarily considered Nyegaard & Co. as a marketing channel and was willing to let the company regress into a center for secondary production. But Nyegaard & Co. was now intensely oriented toward research and new technology and was working to develop primary production through chemical syntheses. Finding other products to market would be one way to secure its position without the support of Glaxo. In an attempt to become less dependent on Glaxo, Nyegaard put pressure on Sterling Drug and Schering AG for the right to distribute their entire product portfolios in Norway. Schering was willing to transfer sales rights for its contrast agents in Norway and Sweden, but Nyegaard already dominated this market so much that this would bring little gain. Nyegaard continued to press Sterling Drug and at last managed to become its representative in Norway.[76] But Sterling had a much less interesting product portfolio than Glaxo, so this did not solve many problems.

There were clouds on the horizon in 1980, but since the Amipaque success and the teaming up with Schering and Sterling Nyegaard could look fairly confidently to its medium-term future. It was a major—and very profitable—player in a group of powerful companies which were developing new concepts for contrast media for the global market. Nyegaard was a key participant in that ambitious process. The firm's biochemical research projects appeared to give more exciting hope for the future. Maybe the days of accepting the possibility of being a peripheral marketing agency for a multinational company were over.

New owners

Brothers Nils and Ulf Blix had come a long way since they formally entered the company's leadership positions in the beginning of the 1960s. At the beginning, Nils was more visible and was better prepared for an economically

[75] NFR, 15, Glaxo. drøftelser: Nils Blix to Douglas Back, May 20, 1980.
[76] Interview with Thor Andersen, March 31, 1993; NFR, 15, Sterling 1979–1980: Ulf Blix to Trout, November 5, 1980.

oriented management position than Ulf, who should provide all the new inventions that were to propel the company to new heights. Well, Ulf had delivered, with help, but he had also grown into a responsible and quite able tactician when it came to forging external relations. He was a man who could take charge of the selling of the company too.

The Blix brothers and Nyegaard approached Norsk Hydro, one of Norway's largest industrial enterprises at the time. But pharmaceuticals did not fit into Hydro's plans. The energy and metal-smelting company Hafslund showed interest and offered NOK 20 million, which the possible sellers interpreted as a polite "No."[77] The possibility of putting the company on the stock exchange was again discussed with Den norske Creditbank, but the bank's estimated value of the enterprise, between NOK 36 and 60 million, was obviously too low.[78] No one seemed to appreciate the full potential of Nyegaard & Co.

The problem was convincing possible investors of the true value of the company. Given the Glaxo negotiations and the rather cautious attitude by the Blix brothers themselves, this was hardly surprising. Why should Norwegian outsiders in unrelated businesses place a high value on Nyegaard? More than anything, this was a matter of whether any buyers could understand how successfully the business had come out of the maneuvering and positioning in the global X-ray contrast media market. The way Nyegaard had bonded with its partners—in a race with another group of companies, had opened up new and significant possibilities and had secured the company's competitive position. It is no surprise then, that the man who could seize these opportunities was a friend of Ulf Blix. After reviewing the whole situation of the potential sale, Nils and Ulf Blix agreed that Ulf should visit his friend and summer neighbor, the president of Norgas, Kåre Moe.[79]

Through their years of friendship, Moe and Ulf had often discussed issues involving Nyegaard, but they had never considered a merger. The thought had never even occurred to Moe. Nyegaard was too different from Norgas, which was the major supplier of industrial gas in Norway, with important operations in welding and ship supplies as well. However, in November 1980, Blix asked Moe whether Norgas would consider merging with Nyegaard. Moe appreciated Nyegaard's true value.[80] Norgas was in a period of expansion and enjoyed good profitability. With a decentralized

[77] Interview with Harald Schjoldager, September 7, 1993.
[78] NUB: "Aksjevurdering–Nyco A/S," appendix to DnC to Odd Heggim, December 5, 1980.
[79] Interview with Ulf Blix, November 30, 1993.
[80] Interview with Ulf Blix, March 9, 1993 and Kåre Moe, March 12, 1993.

organizational structure, it had the administrative capacity to incorporate a company like Nyegaard. Norgas's internal analyses of Nyegaard were extremely positive.[81] On April 1, 1981, the merger took place at an exchange ratio of one Nyegaard & Co. share for two and three-quarters Norgas shares. Calculated by the market value of the shares that the owners received in the new Norgas, the price for Nyegaard & Co. was about NOK 140 million.[82] Nyegaard was interested in Norgas's financial resources and in its planning and control systems, while Norgas asked Nils and Ulf Blix to continue managing the pharmaceutical operations. Nils had to be persuaded to stay on as president.[83] The merger was also a matter of timing. On the one hand, the Blix family wanted to withdraw from the business after the problems that had appeared after the firm's expansion had been temporarily solved. It was now feasible to integrate Nyegaard & Co. into a Norwegian industrial company that had no pharmaceutical expertise.

Thus ended 60 years of ownership for the Blix family. In Nils and Ulf Blix's time, the company had outgrown the capabilities of normal family capitalism. A third generation taking over would have needed a great commitment and willingness to go into uncertain territory should present opportunities be exploited to the fullest. Nils and Ulf Blix had already realized their father's dream of taking the company out into the world with an important and in-house developed drug. Yet, the new challenges that followed that success had not been foreseen.

Conclusion

The remarkable and unqualified success of Amipaque took center stage in the 1970s. The achievement of a very long-term goal left the owners contemplating a future that was demanding and also promising. A nationally oriented company of unproven scientific capabilities had turned into a major international innovator of a product that started an important new product group. Nyegaard had successfully built systems within the firm and networks outside of the business (Hughes, 1989). A great collaborative effort was the result. The collective effort *inside* Nyegaard & Co.

---

[81] Henning Larsen to Kåre Moe, February 6, 1981, borrowed from Sigbjørn Slind.
[82] Borrowed from Sigbjørn Slind: "Prinsippavtale for fusjon mellom Nyco og Norgas"; document for board meeting, case 18/81, Norgas.
[83] Interview with Ulf Blix, March 9, 1993 and Kåre Moe, March 12, 1993; borrowed from Sigbjørn Slind: merger-agreement between Nyco and Norgas.

drove the process; the collaboration with *outside* individuals and institutions was vital to the success of the process. The breakthrough in research in the 1960s came through internal and external research networks, and in the 1970s the success was grounded in commercial alliances with larger multinational companies.

Some of the central people within the company pushing forward this exciting new product had striven for it through decades. Some key figures had been with the company since the war. Rakli, Brekke, Holtermann, Wille, and Tjønneland had all started their employment in Sverre Blix senior's time. All of them participated in developing the "new" Nyegaard of the late 1970s, and they all benefitted from the work of Haugen and Dahlstrøm, among others, hired in the 1950s before the mundane discovery of Isopaque.

It is important to note, however, that the 1970s was also a decade of uncertainties. There were crises in the contrast media research. The competitive situation going into the 1980s was highly uncertain. Glaxo was still, in the late 1970s, taking a legitimate position, arguing that Nyegaard's uncertain situation could be alleviated by its continued role as a Nordic-oriented sales arm of Glaxo products. As strange as it may sound in retrospect, Nyegaard was on the verge of being one of those smaller and medium-sized companies that the new and demanding competitive situation of the pharmaceutical sector shook out of the business.

Being a Norwegian company mattered positively in the 1970s. The company's Norwegian surrounding from the 1960s is aptly summarized by Rolf Torstendahl's concept of participatory capitalism. The company and the state had developed common goals. Through its industrial policy, the Norwegian government became a partner that contributed important financial resources to the preparation of the launch of Amipaque. Nyegaard's main way of hedging for failure in contrast media came with an increasing portfolio of biochemical research projects that to a great degree were supported by the state directly through grants and indirectly via the university sector of Norway. Glaxo and Pharmacia also contributed.

In the challenging 1970s, the process of developing a successful, one-product—or one-technology—research company appeared somewhat completed. The 1980s were likely to be even more demanding as the firm obviously needed to broaden its base of products fairly soon. It would go forward now with new resources and new ownership, seeking to solve the problems of being a successful international pharmaceutical firm in its own right. The success that other Scandinavian firms has achieved in pharmaceuticals suggested that this goal too might be achieved.

References

Ballance, R., Forstner, H., Pogány, J., and United Nations Industrial Development 1992. *The World's Pharmaceutical Industries: An International Perspective on Innovation, Competition, and Policy.* Aldershot: Edward Elgar.

Hughes, T. P. 1989. *American Genesis: A Century of Invention and Technological Enthusiasm, 1870–1970.* New York: Viking.

Lacy Glenn Thomas, I. 1996. "Industrial Policy and International Competitiveness in the Pharmaceutical Industry." *In*: Helms, R. B. (ed.) *Competitive Strategies in the Pharmaceutical Industry.* Washington, DC: The AEI Press, pp. 107–129.

Norgren, L. 1989. *Kunskapsöverföring från universitet till företag: en studie av universitetsforskningens betydelse för de svenska läkemedelsföretagens produkt-lanseringar 1945–1984.* Stockholm: Allmänna förlaget.

Silverstein, A. M. 1989. *A History of Immunology.* Harcourt: Academic Press.

Sindbæk, H. 2019. *De renfærdige. Fortellingen om Novo-Nordisk.* Copenhagen: Politikens forlag.

8
Structure Follows Strategy

The resourceful pharmaceutical companies—one of which Nyegaard & Co. was fast becoming—have at times directed their future with bold moves that implicated their strategies. Merck, Sharp and Dhome and other "big pharma" companies steered their research content to align with important trends within academic research: starting out in organic chemistry in the 1930s, moving on to biochemistry in the 1950s, and then onto the biotechnology bandwagon in the 1970s (Galambos, 1991; Hikino et al., 2007). Biotechnology was a US specialty benefitting from the huge federal input into medical research (Rasmussen, 2014). But the Danish insulin companies used biotechnology constructively, and the Swedish companies put resources into the emerging technology.

Nyegaard purchased the US biotech company Seragen of Boston in 1984. For the first time ever, Nyegaard & Co. tapped into an outside technology base—and on another continent and in a new scientific field. Nyegaard did not do biotech research. Seragen represented a science-centered approach to developing the company, again emphasizing how Nyegaard & Co. used innovation as its tool to develop new directions for the future. The purchase of Seragen did represent some connection with the company's reagents products but also emphasized a looser and less directly commercial continuation and redirection of the old biochemical emphasis.

The first part of the 1980s—under new ownership and old management—became an exercise in applying forward-looking industry-specific thinking. Fueled by continuously excellent financial sales and an increasingly optimistic attitude for what was to be expected when Amipaque were to be replaced by its successor Omnipaque, Nyegaard & Co. aimed to exploit its wealth for constructive purposes. Going into biotechnology reflected what Nyegaard & Co.'s old leadership would want to do, now under Ulf Blix as chief executive officer (CEO). Yet, increasingly, the new owners of Nyegaard & Co. identified their own ideas about how the future should look, and they put emphasis on Nyegaard's commercial possibilities within the contrast media field. This, too, typified the times, as Nyegaard had experienced with Glaxo and as the larger

Norway's Pharmaceutical Revolution. Knut Sogner, Oxford University Press.
© Knut Sogner (2022). DOI: 10.1093/oso/9780192869005.003.0008

Scandinavian enterprises continued to exploit their technology and product paths.

The formation of strategy had center stage in the first part of the 1980s. A combination of anticipation about the results from the Omnipaque sales and increasing confidence because of the ever better financial results shifted the emphasis from getting details right to scanning the horizon for new possibilities. The new owners magnified the strategy emphasis as a consequence of both wanting to learn about the company and the pharmaceutical field and wanting to sort out constructively what to do with all that incoming cash.

Part of a conglomerate

CEO Kåre Moe emphasized systematic development of strategy already at Norgas, and he wanted to apply the same kind of forward thinking in his role as new chairman of the board at Nyegaard & Co. Norgas applied the fairly new concept of "strategic planning," a market-emphasizing approach that primarily US consultants brought to Europe in the 1970s.

The rationale behind the merger between Norgas and Nyegaard represented the new kind of thinking. The many mergers in Norwegian industry after the Second World War, which were quite often government-facilitated, aimed to rationalize industrial structure. Structural rationalization guided post-war industrial development and industrial policy (Hanisch and Lange, 1986). The merger between Nyegaard and Norgas aimed to achieve business development from the changes of the supposedly clever thinking that Norgas managers could introduce for Nyegaard. Nyegaard & Co. was a technologically oriented company that attained impressive results through laborious research—strategy followed research results. Norgas applied market-led thinking and formal decentralization of responsibility through divisionalizing the company in several semi-independent units. Nyegaard became a new unit. Norgas had no comparable activity and no research activities even faintly similar to those at Nyegaard & Co. The merger focused on how the planning and governing systems at Norgas could benefit Nyegaard & Co.

Norgas organized its division Nyegaard & Co. as a formal company and divided Nyegaard itself into product divisions. Nyegaard had traditionally been organized into functional areas and top management worked through different professional staffs. Divisionalizing separates a company into independent profit areas, often specific product areas such as Norgas practiced. Nyegaard & Co. became a pharmacy division within Norgas with the merger of 1981, which, by the summer of 1982, consisted of three subdivisions: contrast media, pharmaceuticals, and reagents. Each division could be considered a small, separate company and was as self-sufficient as possible, run by its specific staff. Corporate management (of Nyegaard & Co.) watched over the divisions primarily through their total financial results, as was the norm at Norgas.[1] In addition, Norgas's president, Kåre Moe, chairman of the board at Nyegaard & Co., maintained close control of the company's divisions.[2]

The setting up of three subdivisions aimed to give each of Nyegaard's different operations a certain autonomy. At the outset, Norgas considered Nyegaard's dependence on contrast agents a possible weakness. Nyegaard's other activities had to be strengthened and greater attention should be paid to pharmaceuticals and reagents.[3] With the creation of subdivisions, each of the three product areas was given equal importance.

Apart from the handful of large Norwegian enterprises with large exports, Norwegian companies hardly practiced divisionalization. Norgas, with Kåre Moe at the helm, introduced the concept in the late 1970s (Nerheim, 1983). Moe came to the company from the Swedish gas company AGA, which made him very familiar with Norgas's key areas of activity. By divisionalizing Norgas, he consciously broke with tradition and established new organizational structures, just as he had done a few years previously at AGA. In particular, he reformed the time-honored union of gas and welding. Moe chose to meet the challenge of a changing market by transferring more responsibility and authority into middle management.[4]

There are usually two reasons for organizing by divisions. One is that a company's size or the nature of its operations make it difficult for top management to maintain detailed control. Norwegian companies were comparatively small and the divisional form less used (Gammelsæter, 1991: 50–56). For Norgas, its diversification supported divisionalization. Divisions were established too in the belief that they allowed a clearer focus in a specific area. Sharper international competition during the 1960s may have emphasized this approach.

[1] Minutes of board meeting, March 14, 1983 introduced this in Nyco; followed up in minutes of the board throughout 1985.
[2] Interview with Sigbjørn Slind, April 21, 1993 and Odd Kåre Strandli, October 2, 1992.
[3] H-N, Actinor archive, Nyco, Nycotron, Nyegaard & Co: "Norgas syn på Nyco's fremtid," unsigned note, January 27, 1982.
[4] Interview with Kåre Moe, April 19, 1993 and Sigbjørn Slind, April 21, 1993.

Strategy and Structure (1962), Alfred Chandler's study of the development of industry in the United States, contributed to this new focus on company organization (Chandler, 1962). Multinational consultant firms such as McKinsey, Arthur D. Little, and the Boston Consulting Group developed the concept further and applied it. While companies had worked with budgets and financial control systems previously, and some initiated long-term planning in the 1960s, consultant firms developed a different system called strategic planning. Long-term planning dealt with relatively simple prognoses, based on former results, which were used to plan future operations. Strategic planning started with the market, not the company (Hax and Majluf, 1984). Strategic planning is an attempt to understand and predict how the market for a company's products will—and may—develop. The company should aim for market shares and assess how those may be reached. By thinking ahead and thinking contextually, possible upturns and downturns in the company's development may be better understood. Strategy is formed by combining an interpretation of market fluctuations with an understanding of the company's strengths and weaknesses related to its markets.

With the coming of strategic planning, the size or nature of the company ceased to be the primary consideration in the decision to divisionalize. Small units, like two of the three subdivisions at Nyegaard & Co., became tools with which top management aimed to improve operations (Hax and Majluf, 1984). The intention was to isolate the various operations in order to improve the insight into market possibilities, improve the overview, tighten cost control, and make it possible to arrive at better decisions.

As Norgas Vice President Svein Ribe-Anderssen emphasized, commercial strategy had to be drafted on many levels: it concerned an arena that a company dominated or wanted to dominate, a product or a group of products that it offered, and the resources and organizational systems that were necessary to achieve dominance. Commercial strategy could be compared to a piece of machinery in which all of the parts were adapted to each other and contributed to the creation of a whole. Ribe-Anderssen emphasized that the point was not size as such but the size of the market arena one operated in. Efficiency and progress followed superiority in one's own arena. Dominance could be traced back to a "superiority" that had been built into the company's organizational structure and/or into individuals within the company. The goal was to arrive at a formulation, a basic strategy, that could create a system superior to that of the competitors and dominate in one's own arena.[5]

There was an explicit connection between the subdivisions within Nyegaard & Co. and the focus on viewing commercial strategy in relation to each product's market. It was important to stay close to the market, and corporate management could not possibly do this. Divisionalizing resulted from a need to declare strategy; the structure should follow the strategy.

Strategy and structure in an old company

Norgas did not control Nyegaard with an iron hand. Norgas was not familiar with the pharmaceutical industry and rather established a corporate policy and an administrative system. It had no intention of taking over management of Nyegaard & Co. This was to remain in the hands of Nyegaard's executives, who had already shown their proficiency.

The new organization represented continuity. Nils Blix continued as president to the end of 1983. After this, Ulf Blix was to take over for a two-year period.[6] The technical director, Ulf Blix had been made vice president of Nyegaard a few years earlier, a position he retained after the merger. He continued to be responsible for the company's research activities. Nils and Ulf Blix both became members of the management group in Norgas.[7] Odd Heggim, who had been in charge of company finances since Bjørn Sinding-Larsen retired in 1970, continued as director of finance. Tore Tjaberg, DVM, was hired as Director of Research in 1983. He came from Oslo's Board of Health as the municipal veterinarian. Tjaberg was assisted by research managers Trond Jacobsen, MS (hired in 1972) for organic chemistry and Lars Aukrust, Dr Philos (hired in 1979) for biochemistry. Jacobsen had always been involved in contrast media research, and he assumed Leif G. Haugen's position when Haugen wanted to return to his old responsibilities, leading patent and trademark operations. Aukrust replaced Bjørn Skålhegg, who had become Director of Research at Swedish Pharmacia. Engineer Odd Kåre Strandli (hired in 1963), who had succeeded Ulf Blix as

---

[5] Minutes of board meeting, March 14, 1983; "Nyegaard & Co. A/S forretningsidé," unsigned note to board meeting March 14, 1983; "Om forretningsidé" by Svein Ribe-Anderssen, March 11, 1983 in "Vedlegg til styremøteprotokoller/1983."

[6] H-N, Actinor archive, Org.-prosjekter Nyco, HT: Tønsberg to Kåre Moe November 19 and 25, 1981.

[7] Interview with Sigbjørn Slind, April 21, 1993.

technical director, became the director of the contrast media division. All other leadership positions were filled with personnel from old Nyegaard.

The new management system made room for the original leaders, so they could continue to work virtually as before. This was a collective and inclusive form of management which integrated conditions far into the lower levels of the company. The earlier ambition to provide a climate for scientific breakthrough was still important. The objective was to develop important new products in close cooperation with physicians. Though market-oriented in this sense, Nyegaard's research policies were not traditionally characterized by deliberate marketing philosophies. Research opportunities came before market opportunities.

The philosophies of Kåre Moe and of Nyegaard's management differed somewhat. Board discussions about research policy made the differences abundantly clear: Ulf Blix and Kåre Moe held different opinions. Moe wanted to place research in the divisions, but Ulf Blix feared that this would lead to short-sightedness and a divided atmosphere. He was also against giving research in contrast media a much better financial basis than the other research categories. Blix believed that the projects had to be *evaluated* and that research should be given top priority. This was how it turned out: Moe gave in. Blix also wanted to keep investments in research at a high level, at least 10–13 percent of turnover, despite the fact that turnover was increasing rapidly.[8]

Kåre Moe yielded because he did not regard himself an expert on the pharmaceutical industry.[9] He and Norgas were learning all the time about what the pharmaceutical industry actually involved. Increasingly, Norgas wanted to concentrate on this industry, the only division in Norgas that showed a large profit. The gas division, which had previously dominated the market in Norway, faced increased competition from Norsk Hydro. When, in 1983, the gas division was sold to Swedish company AGA, Norgas changed name to Actinor. Actinor's main operations were now in pharmaceuticals, welding, and shipping equipment. The sale of the gas division freed NOK 400 million too, and some of that cash was earmarked for opportunities within the pharmaceutical industry.[10]

Actinor clearly expressed its willingness to invest in the pharmaceutical industry in a meeting of Nyegaard's board of directors in the spring of 1984.

---

[8] Minutes of board meeting, May 30, 1983 and November 14, 1983; NFR, 15, D-møter: meetings, August 26 and 27, 1982.

[9] Interview with Kåre Moe, April 19, 1993.

[10] NKT, 502: "Actinors strategiske plan 1984–88."

It decided to invest NOK 200 million in three major projects: a building to house research and development, an expansion of the chemical production capacity at Lindesnes, and the purchase of a US biotechnology company, Seragen. The investment in these three projects equaled Nyegaard's total turnover in 1983. The first two projects followed the logic of the company's expansionary trajectory, while the last one represented radical renewal.

Obviously, the purchase of Seragen reflected Actinor's new attitude after the sale of its gas division.[11] An opportunity appeared, and Actinor-Nyegaard & Co. had cash in hand to match its policy of concentrating on pharmaceuticals. Nyegaard & Co. considered Seragen a natural solution to its clear intention of supplementing its contrast agents with other specialties. Nyegaard & Co. bought into the Boston company Seragen for NOK 50 million in 1984. Seragen was founded in 1979 by researchers from the Department of Biochemistry at Boston University's School of Medicine. It utilized the newest techniques in biochemistry and biotechnology to develop therapeutic and diagnostic products. One of the main ideas was to pass on academic research results to industry, and Seragen had signed many agreements with researchers and universities in the Boston area. In 1984, 73 employees worked on research and development, and of these, 25 had doctoral degrees. In addition, 55 external projects with institutions and researchers in the Boston area were in progress.[12]

Seragen offered two concrete opportunities too. The company specialized in diagnostics and, in order to secure a marketing network, had purchased Dow Diagnostics a few years earlier. Therefore, Seragen could become Nyegaard's marketing channel in the United States, at least for reagents. Seragen also could provide Nyegaard & Co. with new diagnostic products for marketing in Europe.[13] Looking further ahead, other exciting prospects could develop.

The Seragen purchase very clearly fitted into the old Ulf Blix–Søren Laland line of thinking. Professor Søren Laland visited Seragen prior to the purchase, as Nyegaard's consultant. Ulf Blix wanted centralized research and development (R&D) precisely for this kind of action. As part of his battle to keep R&D funds centralized, Ulf Blix explained to the board that the products had to be seen in their *historical* context.[14] Since the 1940s, earnings from Globoid and Nyco Fruktsalt had financed the research in

[11] Board meeting, April 12, 1984.
[12] Board meeting, April 12, 1984; note to board meeting, April 12, 1984, "Seragen Inc.," April 9, 1984.
[13] Board meeting, May 9, 1984.
[14] Board meeting, May 30, 1983.

contrast media, and future earnings from contrast media would pay for other research.[15] This was the old Blix-led Nyegaard & Co. in a nutshell of sorts, where the parts in principle were less important than the whole when seen from a long-term perspective. There ought to be room, meant Blix, for a less profitable activity when the company as a whole was earning money. And the pharmaceutical and reagent divisions were not very profitable. Reagents returned a profit, but only just.

Yet conflict had also been part of Nyegaard's research history. Without Holtermann's determined belief in contrast media, contrast media would not have succeeded because the line would not have been prioritized. The chances were that biochemical research under the influence of father and son Laland would have continued as before. And the purchase of Seragen represented continuation of the old biochemical line in new biochemical apparel. Ulf Blix directed Nyegaard's research policy back onto the track he saw as most interesting, spending what formally was Actinor and Nyegaard money—but clearly operating, and not without justification—with all the legitimacy as "supremo" of the huge influx of contrast media earnings. The purchase of Seragen represented a direction in which Ulf Blix would have taken the company were it not for the Actinor ownership, and the Actinor ownership trusted Blix's judgment about specific issues in general and about specific research-relevant issues in particular.

A concept such as strategic planning would have been inept in these discussions. Any attempt at market penetration with original pharmaceutical products would have to include research and science in a fundamental way. Buying Seragen rested on a combined approach of formulating marketing possibilities with scientific approaches, and the opportunity to integrate Seragen into Nyegaard's reagent division could justify the purchase to some extent. The question remained, though, whether or not the fit and the content stood up to the kind of scrutiny that would lead to further successes down the road.

The challenged divisions

New divisions for reagents and pharmaceuticals represented a market-oriented approach. Reagents were sold in numerous markets almost all over the world, in small quantities, while the pharmaceuticals portfolio

---

[15] Interview with Ulf Blix, March 9, 1993.

constituted those products that sold in Norway, licensed ones, and generic ones as well as those branded generics like Globoid that had a long-term standing in the Norwegian market. This division was somewhat paradoxical from a research point of view, though, for under Bjørn Skålhegg's leadership the research projects in biochemistry crossed these divisions.

The reorganization into divisions mercilessly revealed profitability differences between the three areas. The reagents division was ripe for renewal, and reagents would be reliant on research results in order to prosper. Most of its products sold well, but in practical terms, the excellent profitability of Thrombotest, the other coagulation test products, and AllergenLab (the commercial part of the allergen research) kept the division above water. Seronorm and the other control sera and some other reagents, some of which had been ambitious research projects, were possibly not profitable.[16] Nyegaard & Co. had worked intensely in the area of reagents since 1959 but within narrow fields and without any real strategic goal in the world market.[17] Around 1980, the company had six coagulation tests and seven control sera, while larger reagent producers such as Boehringer Mannheim, General Diagnostics, and Dade each had 20–30 tests of both product groups. Nyegaard & Co. focused on a combination of top quality, high price, and good profitability. In the 1980s, the company still disregarded the strategy of developing a broad range of products.[18]

One opportunity arose when Paul Owren, the inventor of the coagulation test line, wanted to sell his business interests to Nyegaard & Co. He had originally transferred the sales rights for Thrombotest to Nyegaard & Co., but he kept the rights for production of the semi-finished product and established a production company, A/S Trombo. Nyegaard & Co. purchased this company in 1983 and thereby increased revenues and established better market control. Nyegaard had now got the incentive to continue.[19] In the early 1980s, its coagulation tests, mainly Thrombotest, had a market share in Norway and the Netherlands of close to 100 percent. In Sweden and Japan, the market share was 75–80 percent, and it was as high as 60 percent in Denmark, Austria, and Singapore and 50 percent in Finland.

[16] NTA, 1135, McKinsey: Summary of Steering Committee Presentations, January 31–February 1, 1984, Diagnostics.

[17] NBA, 3. Skuff. budsj: Bjørn Skålhegg to Hugo Holtermann, October 30, 1968; NFR, 15, D-rådet: meetings, November 26, 1976; August 4 and November 3, 1978; January 19 and November 30, 1979; February 22 and March 21, 1980; NFR, 15, A-rådet: May 24, 1976.

[18] NBA, 4. skuff. Reagensrådet: "Sammendrag fra Diskusjonsmøte . . . Reagenser på Nyco i 1980-årene" by Carl Gilhuus-Moe, October 30, 1980 (with appendix).

[19] Minutes of board meeting, September 8, 1983 and February 9, 1984; "Trombo A/S," unsigned note to board meeting, September 8, 1983.

The rest of Western Europe should represent opportunities for expansion with 20 percent market share or less, while sales in the United States and Canada were negligible. The company worked to increase its market shares, although it was difficult to imagine a magnificent upside.[20]

At Seragen, the company of opportunity, the situation rather quickly turned out not to be as promising as Nyegaard & Co. had foreseen. This surprised Nyegaard's management, which expected several promising projects to be underway, and that might still be the case. Professor Søren G. Laland had made an exhaustive study of the company in Boston and confirmed that the key researchers and their projects were reliable. The problem appeared to be in the sales activities for diagnostics. Seragen's product line did not show the expected immediate profit, and the opposite picture began to emerge: profitability was nowhere to be seen. In conflict with previous agreements, Seragen had spent all of the NOK 50 million that Nyegaard & Co. had put into the company on its diagnostics section with little return. Nyegaard therefore assumed full ownership and completely reorganized Seragen. It maintained the research projects but disposed of the diagnostics division—one of the main arguments for going in.[21] Nyegaard & Co. had analyzed the situation poorly and bought Seragen on the basis of an inadequate analysis.

Given that Nyegaard's biochemical activities in itself had never achieved any form of research success that led to internationally marketable products, the Seragen purchase represented a remarkable optimistic approach. Given, too, that the biochemical research department only the year before the Seragen venture had lost is leader, Bjørn Skålhegg, very few, if any, in that part of the company had much experience to steer foreign companies, lead research in other companies on other continents, and build the necessary alignment between the two companies, Nyegaard and Seragen. Even if Skålhegg had not yet achieved the kind of accomplishments that Holtermann had, he was highly respected and, as mentioned, got a better job at Pharmacia than the one he had with Nyegaard. The whole Seragen venture smells of somewhat optimistic superficiality, maybe superficiality of the kind that had appeared previously with the biochemical research activities.

On the whole, the first part of the 1980s were not good years for the reagent division. Its oldest product, Thrombotest, was still its most

[20] Ibid.
[21] Board meetings, March 14, May 9, and June 20, 1985; note to the board: "Rapport vedrørende Seragen Inc." by Stein Annexstad, John Giverholt, and Tore B. Tjaberg, April 12, 1985.

important. Although the small AllergenLab was doing well as a free standing unit, it was a small operation and benefitted from the costly bigger allergen research project. The projects that were intended to result in expansion and innovation, the test Sterognost and the Seragen portfolio, had not been successful. The reagent division was marked by stagnation during these years, and in that sense its development mirrored that of the pharmaceutical division. The pharmaceutical division was, by definition, a rest category once contrast media and reagents had been removed and had renewed itself with licensed products. After the loss of the Glaxo products, it had a run down appearance.

The commercial results of the extensive allergen research project gave little reason to rejoice. Pharmacia's endeavors had long been a source of discontent.[22] It experienced trouble conquering the world. Nyegaard's purified products depended on hyposensitization as a method of treatment, but physicians increasingly preferred to use new medications that reduced symptoms. In the end, Nyegaard & Co. sold all of its rights to the allergen project to Pharmacia.[23] As mentioned previously in chapter 7, the metaphase project was in decline too and eventually ended. Peptide research continued, though, but results were not yet of the sort that led to new products.

The division as a whole ran at a loss. Although product profitability varied, no product did especially well. This did not surprise. The Glaxo products lost in 1981 had given the company an impressive facade and good earnings. These exceptional, newly developed pharmaceuticals generated high profit margins also for Nyegaard and they could not easily be replaced.[24] That Glaxo's products had replaced Schering Corporations in the late 1960s proved an unexpected windfall but a windfall that Nyegaard had adapted to. The expansion of research into therapeutics reflected that. Nyegaard & Co. was left with research projects which were ambitious by global standards and with an outdated product portfolio targeted on the domestic market

However, the relationship with the state—previously so damaging—was again turning for the better. The weakness of Nyegaard's pharmaceutical division in the 1980s reflected a general distrust of the state. After

[22] NFR, 15, Pharmacia 1971–1979. I: Allergengruppen v/Skålhegg to Direksjonen, March 6, 1980; Lars Aukrust/Tove Måseide/ Øivind Grimmer to Ulf Blix and Bjerke Paulssen, March 9, 1982 with appendix by Dale, February 19, 1981 and Øivind Grimmer/Tove Måseide/Lars Aukrust undated.
[23] Interview with Øivind Grimmer, February 16, 1993.
[24] NTA, 1135, McKinsey: "Identifying and Evaluating Alternative Strategies for Growth," final report volumes I & II, McKinsey & Co., March 21 and April 12, 1984.

1960, the company had experienced the situation as improved and moved relentlessly forward, but the great inflation of the 1970s again increased costs and ate profits. After 1975, the Norwegian pharmaceutical industry's two trade organizations tried urgently to make clear to the government the problems that price regulation created, and in January 1982 their argument was accepted. The principle of negotiating for *general* price increases was adopted.[25] This was a turning point in the relationship between industry and government. Price negotiations no longer took place between the government and each individual company for each individual product but between the government and the industry's trade organizations. This marked the end of an era.

The timing of the change can be credited to constant pressure from NOMI and No-Re-Farm, respectively the organization for the Norwegian industry and the organizations for foreign interests. Both protested that prices were not being increased in line with cost increases. This could be documented. NOMI commissioned a study by the Production Engineering Research Institute (PROFO) to show the relationship between cost structure, productivity, and sales prices. PROFO's study demonstrated that from 1967 to 1979 prices had not compensated for cost developments, despite improvements in productivity.[26] Director General of Health, Torbjørn Mork, and the Norwegian Medicines Control Authority raised a number of prices after written applications from the industry.

Mork had long resisted the industry's entreaties. Negotiations with No-Re-Farm were especially tough, but Mork was more willing than his predecessor, Evang, to involve the Ministry of Industry in issues concerning the Norwegian pharmaceutical industry. He was reluctant to change, though. Not until the end of 1981 did he allow the national and international industry to make general price increases.[27] That Conservative Party member Leif Arne Heløe had just become Minister of Health and Social Affairs in 1981 may have had an influence, but officially it was due to the Director General of Health, Labour Party member Torbjørn Mork.

---

[25] HD, N124, 1981: Egil Willumsen to NOMI, January 28, 1982; HD, N124, 1981–1983: Leif Arne Heløe to No-Re-Farm, January 21, 1982.

[26] HD, N124, 1981: NOMI to H-direktoratet, July 6, 1979, August, October 8, and November 24, 1981.

[27] HD, N124, 1976–1978: meeting I-dep., January 29, 1976; HD, N124, 1981: NOMI to H-direktoratet, July 6, 1979; August 27, October 8, and November 24, 1981; NOMI to SLK, February 5, 1981; NOMI to H-dir., April 24, 1981; Torbjørn Mork to NOMI, June 4 and September 2, 1981; HD, N124, 1981–1983: several notes and letters, especially: Mork to No-Re-Farm, September 23, 1981; No-Re-Farm to Heløe, November 13, 1981.

This breakthrough was of great importance to Norwegian industry. Conservative Minister of Industry Jens H. Bratz reminded the Health Directorate that for Norwegian firms to compete with foreign industry, a firm national foundation was needed for the financing of research and development. The Norwegian Union of Chemical Industry Workers also supported Norwegian industry's position.[28] The trade unions and the pharmaceutical industry joined forces against the government. The pattern corresponded with broader developments in the same period. In the mid-1970s, governmental systems, established in an era of consensus and economic wealth, came under pressure when the world economy found itself in crisis. New partnerships developed, and in various sectors the labor movement and industry joined forces against the government and its established policies (Torstendahl, 1989).

The new state policies somewhat opened up for a renewed look at the Norwegian market. The combination of existing therapeutic research projects, financial wealth, an increasingly creative Norwegian medical ecosystem, and an emphasis on strategy thinking, somehow led to a cautious expansion of the pharmaceutical division. In 1985, Nyegaard & Co. merged with a former competitor, AFI (A/S Farmaceutisk Industri).[29] AFI was founded in 1918 and had been one of the four industrial companies in Norway which dealt solely with pharmaceuticals. Like Nyegaard & Co., AFI found it increasingly difficult to acquire attractive foreign products, but unlike Nyegaard it had not managed to develop important products of its own. The 1970s had been particularly difficult and AFI was financially very weak when purchased by Nyegaard & Co. in 1985.

Actinor paid AFI's owners about NOK 30 million in Actinor shares. Nyegaard & Co. bid against Norwegian company Apothekernes Laboratorium (AL) for AFI, and the purchase was settled in a final, informal round of bidding. AL probably recognized the same potential in AFI that Nyegaard & Co. had seen. AFI provided a chance to develop a more attractive product range and a merger could lead to gains in efficiency. After the merger, 30 of the 190 AFI employees became redundant, but Nyegaard found work for them in other areas of the corporation. With this acquisition, Nyegaard & Co. became the largest domestic supplier to the Norwegian market with a market share of 8 percent. The acquisition of AFI gave a sorely needed

---

[28] HD, N124, 1981–1983: Jens H. Bratz to S-dep., January 29, 1982; Heløe to Norsk kjemisk Industriarbeiderforbund, January 27, 1982.

[29] The following: board meetings, February 14 and September 5, 1985; note to the board, September 5, 1985: "Resymé vedr. STP 1986–1990 for Nyco-AFI," August 21, 1985.

boost to the pharmaceutical division as such. Nyegaard & Co. also used AFI's buildings located close to Nyegaard. Nyegaard's board members did, however, disagree on the purchase of AFI. Two of the eight opposed the acquisition, believing that there were better ways to use resources than to invest in an old and tired organization.

Dissent over the purchase of AFI in 1985 and the hasty acquisition of Seragen in 1984 reflect an important fact about Actinor and Nyegaard & Co. The idea of heavy investments in pharmaceutical companies was still in its infancy, and there were no obvious tactical solutions. Seragen and AFI were opportunities, but both purchases indicate they were made because the finance was available and because they could be fitted into a corporate growth strategy. Neither division seemed particularly promising after the uncovering of the Seragen challenges. The short-term future still belonged to contrast media.

From strength to strength

The preparations for the launch of Omnipaque seemed to have been immaculate as the new product immediately sold excellently. Moreover, in markets—primarily Japan—where Amipaque was launched quite late, that, too, sold excellently in the first half of the 1980s. The two non-ionic contrast media conquered the global market, and for each year the turnover and the income increased significantly.

As is shown in Table 8.1, these new products represented turnover comparable to the combined sales of pharmaceuticals and reagents in the

Table 8.1 Operating revenues in product areas in million kroner, 1979–1985; fixed prices: 1985 = 100 (SSB consumer price index)

	Pharmaceuticals	Reagents	Contrast media
1979	82	52	99
1980	79	54	119
1981	76	58	118
1982	67	54	129
1983	63	57	143
1984	64	61	239
1985	67	67	327

Source: Nycomed.

first years of the 1980s, and their significance in these years was first and foremost their high profit margin. When sales volume increased dramatically, especially in 1984 and 1985, profit margins kept pace. In 1985, turnover of contrast media was about five times larger than in either of the other divisions. The combined impact of the new technology and the new price level commanded by non-ionic contrast media worked to Nyegaard's advantage.

One bi-product of Amipaque's launch as a myelographic medium was the new price level for vascular contrast agents like Omnipaque. Amipaque's price level, originally constructed by Holtermann, had been formally set in 1974, with its new characteristics as justification for its elevated level compared with old myelographic mediums. Amipaque was the first contrast agent that could be injected into the entire spinal canal, and no one could foresee its market reception. Myelographic examinations also required smaller amounts of contrast medium than vascular examinations, so the high price of Amipaque in volume terms compared with vascular media did not mean that the prices of the respective examinations were directly comparable. Calculated in terms of its iodine content, Amipaque's price was 20 to 40 times higher than the other contrast agents on the market, so the shift was certainly not negligible.[30]

From 1979, when radiologists started to use Amipaque in certain vascular examinations, they increasingly came to prefer this expensive product to regular ionic contrast agents. European sales figures in Table 8.2 for 1979 illustrate this, although US sales at the time were affected very little. In Japan, they quickly started to use Amipaque extensively for vascular purposes, and sales increased considerably in 1984 and 1985.[31] The vascular use of Amipaque clearly indicated that Nyegaard—and Bracco—could justify a price level for the new vascular agents that lay in between that of the older contrast agents and Amipaque. Nyegaard and Bracco introduced new and improved vascular contrast agents, Omnipaque and Iopamidol, respectively, when the use of Amipaque as vascular agent proved that radiologists thought that a higher price than ionic media was justified. Nyegaard and Bracco communicated about setting this new price level for vascular contrast media too.[32]

---

[30] Interview with Thor Andersen and Svein Nilsen, January 31, 1992; NKT, 629, reiserapp: "Addendum til referat fra besøk hos Winthrop Labs" by Bjørn Erik Holst, September 1, 1981.

[31] Odd Kåre Strandli to Stein Annexstad, February 11, 1985; appendix to the board meeting's protocol, February 14, 1985.

[32] I do not have a written source for this information, but this was made clear to me by a high-level Nyegaard employee in a meeting in the early 1990s.

Table 8.2 Revenues of non-ionic contrast media in million kroner, 1977–1985 (current prices)

	Amipaque			Omnipaque
	Europe	USA	Japan	Europe
1977	8	–	–	–
1978	18	4	–	–
1979	25	19	–	–
1980	33	29	–	–
1981	35	25	11	–
1982	37	33	7	11
1983	20	34	11	46
1984	13	31	49	119
1985	11	33	65	201

Note: Europe includes small non-European revenues.
Source: Nycomed.

Table 8.3 Key figures in the accounts, 1980–1985; operating revenues (OR) in million kroner; fixed prices: 1985 = 100 (SSB consumer price index, net operating profit (NOR), and income before taxes (IBT) in percent of OR); solidity (SOL) in percent of assets

	OR	NOP	IBT	SOL
	Year	Million	Percent	Kroner
1980	274	24	24	29
1981	272	23	24	42
1982	285	24	27	54
1983	295	16	16	–
1984	406	25	25	–
1985	510	23	22	–

Note: Royalties included.
Source: Nycomed.

Market developments yielded impressive financial results, both in terms of sales volume and profitability. Nyegaard's relative profitability declined in 1983 (Table 8.3), perhaps due to the replacement of some of Amipaque's profitable sales in Europe by Omnipaque sales. Profitability rose again in 1984, partly because of a sharp increase of Amipaque sales in Japan. A second factor was that the sales volume of Omnipaque increased steadily. Omnipaque gradually came to dominate the company's total sales, including pharmaceuticals and reagents.

After Norgas merged with Nyegaard & Co., all of the products in the field of contrast agents enjoyed substantial success. Amipaque not only meant a new technology but it also raised the price level for all non-ionic contrast agents. Physicians eventually chose Omnipaque for vascular areas because they preferred an expensive substance that was excellent to an ionic one which was cheap but just acceptable. Nyegaard's initial pricing of Amipaque was important in creating a new and attractive international market as well as in reviving interest in research. Nyegaard created both a new technology and a new market. These were indeed exciting times, but something started to emerge as a thought: Since everything was going so smoothly and seemingly effortlessly, maybe an increased effort and clearer priorities would achieve even more?

A new company?

Kåre Moe and his team of Actinor managers started to think that Nyegaard was not fully exploiting its commercial potential. It may not have been easy to fully predict Nyegaard's positive development. After 1982, many elements fell into place. Omnipaque found a high price level and proved itself as a product that would replace older contrast agents. Actinor, a company actively engaged in strategic planning and new to the pharmaceutical industry, wanted reliable evaluations of future prospects. Kåre Moe therefore asked Nyegaard & Co. to bring in the multinational consultant firm McKinsey, a company he was familiar with from his years at AGA and Norgas to help develop strategic planning.[33]

In late 1983, McKinsey and Nyegaard's management began to analyze the three divisions, their market prospects, and Nyegaard's position in these markets. The examination of the three divisions concluded that the pharmaceutical division, in its present state, had no future unless it became part of a larger entity. This somewhat supported the AFI merger. In the reagents division, coagulation tests were considered the most promising, and in the contrast agents division, there were still untold possibilities.[34]

The McKinsey analysis implied that Nyegaard & Co. could expect a new and vastly larger world market in contrast media to unfold. This contributed to a new company awareness, particularly in regard to

[33] Interview with Kåre Moe, April 19, 1993.
[34] NTA, 1135, McKinsey: "Identifying and Evaluating Alternative Strategies for Growth," final report volumes I & II, McKinsey & Co., March 21 and April 12, 1984; board meeting, March 21, 1984.

exploiting the opportunities inherent in X-ray contrast agents.[35] Nyegaard's management calculated with McKinsey that in 1983, there were between 32 and 42 million X-ray examinations using contrast agents worldwide and that by 1990 there could be as many as 68 million. In all probability, prices would not fall. They concluded that Nyegaard & Co. could expect a far higher income than anyone had envisioned.[36]

McKinsey also recommended that *X-ray* contrast agents should be followed up with other contrast agents, particularly those involving the newest technology, magnetic resonance. Research that had already been started in this field should be expanded. Alongside Schering AG, Nyegaard & Co. had the best research competence in the world, and it would be easier for them than for others to make use of this new technology. In addition, McKinsey meant that Nyegaard could sell catheters along with contrast agents, as the subsidiary in England already did. Customers purchasing X-ray contrast media also bought catheters as they were used to inject the contrast agents.[37]

McKinsey's analysis indeed identified income opportunities for X-ray contrast agents, but they also gathered a list of potential threats. Nyegaard's main licensees, Schering AG, Sterling Drug, and Daiichi, were all favorably positioned by their connection to Nyegaard. They had good control of their markets and would eventually be able to introduce their own contrast agents and displace Nyegaard's products. Their license agreements with Nyegaard & Co. generated huge revenues for them, too, which they could invest in research activities and in new product agreements which could conflict with Nyegaard's interests. Schering AG in West Germany was already well on its way and was investing heavily. As well as developing products that would compete with Omnipaque, Schering AG was working on totally new contrast media for magnetic resonance.[38]

The McKinsey assessment outlined a broad "Imaging Strategy." Nyegaard & Co. had tremendous potential, but significant sums had to be invested before this could be realized. Most importantly, Nyegaard & Co. could look forward to an income never before imagined. Second, it was in a unique position in relation to its licensees and the possibility of forging these relations in a new and—for Nyegaard—more profitable way.

---

[35] Interview with Odd Kåre Strandli, October 2, 1992.
[36] NTA, 1135, McKinsey: "Identifying and Evaluating Alternative Strategies for Growth," final report volumes I & II, McKinsey & Co., March 21 and April 12, 1984; board meeting, March 21, 1984.
[37] Ibid.
[38] Ibid.

Nyegaard & Co. had Omnipaque, but it also had two other substances that were at least as good: Iopentol (Imagopaque) and Iodixanol (Visipaque). Nyegaard & Co. saw that this strength represented a threat to the licensees and that it could be utilized by developing Nyegaard's own marketing network. Nyegaard's managers expressed uncertainty about how to handle this potential threat since they agreed among themselves that the company should not ruin its friendly relationships with Sterling Drug and Schering AG. They would have to negotiate on a "win–win" basis. Nyegaard & Co. should receive a larger portion of the total sales income, and licensees would in return be given Nyegaard's new products and technology as soon as they were ready for the market. Nyegaard & Co. would put all of its effort into developing new products, especially in the field of magnetic resonance.[39]

McKinsey introduced an entirely new line of thought. When Nyegaard & Co. had developed Amipaque, the company waited until everything was ready before arranging external license contacts and contracts. In the case of Omnipaque, Nyegaard brought Schering AG and Sterling Drug in at an earlier stage of development because of the need to get the product on the market before Bracco's product was launched. This occurred *after* Nyegaard & Co. had created a new and patented technology, so things worked well. The McKinsey study in 1984 pointed out that Nyegaard & Co. would need a much more clearly defined program for the future if it were to continue its success.

The greatest challenge, in McKinsey's opinion, was management. Rajat Gupta, the leader of the McKinsey group, emphasized Nyegaard's enormous potential and pointed out that the problem would be to find enough expertise to carry out future objectives. Human resources would be the greatest bottleneck in the years to come, and it was extremely important to strengthen management both in quantity and quality. This was particularly important in the development of contrast agents and in avoiding any weakening of resolve in other sectors. The opportunity needed to be seized immediately.[40]

The McKinsey process was reminiscent of Holtermann's quest in the 1960s; contrast media had to be prioritized. Of course, there were differences, not least because one built upon the other. McKinsey introduced market thinking and Holtermann emphasized research

---

[39] Ibid.
[40] Board meeting, March 21 and April 12, 1984.

opportunities. However, McKinsey highlighted research too and Holtermann had had a clear idea about the market. McKinsey did introduce new methods with which to analyze the market, but the question remains: Would a possible Norwegian CEO other than Ulf Blix, one who for decades had been enthusiastic about contrast media, have developed a company that to such a degree was taken by surprise by McKinsey's findings? Probably not.

Taking charge

When McKinsey presented its final reports in the spring of 1984, Actinor had owned Nyegaard & Co. for three years. Actinor had been careful with Nyegaard & Co., practicing flexibility. Although Actinor had introduced new organizational policies, Nyegaard's management kept a relatively free hand. In the spring of 1984, three conditions led Actinor to change its policy regarding Nyegaard & Co. The first was that Actinor planned to concentrate fully on the pharmaceutical industry. Second, Actinor had now become familiar with Nyegaard & Co., and third, the time had come to take advantage of the potential of contrast agents.

Kåre Moe wanted Nyegaard's new CEO succeeding Ulf Blix to come from outside the company. He was not certain that the closely woven management team at Nyegaard & Co. would exploit the full potential in the field of medical imaging. He selected Stein Holst Annexstad from Dyno Industries (a chemical company, specialized in explosives) to come in as vice president under Ulf Blix in the spring of 1984 and then to become CEO as of January 1, 1986.[41] Stein Annexstad was well aware that he was the owner's representative. He had been hired explicitly to ensure that Nyegaard's potential in contrast agents was put to work.[42]

Kåre Moe saw great inconsistency between total concentration on contrast agents and the way Nyegaard's management functioned. Left to itself, Nyegaard & Co., as a technologically oriented company, would probably have continued its broad and innovative work in therapeutic products and contrast agents. Bringing in the services of McKinsey set the company on a different track. The McKinsey analysis and board meeting debates showed that Nyegaard & Co. could choose between two strategies. Contrast agents could be given priority and allocated substantial resources, but

[41] Interview with Kåre Moe, March 12, 1993.
[42] Interview with Stein Annexstad, June 4, 1993.

the company's other operations would suffer.[43] The second option was to give all parts of the company an equal footing and to allow for relative freedom within each unit. Only after some time had passed would the company decide what to do next. In other words, reagents, therapeutics, and a pharmaceutical unit would continue to be financed as in the past, alongside contrast agents. The strategies reflected contrasting corporate viewpoints: If the second option was chosen, contrast media operations would continue in compliance with licensee terms in the belief that research and product development would create new products in the future. This strategy incorporated an element of chance, but it had led to the success of contrast media in the first place (possibly for other reasons than loose reigns). The first choice involved tying up organizational and financial resources in contrast agents with a relatively good guarantee of substantial financial return.

Kåre Moe and Stein Annexstad decided to implement the first option when, in May 1985, it was formally decided that Annexstad would succeed Ulf Blix. Not all of the solutions had been found, but the board had already set important premises. Contrast agents were to be given highest priority. The contrast agents division became the cornerstone of a new international division. There was a major campaign to recruit new personnel and research for contrast media purposes would absorb a much larger portion of the budget.[44] The pharmaceutical and reagent divisions and newly bought AFI were placed under the new Scandinavian division. The creation of two new divisions (Scandinavian and international) was the new administration's response to the board's indication that Nyegaard & Co. needed to develop two different cultures. Research and development continued in the international division but ceased as such in the other division, whose products could not support the costs involved. The task of the Scandinavian division was to focus on marketing activities and to improve cost efficiency.[45] The other research activities at Nyegaard & Co. did survive the reorganization rather well. A central research organization was formed around Nyegaard's expertise in biochemistry.[46] This was to provide new products for the future, but it was decoupled from the Scandinavian division.

---

[43] Board meeting, March 21, 1984; "Nycogruppens STP 1985–89" by Thor Andersen, September 25, 1984; notes after board meeting, September 12, 1984.
[44] Board meeting, December 12, 1985.
[45] "Nycogruppens STP 1985–89" by Thor Andersen, September 25, 1984; notes after board meeting, September 12, 1984.
[46] "Strategic plan for Nyegaard's New Ventures R&D," November 13, 1985 and "Opprettelsen av FoU nye områder . . .," both by Lars Aukrust, November 6, 1985; notes to the board, November 21, 1985.

Needless to say, the changes affecting the Scandinavian division were not popular with everybody. For many of the employees of the reagent division, becoming part of the Scandinavian division was not easy.[47] Since the mid-1960s, reagents had been an important research area; now it became a part of "distribution business."[48] The division's director, Carl Christian Gilhuus-Moe, left Nyegaard & Co. and Bjørn Flatgård became the leader of the Scandinavian division. Flatgård had no background in the pharmaceutical industry but came from Actinor. He had been chosen because of his qualifications as a manager.[49]

The establishment of the two divisions showed important differences in Nyegaard's situation. For Nyegaard & Co., it was a novelty that the highest level of administration set the guidelines for the company's activities. In the original company, decision-making sometimes generated from the lower echelons, and this reversed decision-making process had contributed to the development of contrast agents. Actinor shaped Nyegaard & Co. anew. The earlier Nyegaard administration had not considered leaving the field of contrast media, but its inclination was to give it no higher priority than the company's other undertakings. The new international division did build on the "old Nyegaard & Co.," trying to give new focus and direction to the work that had already been started by Nyegaard & Co. However, the Scandinavian division was a new concept and had little in common with the former Nyegaard & Co. Efficiency and cost control reigned in this division, as it had at Nyegaard & Co. during the 1950s. But this time around, cost cutting was not to be inspired by a fundamental ambition to develop new products.

Conclusion

During Actinor's reign at Nyegaard & Co., the emphasis of the company's direction was radically shifted. The aim was no longer only to look for innovations in general but also to develop a commercial strategy that would

[47] Interview with Øivind Grimmer, February 16, 1993; Stein Annexstad, June 4, 1993; Svein Ribe-Anderssen, May 28, 1993.
[48] "Betenkning vedrørende reagensvirksomhetens organisering" by Stein Annexstad, November 20, 1985; note to the board, November 21, 1985.
[49] Interview with Stein Annexstad, June 4, 1993.

secure more income from its existing contrast media business, as well as position the company for future developments within the same field. Innovation that had for so many years been seen as a tool with which to change the company's fortunes was to be used for purposes not foreseen those many years ago. Actinor aimed to reshape Nyegaard & Co. as one of the international pharmaceutical companies, one that had its eye as much on markets as on research.

Surprisingly, this new emphasis on market considerations led to a reappraisal of the traditional Norwegian pharmaceutical business. Making low-volume pharmaceutical products had been the starting point of it all, and it had been difficult and thankless at long periods when profitability was low or non-existent. Paradoxically, just when the global market transformed the contrast media business to a great international success, a different policy from the Norwegian pharmaceutical authorities opened up the possibility for exploiting the traditional Norwegian business in a new way consolidating the Norwegian generic market. Seen together with a Norwegian medical ecosystem that for some time—and increasingly through the 1980s—developed scientific ideas that could be advantageous for Nyegaard, the whole "home market" situation could be seen as much more encouraging that in previous decades. Strategic planning could be used also to develop the pharmaceutical business in new ways.

How much did the focus on strategic planning—on identifying market opportunities—really represent a change? Appointing outsider Stein Annexstad with the explicit agenda of prioritizing contrast agents could have been done without the strategy jargon. Identifying the inherent and concrete opportunities within contrast agents could easily have been achieved without McKinsey, although the thoroughness of its work should not be underestimated. The very real differences that could be observed between the research achievements of the contrast media group and the biochemical line was clear for everybody to see—even without the knowledge of the extensive and fruitless liver research of the 1950s and 1960s. But, regardless of inadequacies and crystal-clear prospects, the old Nyegaard had been a very functional whole that had grown together over a long time. Kåre Moe, CEO of Actinor, wanted change, and he took the leadership baton from Blix's hands (after he had fully served his period) and gave it to someone from the outside who he knew would think differently about internal priorities.

References

Chandler, A. D. 1962. *Strategy and Structure: Chapters in the History of the Industrial Enterprise.* Cambridge, MA: The MIT Press.

Galambos, L. 1991. "Values." *In*: Sturchio, J. L. (ed.) *Values & Visions: A Merck Century.* Rahway, NJ: Merck, Sharp and Dohme, pp. 5–156.

Gammelsæter, H. 1991. *Organisasjonsendring gjennom generasjoner av ledere: en studie av endringer i Hafslund Nycomed, Elkem og Norsk hydro.* Molde: Møreforsking Molde.

Hanisch, T. J. and Lange, E. 1986. *Veien til velstand: industriens utvikling i Norge gjennom 50 år.* Oslo: Universitetsforlaget.

Hax, A. C. and Majluf, N. S. 1984. *Strategic Management. An Integrative Perspective.* Englewood Cliffs, NJ: Prentice Hall.

Hikino, T., Zamagni, V., and Galambos, L. 2007. "Introduction." *In*: Galambos, L., Hikino, T., and Zamagni, V. (eds) *The Global Chemical Industry in the Age of the Petrochemical Revolution.* Cambridge: Cambridge University Press, pp. 1–20.

Nerheim, G. 1983. *Gassflamme og lysbue: perspektiver på et sveisefirmas historie: Norgas AS 1908–1983.* Stavanger: Universitetsforlaget.

Rasmussen, N. 2014. *Gene Jockeys: Life Science and the Rise of Biotech Enterprise.* Baltimore, MD: Johns Hopkins University Press.

Torstendahl, R. 1989. "Teknologi och samhällsutveckling 1850–1980. Fyra faser i västeuropeisk industrikapitalism." *In*: Nybom, T. and Torstendahl, R. (eds) *Byråkratisering och maktfördelning.* Lund: Studentlitteratur, pp. 85–102.

9
Transformed Surroundings and New Priorities

The 1980s was a major period of corporate restructuring in the western world. The process, which left a strong footprint in the pharmaceutical industry, extended well into the 1990s. Very large, international firms emerged in an industry that had been largely national at its core. The merger movement was obviously influenced by the general trend in the 1980s of shareholders asserting their power in order to restructure businesses. For the pharmaceutical industry, this reorganization very often took the form of mergers that created much larger entities which sought economies of scale in international marketing operations, broader-based research efforts, and attempts to spread the risks of innovation (Kumar, 2012). For some firms, these were protective moves to counterbalance the decline in the 1990s of important innovations in the industry (Henderson and Cockburn, 1996).

For the Scandinavian pharmaceutical industry, this merger movement had deep implications. The two large Swedish companies Pharmacia and Astra merged in 1995 and 1999, respectively, with US Upjohn and British Zeneca. Pharmacia Upjohn subsequently merged with Pfizer. In short, the Swedes took full advantage of the trend toward international mergers. The Danes followed their own path: the two adversaries Novo and Nordisk joined forces in 1989 to form a single, large Scandinavian-owned pharmaceutical company. Meanwhile, the business that was once Nycomed—which, from 1986, was the new name of Nyegaard & Co.—merged with British Amersham in 1997.

From 1986 to 1997, Nycomed's development was characterized by a puzzling duality: On the one hand, the company created and experienced great commercial success, both through its contrast media sales and through numerous acquisitions used to develop its business. Nycomed realized a lot of the commercial potential that had previously been identified but not exploited. On the other hand, it was caught in several consolidation

Norway's Pharmaceutical Revolution. Knut Sogner, Oxford University Press.
© Knut Sogner (2022). DOI: 10.1093/oso/9780192869005.003.0009

processes, starting when it was purchased by the Norwegian company Hafslund in 1985 and ending with the merger—as the financially strong but
organizationally "weak" partner—with British Amersham in 1997.

In an unfriendly takeover in 1985, conglomerate Hafslund bought Actinor. Hafslund was a traditional energy-producing company that had diversified. Hafslund, rechristened Hafslund Nycomed in 1988, went wholeheartedly into the pharmaceutical business, and therefore a new group of
Norwegian owners and managers came to dominate Nycomed into the
1990s. They continued some of the processes established under Actinor
but with an emphasis much more clearly directed at creating shareholder
value and catering to a stock market agenda. The willingness to merge
Nycomed into a foreign company—after establishing a very favorable
commercial position—indicates that in a world of stock listings, the dynamic of measuring a company's worth on a short-term basis brings in
a volatile component. The company and its management is measured
according to alternative investments in the short term, and statements
about the fruitfulness of longer-term horizons ring hollow in the ears of
investors.

The challenges of the contrast media community

Of all the various activities Nyegaard & Co. could do to better its business
position in the short and long run, one stood out in 1985: renegotiate its
contracts for non-ionic contrast media with Sterling Winthrop and Schering AG. Nyegaard had to appropriate more of the income generated from
Omnipaque. McKinsey's consultants and the leaders from Actinor and
Hafslund criticized Ulf Blix and Nyegaard's older leadership about these
contracts.

The new leaders possibly underrated the impact of Holtermann's ploy of
launching the new non-ionic contrast media, first as myelographic media,
then as a vascular product. Blix had followed up, and it turned out bril-
liantly. Nyegaard had been able to sell a new niche product and to make
deals with the larger companies capable of giving the product a strong position in the non-ionic market. The fact that the small Italian Bracco headed
to market in the 1970s with a comparable non-ionic product to Omnipaque
may have unnerved the two larger companies. Rather than stalling the new
concept of non-ionic contrast media, however, the large licensees launched

and supported it with their large and respected staffs in the world's most important markets.

The year 1985 was an opportune time to change the firm's contracts. When the renegotiation discussion started, 67 percent of all contrast media volume came from sales to Schering.[1] In the foreseeable future, something in the region of 70 percent of sales would be going through the big three distributers: Schering AG, Sterling Winthrop, and Japanese Daiichi.[2] They earned very healthy profits, and they kept and improved their positions in their respective markets.

Schering AG had already exploited the situation by launching its own non-ionic contrast medium, Ultravist. At the very time Omnipaque proved a great success for Schering AG on the German market (the world's third largest home market for pharmaceuticals), Schering AG added its own in-house-developed, non-ionic contrast medium to its portfolio. Schering had previously informed Nyegaard that it would price Ultravist at 10 percent more than Omnipaque and that Schering had no intention of competing with Omnipaque but that Ultravist was needed vis-à-vis other products on the market such as Hexabrix and Iopadimol. In April 1985, Schering informed Nyegaard that Ultravist would be sold at the same price level as Omnipaque and explained that the launch of the product had already taken place. Schering AG was keen to establish a business in the United States, but the Norwegian reaction was acidic: "We are as you will understand, deeply concerned about the situation for Omnipaque. Nyegaard can as we also stated during the meeting, not just let the product be cannibalized."[3]

Ulf Blix—the outgoing chief executive officer (CEO)—followed up with a personal letter to his long-term associate, Wolfgang Degen, in Schering. Blix criticized the process and Schering's outreach with suggestions for future collaboration:

I shall not comment here on your proposal for a new [income-sharing] formula, because I think the effects of a diminished sale of Omnipaque by cannibalization may be harmful for future collaboration regardless of purely economic arrangements. If such cannibalization takes place to an extent which we consider unfair, there will of course be consequences with regard to future products, since we

[1] RA, Nycomed, 1st part. Aa-L0002, styreprotokoll 1981–1986: board meeting in Nycomed, September 5, 1985.

[2] Which was the situation in 1988. RA, Nycomed, 1st part. Ab-0026, Nycomed board meetings etc. 1988–1992: minutes from meeting in Nycomed Imaging's council, December 2, 1988.

[3] RA, Nycomed, 2nd part. E0009: Odd Kåre Strandli to Fragner, May 14, 1985.

> will be looking at such cannibalization as a breach of confidence. Also we have
> new products in the pipeline, which we, in such case, would feel forced to launch
> in Germany and your other exclusive territories through other channels. [...]
> The decisive factor in this issue will of course not be in the formula we arrive at,
> but Schering's attitude to best effort in the best sense of the word, which means
> your positioning of the two products in question.[4]

Blix reminded Wolfgang Degen about the need to establish a common spirit behind contractual arrangements. Nyegaard had given Schering exclusive rights to market Omnipaque, which came with the responsibility to honor the intent of the contract and represent Nyegaard's interests. No doubt, Schering misused its size and market presence by behaving the way it did with the launch of its own product. Nyegaard could now exploit its position as a global leader with a head start and patent protection in contrast media chemistry. It had two new products: Visipaque (Iodixanol) and Imagopaque (Iopentol). Imagopaque was a comparable product to Omnipaque, Iopadimol (Bracco), and Ultravist (Schering AG). Visipaque had lower osmolality than these other products and possibly represented another new generation of non-ionic contrast media. Blix leaned on Degen:

> Apart from the possible effects on the Schering/Nyegaard relationship, I will also
> remind you of the effects on the closed society of the few firms engaged in imaging
> research. If one wants to keep a door open for future collaboration with other
> firms, the image of being reliable is perhaps the key factor.[5]

Strong words, indeed, but Nyegaard behaved cautiously with Schering.[6] Noticeably absent from this serious interchange was the threat of legal action. The board of Nyegaard concluded that its only real advantage was its range of research projects new and old.[7] The board also assumed that Schering would keep Omnipaque sales stagnant and let new business go to its own product. For the chairman of the board (the outgoing former head of Actinor, Kåre Moe), this kind of situation further legitimized additional investment into contrast media research.

Nycomed, as Nyegaard & Co. was named from 1986, did not manage to stop Schering from competing, but it quite possibly prevented additional

---

[4] RA, Nycomed, 2nd part. E0009: Ulf Blix to Degen, May 28, 1985. Original underlining.
[5] Ibid. Original underlining.
[6] See, e.g. RA, Nycomed, 2nd part. E.0020: Hafslund Nycomeds STP 1990–1994, September 19, 1989.
[7] RA, Nycomed, 1st part. Aa-L0002, styreprotokoll 1981–1986: board meeting in Nycomed, September 5, 1985.

damage. In 1990, the two companies signed a deal that was adjusted in Nycomed's favor.[8] Even during these years of strained business relationship, the communication between the companies evolved in a positive way.[9] Nycomed learned that Schering, once again, had turned its full attention to contrast media. In addition to Ultravist, Schering also developed contrast media for new imaging technologies, primarily magnetic resonance imaging (MRI). Here, Schering was ahead of Nycomed.

The Schering situation may have been catalytic in shaping an even firmer way forward; here are Stein Annexstad's words to the board of directors in March 1987:

> During the latter half of 1986, Nycomed adopted a new strategy that calls for both concentration and selective widening of its business horizon: Concentration on medical imaging; and a wider business horizon in the sense of including substitute imaging technologies to X-ray such as nuclear magnetic resonance (MRI) and ultrasound. Diagnosis, and control are considered to be basic parts of the Nycomed business idea, commercially targeted however, mainly at the Scandinavian market.[10]

He also mentioned the importance of getting more "added value downstream" and referred to ongoing negotiations with Sterling Winthrop. It was now also time to let Seragen in Boston go. Just a couple of months later, Seragen was sold.[11]

Nycomed had established a new and lucrative market and through its portfolio of products could renegotiate contracts to reap major benefits from the growing market for non-ionic contrast media. The longer-term threat to this market in the form of new imaging technologies was also an opportunity for a company with substantial income to spend on research and development. To support this new line of research, the company had to hire people and further strengthen its human capital.[12] Research to find new contrast media for ultrasound and MRI respectively entailed

---

[8] RA, Nycomed, 1st part. Ab-L0026, Nycomed board meetings etc. 1988–1992: board meeting, March 20, 1990.

[9] RA, Nycomed, 1st part. Ab-L0025, Nycomed board meetings, 1986–1987: the Nycomed group's STP 1987/91, addendum to board meeting, September 3 and 4, 1986; Stein Annexstad to the board of directors, March 26, 1987.

[10] RA, Nycomed, 1st part. Ab-L0025, Nycomed board meetings, 1986–1987: Stein Annexstad to the board of directors, March 26, 1987.

[11] RA, Nycomed, 1st part. Ab-L0025: Nycomed board meetings, 1986–1987: "Forslag til møteprotokoll," September 17, 1987.

[12] RA, Nycomed, 1st part. Ab-L0025: Nycomed board meetings, 1986–1987: "Forslag til møteprotokoll," September 4, 1986.

wholly different chemistries than for X-ray contrast media. Nycomed lagged behind Schering AG in these new modalities and consequently signed a licensing agreement for the ultrasound product Albunex with a US company. It then purchased the Californian company Salutar, which had several substances suitable for various purposes in MRI, in 1989.[13] Nycomed was making the most of its advantageous financial position.

The firm pressed forward in the "friendly" atmosphere of the contrast media business. The complex relationship with Schering AG reflected the view that friendliness with other contrast media companies was beneficial. That the Italian company Bracco became such a major competitor had been treated in the same friendly manner. Bracco found a hole in Nycomed's patents, but apparently the hole was not big enough to prevent a friendly settlement that gave Nycomed a royalty of Bracco's sales.[14] Rather than develop a dispute that would find its solution in court, Nycomed thereby not only settled a difficult situation but also established a business understanding with its biggest competitor.

Sterling Drug was Nycomed's main "ally." That relationship reflected many years of close communication and increased cooperation. That said, Sterling enjoyed great profitability in the United States from its Omnipaque deal and was in an increasingly vulnerable position as the only established contrast media company without a state-of-the-art product of its own. As a result, Nycomed succeeded almost beyond expectations in its negotiations to get a better deal.[15] It threatened to establish its own US sales organization based on Imagopaque and Visipaque. In the summer of 1987, it was able to sign a new deal bringing in much more royalty from Sterling's sales.[16] The deal gave Sterling the "right of first refusal" for new products[17] but gave Nycomed an estimated extra NOK 200 million a year in the first year and with more to come as sales were expected to increase (Aaserud, 1987). Clearly, matters were turned to Nycomed's advantage.[18]

The company's position within the community of contrast media companies was now comparable to that of former leaders Schering AG and Sterling Drug. When Nycomed launched its first contrast medium for MRI,

[13] RA, Nycomed, 1st part. Ab-L0026: Nycomed board meetings, 1988–1992: "Referat fra styremøte," February 6, 1989.
[14] Interview with Carl Christian Gilhuus-Moe, August 22, 2019.
[15] Interview with Dagfinn Hansen, March 10, 2020.
[16] RA, Nycomed, 1st part. Ab-L0025: Nycomed board meetings, 1986–1987: "Forslag til møteprotokoll," June 16, 1987.
[17] RA, Nycomed, 2nd part. E.L0020: Hafslund Nycomeds STP 1990–1994, September 19, 1989.
[18] RA, Nycomed, 1st part. Ab-L0026: Nycomed board meetings, 1988–1992: "Referat fra rådsmøte i Nycomed Imaging," December 2, 1988.

a product developed by Salutar and given the name Omniscan, meetings were held between the heads of the three companies. Schering AG claimed that Omniscan infringed on its US patents, but all of the companies agreed that they had to find a "business solution." This not only meant that they would not want to go to court but also included other business matters that concerned the three companies. That this, either explicitly or implicitly, also included Schering AG's ambition to enter the US market with its X-ray contrast media Ultravist made matters complicated.[19] The solution brought a payment from Nycomed to Schering AG; Sterling could thereafter launch Omniscan in the United States in 1993. But along the way, Schering AG nevertheless filed a suit against Sterling—at the same time as Schering AG reached out to Nycomed and suggested tighter collaboration.[20]

By the very beginning of the 1990s, Nycomed had advanced significantly as an international player within both its X-ray contrast field and the emerging broader-imaging area. By a combination of rich financial resources, renegotiations of contracts, research results, licenses, and acquisitions, in particular the building of a European marketing network through the purchase of French Ingenor and Austrian-German CL Pharma, Nycomed may arguably be said to have become the leading global company in its field. Still, the firm had two particularly noteworthy weaknesses. Nycomed was strong in X-ray contrast media but not so much within the newer modalities like ultrasound and MRI. Nycomed's products had penetrated all important global markets, yet the end-user sales were mostly dealt with by licensees. That precluded Nycomed from both substantial income and direct user contact, something that could be a real disadvantage when the new imaging technologies fully emerged.

New shareholders, new leaders

The merger of Nycomed with Actinor had been friendly and cautious, yet had happened on the doorstep of a new shareholder activism that also affected the Oslo stock exchange. Hafslund's purchase of Actinor in 1985 was possibly the first significant unfriendly takeover in the new shareholder-centered world of Norway in the 1980s. Hafslund, as owner of

---

[19] RA, Nycomed, 1st part. Ab-L0026: Nycomed board meetings, 1988–1992: "MRI Patent Situation in the United States, vedlegg til styremøte," April 23, 1991.
[20] RA, Nycomed, 1st part. Ab-L0027: "Styremøte," January 22, 1992.

Nycomed, meant an increased emphasis on shareholder values. Becoming more international, the firm was perforce becoming less Norwegian too.

Hafslund was an old and wealthy company with a core business in electricity production and, in 1983, had been targeted by Tharald Brøvig and Terje Mikalsen, two wealthy investors with a background in shipping and industry. At the time, they were very successful investors in Norsk Data, a minicomputer company stock-listed in New York. They bought into Hafslund as an undervalued company, and as new members of the board of directors they met a company management that was indeed working for reorganization (Næss, 2012).[21] Hafslund looked to buy other companies and had for some time zoomed in on Actinor to get hold of Nycomed. Mikalsen and Brøvig thought this an interesting avenue and supported the purchase that was finalized in early 1985.

Hafslund had to rearrange itself before it could start to dominate Nycomed, though. There was a lot to sort out in the merged conglomerate. Stein Annexstad had Hafslund's trust and recognized that it was very much up to him and his leadership group to blend Nycomed into the Hafslund organization.[22] Hafslund's board did find it necessary to change the enterprise's CEO, and in the fall of 1987 Svein Aaser, a 41-year-old business economist with extensive managerial experience replaced Emil Eriksrud as head of Hafslund. Under Aaser, in late 1987, Hafslund declared itself a pharmaceutical industrial company fully integrated with Nycomed: "The main goal is to use all available resources to realise Nycomed's potential," the board declared.[23] In May 1988, Hafslund changed its name to Hafslund Nycomed; in June, the large shareholder Terje Mikalsen became chairman of the board, and over subsequent years a lot of the non-pharmaceutical activity was sold off (Næss, 2012).

CEO Svein Aaser immediately forged ties with Stein Annexstad. Annexstad supported Hafslund's aim to concentrate on pharmaceuticals and became number two in the emerging organization.[24] Annexstad then worked to reposition Nycomed within the international contrast media community. On the face of it, Annexstad and Actinor had changed the course of Nycomed in a direction that supposedly would blend well with Aaser and Hafslund. Says Annexstad about his troubled alliance with Aaser:

---

[21] Interview with Terje Mikalsen, August 14, 2018.

[22] "Noen erindringer fra Nycomed 1985–1991" by Stein Annexstad, January 25, 2020, unpublished PM with the author.

[23] RA, Nycomed, 1st part. Ab-L0026: Nycomed styremøter, 1988–1990: "Forslag til møteprotokoll," November 24, 1987.

[24] Interview with Stein Annexstad, December 16, 2014.

This should prove to be unfortunate for me personally in the short term and in my opinion industrially in the longer term. Not much time went by before it emerged that for Aaser it was more important to build his own position than to develop Nycomed along the industrial-strategic parameters we had established.[25]

In early 1991, Annexstad resigned. Before that, his position as head of Nycomed AS, in all practicality the administrative head of pharmaceuticals in Actinor and Hafslund, was transformed. First, Aaser increasingly became active in pharmaceuticals, and in 1990 he recreated the modest Scandinavian division as the ambitious Nycomed Pharma and the start of a major generics business. He made Nycomed Pharma the equal of Nycomed AS (subsequently rechristened Nycomed Imaging).

Aaser took charge of Hafslund Nycomed. He was a very assertive leader and was described by some of those working close to him as able, operative, restless, and control concerned.[26] He replaced Annexstad with one of those McKinsey consultants who had studied the contrast media strategy, Gert W. Munthe. Aaser's determined path into generics was alien to Nycomed's culture and to Annexstad's thinking. Ever since the end of the Second World War, the business had striven to get out of generics and into selling original pharmaceuticals. It had sought close and articulate relationships with the medical sector that was concerned with bringing new and improved pharmaceuticals to patients.

Hafslund Nycomed was a construction of the new, shareholder-oriented times of the 1980s. "Nobody is whistling in the hallways anymore," an old Hafslund employee said (Næss, 2012: 206). This was part of the unanticipated price of becoming an international business. As a result of bringing to the surface all that was good about the company, Hafslund Nycomed became the darling of the stock market. Every year, sales increased and the profit rates were extremely high. Omnipaque sales increasingly dominated the company. Hafslund Nycomed became the second most valuable company on the Oslo stock exchange in the years around 1990, just somewhat below the conglomerate Norsk Hydro. Much was done to promote the Hafslund Nycomed shares. In September 1988, the Norwegian government granted permission to raise the possible foreign ownership share from

[25] <Noen erindringer fra Nycomed 1985–1991" by Stein Annexstad, January 25, 2020, unpublished PM with the author.
[26] Interview with Gert W. Munthe, December 5, 2012; interview with Stein Annexstad, December 16, 2014.

20 percent to 33 percent.[27] In June 1989, the shares became tradeable at the London stock exchange. New capital was raised.[28] Listings in Frankfurt, Vienna (both 1990), and New York (1992) followed.

Large shareholders Mikalsen and Brøvig clearly led the way in internationalizing the shares. Hafslund Nycomed followed a similar pattern to Norsk Data, the company that Mikalsen and Brøvig developed from the board room in parallel with Hafslund Nycomed. No doubt they had the full support of CEO Aaser.[29] And they did not push something that went against the financial forces of the day. Investment bank Merrill Lynch wholeheartedly bid in the spring of 1992 to organize the New York listing of Hafslund Nycomed (Ramel, 2011: 181 and 223f). Merrill Lynch courted Aaser, who was one of a select group of Nordic top managers that were invited to exclusive fishing and hunting trips.

By the early 1990s, Hafslund Nycomed was clearly one of those companies that prioritized maximizing shareholder value (Lazonick and O'Sullivan, 2000). Although that is not a precise term, it covers a lot of what happened in the organization. Great attention was given to the share price, for the sake of the shareholders but also to prevent takeovers. Hafslund Nycomed also sought alignment of shareholders and top management through an options program in which the executives received the right (i.e. option) to buy shares at today's value at a future date. The goal was to secure managers' interest in the rise of future share prices.

It is in this shareholder value context that Aaser's talk to the board in early 1991 must be interpreted.[30] After yet another record-breaking year of turnover and profit achievements, his message was rather cold: "We need to develop, or have access to, new products in addition to our current product portfolio rather soon."[31] This was because of the market expectations of the future share value, and he emphasized that the current portfolio of products in the pipeline was somewhat uncertain. New products are always uncertain. What he did not say, or at least his presentation does not state, is that to achieve a market success of the magnitude of non-ionic contrast media *again* would be a very tall order.

Aaser challenged his organization to achieve better results. For some of the older employees, the middle management of Nycomed, the new focus

[27] Annual report, 1988 (Hafslund Nycomed).
[28] Annual report, 1989 (Hafslund Nycomed).
[29] Interview with Terje Mikalsen, August 14, 2019.
[30] Hafslund, Hafslund Nycomed styresaker, January 2, 1991–December 11, 1991, Sak 51/91 på styremøtet: Svein Aaser's notes.
[31] Ibid.

on profitability was hard to swallow. One of these employees was engineer Leif G. Haugen, head of research Hugo Holtermann's right-hand man in the 1960s, himself for a time head of research. In 1992, he was responsible for the company's patents and a member of the board as employee representative:

> The saying that is rushing around in my head, is that we do as we do and we plan like this and that *because we must earn money*. Yes, we must, but the thought sequence is wrong for me. I feel that this wholly unnecessarily leads me to a colder and less motivating climate. So I turn it around and try the thought of the opposite sequence: We must earn money *because we want to do this and that*. We want to create and sell products that the world around us really needs
>
> (Næss, 2012: 205).[32]

Haugen was part of the research team that had brought the non-ionic contrast media forward. Old Nycomed—or Nyegaard & Co.—had been a broadly oriented, scientifically minded company. Pharmaceutical enterprises in Norway used to be a target for being profit-seeking rather than ethical, and the clear turn of the 1960s to establish a research base and a foundation in original products had been important for company morale. Haugen's statement says something about the pride that he and his colleagues had had all those years ago. *They* had seen their company as an ethical business: One that had important tasks to accomplish—like developing new drugs.

It was almost impossible to call Hafslund Nycomed an unethical company. It operated with the strictest standards and aimed to develop new drugs. But it aimed more explicitly to create shareholder value, concerned itself about financial targets, and developed a broader industrial agenda to supplant its research core. There was, of course, no turning back to the old company. But placing "value creation before medical agenda" constituted a new set of goals and an attempt at creating a new company culture.

Corporate strategy and the direction of research

Hafslund changed much about the overall direction of Nycomed's business but seemingly never touched research before the 1990s. For Hafslund,

---

[32] My translation.

Nycomed research was of the utmost importance, not least for creating shareholder value by informing the stock market about exciting pipelines of new products. There are basically two versions of how successful this undertaking eventually was: The research organization brought forward new products like Imagopaque and Visipaque that were of the utmost importance to the company. However, these two products stemmed as chemical molecules from Holtermann's days (he is himself named in the Visipaque patent). Nothing of equal importance was ever achieved by the huge and richly funded research organization.

Research is fraught with uncertainty. Hafslund Nycomed was certainly not alone among pharmaceutical companies in coming up short in the 1990s and early 2000s. Part of the reason why so many pharmaceutical companies merged at this time was because of their lack of in-house innovation. Mergers meant building larger corporations with larger research portfolios, hedging for research uncertainty by pooling products and seeking economies of scale and scope.

Did Hafslund do damage? Nycomed's research organization actually knew very little about why Hugo Holtermann succeeded in the 1960s. Holtermann was never asked to explain his road to success.[33] The King of Norway made Holtermann Knight of the Royal Order of St Olav for his services to Nyegaard only after the independently written history of Nyegaard/Nycomed was published in 1994 (Amdam and Sogner, 1994). Everybody seemed to believe that Torsten Almén was the inventor. Even though Almén mattered, Holtermann was the planner, the organizer, and the chemical thinker behind the success.

In the aftermath of the 1969 breakthrough, Nyegaard and Nycomed became preoccupied with important development tasks and the organic chemistry part of the research and development (R&D) organization shifted emphasis from inventiveness to development. Again, Blix's reluctance to continue an inventive line within the successful group of organic chemists is a puzzle, although he always seemed to want to prioritize biochemistry. Holtermann's successors in leading this research, principally Leif G. Haugen, Trond Jacobsen, Åse Aulie Michelet, and Arne Berg, prepared Omnipaque, Imagopaque, and Visipaque—and were involved with a host of other molecules (some of which made it to the market). This kind of development work did not diminish in importance in the 1990s, and even

---

[33] Several conversations with the author; see interviews in the notes to Chapter 4. The theme came up because the author asked about it.

products that were on the market demanded attention from the research department.[34]

Much of the return to inventiveness in organic chemistry in the late 1980s concerned new imaging modalities like MRI and ultrasound. Clearly, the most important task in the years ahead was "to continuously feed the Development Organization with new good projects which will turn into new profitable products."[35] The purchase of Salutar in 1989 led to continuation of its research on MRI in California, while another MRI research unit was established that same year around Torsten Almén in Malmö, Sweden. Nycomed had its own MRI and ultrasound research in Oslo too, and the brand new research facility named after the Blix family opened up in 1990. All of this built on Nycomed's very successful research on X-ray contrast media, and in 1989 the firm tried to advance its organic chemistry research through a decentralization strategy, which was also an internationalization strategy:

> The organising is based on a sensible partition of the R&D milieus through the establishment of R&D satellites outside the huge concentration in Oslo/Storo. The goal is for the milieus in the satellites to have better/optimal possibilities for innovation and idea generation. The satellites will be located with interesting groups.[36]

As of 1989, the board again discussed whether too much emphasis was being placed on imaging research. Another important line of products would be attractive and an insurance against setbacks within imaging.[37]

Hafslund inherited a broad approach to research that had room for therapeutic projects as well as those devoted to imaging.[38] Ulf Blix had seen biochemical research as the company's "inventiveness avenue," and Stein Annexstad had carried the approach forward. Annexstad did scale down the already limited research into reagents and did not take the opportunity to take a bigger role in developing the products that Owren and Eldjarn had introduced.[39] But he renewed the research portfolio. Several new projects

[34] RA, Nycomed, 1st part. Ab-L0027, strategic plan 1991–2001, the Nycomed development program, vedlegg til styremøte, June 25, 1991.

[35] Ibid.

[36] RA, Nycomed, 1st part. Ab-L0026, Nycomed styremøter etc. 1988–1992: Vedlegg til styremøte, September 19, 1989, STP FoU, 1990. My translation.

[37] RA, Nycomed, 1st part. Ab-L0026, Nycomed styremøter etc. 1988–1992: board meeting, September 19, 1989.

[38] Interview with Geit Gogstad and Gunnar Sælid, January 24, 2020.

[39] Interview with Øivind Grimmer, December 18, 2014.

concerned peptides. The most important and extensive of these was the one that involved Professor Ole Didrik Lærum, later chairman of the Norwegian Research Council. The project entered Nycomed in the beginning of the 1980s and went through several stages. From the mid-1980s, they seemed to have found a peptide that stimulated the bone marrow's capacity to produce white blood cells and therefore could facilitate tougher treatments of chemotherapy.[40] There were also a couple of other projects in immunology and cancer treatment. The Nycocard concept was a fairly big Scandinavian commercial success involving quick tests to be used at doctor's offices.[41]

When Svein Aaser took command of the research strategy in 1991, he emphasized the need for something new—"a quantum leap." Aaser—with the help of consultants Arthur D. Little—viewed the corporation's research activities as too scattered, lacking synergies between the imaging and the therapeutic areas; it had reached, he concluded, a total expenditure that was at the limit of what the company could afford.[42] Arthur D. Little regarded the therapeutic projects as highly promising but noted that the current portfolio was "very diversified, and resources are thinly stretched on too many projects. [. . .] the current R&D base is insufficient to give a thrust in innovative therapeutics."[43] The main peptide project and the other therapeutical studies pooled in the company Bioreg survived the process of re-examination.[44]

Aaser's research evaluation process represented a logic that was new to Nycomed. The call for sourcing competence, networks, and alliances in the global locations with the highest prestige and the emphasis on "the forces driving the industry," was novel stuff.[45] This meant challenging the Oslo location of central research that historically had been built up around Norwegian researchers who primarily collaborated with Norwegian universities and hospitals—but which had been connected, since the interwar period, to research networks in Europe and the United States. Aaser rocked the collaborative "boat" that the brothers Blix built to create a common

[40] Interview with Geir Gogstad, December 4, 2019 and interview with Tore Skotland, March 26 and April 6, 2020.

[41] Interview with Geir Gogstad, December 4, 2019.

[42] Hafslund Nycomed styresaker, January 2, 1991–December 11, 1991, Sak 51/91 på styremøtet: Svein Aaser's introduction; RA, Nycomed, 1st part. Ab-L0027: Hafslund Nycomed AS corporate strategy 1992–1994, Horizon 2001, October 30, 1991.

[43] RA, Nycomed, 1st part. Ab-L0027: Hafslund Nycomed AS corporate strategy 1992–1994, Horizon 2001, October 30, 1991.

[44] Ibid. Interview with Geir Gogstad, December 4, 2019.

[45] RA, Nycomed, 1st part. Ab-L0027: Hafslund Nycomed AS corporate strategy 1992–1994, Horizon 2001, October 30, 1991.

destiny. The road to research success had indeed been to collaborate internationally, but this strategy was always based on a logic that took the Oslo location as the foundation.

Nycomed's own success recipe of the 1960s and beyond pointed in a different direction to the one proposed by Aaser: It was market oriented (for the myelographic market) and went explicitly against "the forces driving the industry." Holtermann wanted to do research in an area where no one else was working. First among his motivations, though, was to utilize company capabilities and to use national and international networks. He aimed to create an avenue to a new path—what might become a trend itself, a micro trend.

Hafslund Nycomed under Svein Aaser was moving away from creating new room for research-directed strategies. Terje Mikalsen, the chairman of the board, emphasized his own frustration with the lack of research results.[46] He was skeptical about therapeutic drugs. They represented extremely costly testing and very risky development. He thought the company needed to develop more broadly and take industrial opportunities. From 1991, Hafslund Nycomed no longer formally employed a research director.[47] Trond Jacobsen, who had a contrast media background, had until then held this position; he continued in top management, but he was given new tasks in business development.

For key members of the research staff, the changes felt dramatic. A few years later, in early 1996, Gunnar Sælid, vice president of therapeutic research within Hafslund Nycomed, gave a very critical account of how research had been moved around in the organization, disrupting continuity. Top management, he said:

> [. . .] do not have the necessary knowledge of what the international pharmaceutical industry is about. This has been accentuated by the gradual development of minimal real communication with the expertise within the organization. The Corporation has not had a unifying R&D leadership during the last six years.[48]

Sælid obviously aimed to promote therapeutic research rather than imaging research. But he made several pertinent points about the imaging

---

[46] Mikalsen to Knut Sogner, March 31 and April 4, 2020.
[47] Annual reports (Hafslund Nycomed); also interview with Geir Gogstad and Gunnar Sælid, January 24, 2002.
[48] Sælid til Mikalsen, February 12, 1996 (document with the author).

research that later came to be true, such as the possibility that Visipaque would not become comparable in commercial importance to what Omnipaque had been and that MRI and ultrasound products for very specific purposes were overvalued as important commercial avenues, concluding that very little had come out of prioritizing imaging research. He did not criticize prioritizing imaging research as such but rather top management shortcomings. To formulate this kind of critique and send it to the (outgoing at the time) chairman of the board was a bold move on the part of Sælid and underlines the frustration felt in research.[49]

Hafslund Nycomed had become a hierarchical company run by business economists and clearly influenced by the board of directors. Research was still important but no longer as a driver for future strategy. Hafslund had changed Nycomed, with emphasis on what management and the board thought the stock market saw as relevant.

A stock-listed pharmaceutical company of some magnitude

For a long time, Hafslund's leadership enjoyed Nycomed's large turnover and its great profitability. A lot was ploughed back into research and the strengthening of the market apparatus. The continued investment in the chemical plant at Lindesnes in Norway increased capacity and improved the economics of production. Until the very late 1980s, however, Nycomed's great success was hidden within the bigger conglomerate Hafslund Nycomed. Hafslund unloaded most of its other activities except for its original electricity business. But, increasingly, the future loomed with unanswered questions about what to do with all that income.

Table 9.1 shows three important trends. First, Hafslund Nycomed (column 1 + 2) was gradually dominated by pharmaceuticals (columns 3, 4, 5, and 6). Second, when Nycomed Pharma came up to speed in 1990, it quickly filled the void left by the other businesses sold by Hafslund. Third, and most importantly, even though the actual turnover of the Imaging business never dominated the overall turnover, its profitability did. These profits made it possible to redirect the company so rapidly.

Hafslund's main strategic initiative was the creation of Nycomed Pharma. In 1988, it added Danish Pharma Medica, a specialist in skincare.

---

[49] Interview with Geir Gogstad and Gunnar Sælid, January 24, 2020.

Table 9.1 Turnover and results in Hafslund Nycomed, 1985–1995

	Turnover result		Imaging result		Pharma result	
	(1)	(2)	(3)	(4)	(5)	(6)
	1,940	300	621	165	–	–
1986	2,526	379	831	186	–	–
1987	2,114	487	875	337	305	21
1988	2,611	789	1,219	553	345	38
1989	2,972	1,241	1,460	888	423	70
1990	4,340	1,562	1,793	1,095	978	123
1991	5,519	2,192	2,097	1,317	2,469	482
1992	5,843	2,305	2,370	1,501	2,674	562
1993	6,579	2,276	2,526	1,562	3,186	543
1994	7,819	2,433	3,172	1,668	3,346	623
1995	9,682	3,110	5,133	2,329	3,281	616
1996	–	–	4,636	1,822	3,169	500

Source: yearly reports.

Then, the larger European generic strategy emerged in 1989 with the purchase of CL Pharma (Chemie Linz Pharma), primarily to get a German foothold to sell X-ray contrast media. CL Pharma possessed a largely generic portfolio and a marketing organization for central Europe and therefore an opportunity to develop a European strategy for generic drugs.[50]

Over the next several years, Nycomed Pharma grew into a substantial business as a result of a number of purchases: Collett-Marwell Hauge AS (Norway, 1990), DAK-Laboratoriet A/S (Denmark, 1991), Benzon Pharma A/S (Denmark, 1991), Kebo Care's hospital div. (Norway 1991), Hydro Pharma (Norway, 1992), Laboratorios Leo, S.A. (Spain, 1992), and Christiaens International B.V. (Belgium/Netherlands, 1992). Even by 1991, Nycomed Pharma had achieved a higher turnover than Nycomed Imaging. Nycomed Pharma's profits were far below Nycomed Imaging's, but it was profitable and relatively stable. With strongholds in Norway, Denmark, Austria, Germany, and Benelux and a portfolio of generic drugs to exploit for new markets, Nycomed Pharma made inroads in the rest of Scandinavia and other parts of Europe and consciously built a Russian marketing organization. It rationalized the many "me too" drugs in the portfolio, used an increasingly international marketing organization to exploit particular drugs, and modernized production. Top managers from the purchased

---

[50] Conversation with Bjørn Flatgård, November 5, 2019.

companies gained positions in the top management of Nycomed Pharma.[51] Employees had to leave too, also in Norway.[52]

In these several ways, Hafslund Nycomed mirrored general trends in the pharmaceutical industry. In 1985, the 10 largest pharmaceutical firms in the world accounted for 20 percent of sales, while in 2002 the ten largest firms accounted for 48 percent (Kumar, 2012). Between 1985 and 2007, 51 large companies consolidated into 10 companies. Some of Nycomed's old partners were involved in these processes. SmithKline Beecham, collaborator in a research project, resulted from an early merger between three companies. Glaxo's hostile 1995 takeover of Burroughs Wellcome to create Glaxo Wellcome in many ways was typical of the time: A company (Glaxo) with a huge multibillion product success (Zantac) merged with another (Burroughs Wellcome) with its own successful product (Zovirax). Eventually, GlaxoSmithKline emerged, as did several other huge, research-based international pharmaceutical companies containing former national companies. Consolidation also took place in generics.

Several factors contributed to the merger movement in pharmaceuticals (Kumar, 2012). The shareholder activism and the pursuit of greater profitability that characterized the 1980s and beyond obviously changed the climate for business development. Companies looked to expand their competence bases. There was a shift from an optimistic outlook in the acquisitions in the 1980s to a more defensive motivation in the 1990s. There were fears of an end to an era characterized by successful innovation and high earnings. New organizations for purchasing drugs also emerged in these years, putting pressure on prices. Especially in the United States, the emergence of so-called pharmacy benefit managers (PMBs) affected the industry's vision of the future negatively. PMBs rapidly became quite powerful and represented "a rude awakening" to the industry according to Nycomed Imaging's sales director.[53]

Hafslund Nycomed's actions mirrored developments in the international industry. For every success won in increased income and profits, the challenge of establishing longer-term success formulae became bigger. Financial services organizations reminded investors—and the Hafslund Nycomed managerial team—that "Life after Omnipaque" could be challenging.[54] The firm filled its pipeline with new contrast media for X-ray

[51] Conversation with Bjørn Flatgård, November 5, 2019.
[52] Email from Geir Gogstad to Knut Sogner, January 29, 2020.
[53] Interview with Dagfinn Hansen, March 10, 2020.
[54] Hafslund, Hafslund Nycomed styresaker, December 15, 1993–February 9, 1994: report, "Life after Omnipaque" by NatWest Securities, December 15, 1993.

and for MRI and ultrasound too. But the future remained uncertain and certainly less rosy than before. Increased price competition and the threat of generics loomed.[55]

Hafslund Nycomed talked with Sterling for several years about creating an alliance, possibly a joint venture.[56] Through the talks with Sterling Winthrop about collaboration, Svein Aaser was well acquainted with both top management and Sterling Winthrop's business position. When, in March 1994, he heard of the possibility that Eastman Kodak (which had acquired Sterling Drug in 1988) was considering selling Sterling Winthrop, he contacted its CEO, George Fisher, only to hear that Sterling Winthrop's European alliance partner, French Sanofi, had the right of first refusal. Aaser knew Sanofi's CEO Jean-Francois Dehecq quite well from having established a prior relationship with him and had fairly easy access to negotiations. Sanofi, as it turned out, was eager to sell the contrast media business.[57] Hafslund Nycomed was able to buy it and, as a result, its market share in contrast media jumped from roughly 20 percent to 80 percent.[58] Schering AG and Daiichi were still important representatives, but the Sterling purchase added 1,400 new employees, many representing the specialized national sales organization for contrast media in the United States. Hafslund Nycomed also acquired a research organization as well as production plants in Puerto Rico and Rensselaer, New York.[59]

The acquisition was a triumph commercially and organizationally, but there were serious concerns about the company's future. Success came with a bittersweet flavor. With pressure on prices, patents for Omnipaque and Bracco's Iopadimol running out, and a new competitive climate looming, the board and top management were worried about their underwhelming R&D pipeline. They were facing a new reality, one in which mergers and acquisitions played an important part.

The imperative of shareholder value

In 1995, an important group of shareholders opposed the proposed merger of Nycomed with the US pharmaceutical company Ivax. Earlier that fall,

[55] Hafslund, board of directors: meeting, November 4 and 5, 1992.
[56] Hafslund, board of directors: meeting, March 15 and 16, 1994; meeting February 9, 1994; meeting, December 15, 1993; meeting, November 10 and 11, 1993; meeting, October 6, 1993.
[57] The following is based on interview with Svein Aaser, August 1, 2019; interview with Jan Fikkan, February 7, 2019; and a lengthy article, Egenes and Ottesen (1994).
[58] Hafslund Nycomed's yearly report for 1994.
[59] Hafslund, board of directors: meeting, October 5, 1994.

the board had unanimously approved the deal, but when the significant group of shareholders disapproved, the extraordinary general assembly to vote on the merger was called off.[60] CEO Aaser and chairman of the board, Terje Mikalsen, were driving the merger proposal. In September 1994, Aaser had promised something big for the future in an interview with the Norwegian business daily *Dagens Næringsliv*. He foresaw that in five years Hafslund Nycomed would double its turnover and still be paying its customary 15 percent return on equity (Dagens Næringsliv 1994). Although in the interview he clearly implied that Hafslund Nycomed would continue as an independent corporation, a couple of months later the board opened up for the possibility of outright sales of either Nycomed Imaging or Nycomed Pharma or demerging the energy unit Hafslund.[61]

Aaser relentlessly pursued internationalization. When the general assembly elected two new members of the board in the fall of 1994, two Norwegian stalwarts from the old board went out: Tharald Brøvig and Professor of Medicine, Asbjørn Aakvaag. New members were Jacques F. Rejeange, an experienced pharmaceutical industrial manager and incoming CEO of Sterling Winthrop, and Michael von Clemm, an investment banker who, at the time, was chairman of Merrill Lynch Capital Markets (Ramel, 2011: 180ff). Von Clemm, in his role at Merrill Lynch, had previously courted Svein Aaser and other Norwegian top managers. The new board immediately forged relations with Merrill Lynch and Goldman Sachs to discuss the future of Nycomed Imaging.[62] The investment bankers initiated talks with pharmaceutical firms that could be interested in collaborations and mergers. The top management of Hafslund Nycomed and US Abbott Laboratories met and talked for several months in 1995, but eventually they did not find enough common ground.[63]

Merrill Lynch also organized the talks with the US generics company Ivax.[64] Ivax, which was founded in 1987, had grown rapidly by US acquisitions. The idea of the merger involved demerging the energy business (the original Hafslund) as a new and stock-listed company. Nycomed and Ivax agreed on a valuation that saw them as equal, but Ivax Nycomed would become a US company registered in the state of Florida. The global headquarters would be in London, England, with two other main

---

[60] Hafslund, board of directors: meeting, November 15 and 16, 1995.
[61] Hafslund, board of directors: meeting, November 29, 1994; December 19, 1994; February 1, 1994.
[62] Hafslund, board of directors: meeting, November 29, 1994.
[63] Hafslund, board of directors: meeting, March 16, 1995 and June 28, 1995.
[64] Hafslund, board of directors: meeting, September 6, 1995.

offices in Miami, Florida and Oslo, Norway, respectively. Ivax Nycomed would start out with over 13,000 employees in more than 40 countries and be the world's largest generics company as well as the largest in contrast media. Eight thousand of these employees came from Ivax, which, in 1994, had a turnover of 1.13 billion dollars and profits of 90 million. Ivax had four times been on Forbes' list of the 100 fastest growing US companies.[65]

The main goal of Ivax Nycomed was consolidation of the global generics segment. Aaser argued that the two companies had complementary geographic locations as well as well-fitting product portfolios, which meant a lot of products that could be exchanged and developed for new markets. He also maintained that going for such a generics solution would be beneficial to the research-based contrast media company. Chairman Terje Mikalsen saw Ivax Nycomed as an avenue for broader industrial development by seeking value through other means than research.[66] He foresaw that the merged company would develop ingenious, world-leading distribution systems. Aaser would become CEO of the merged company, and Ivax's CEO, Philip Frost, would be chairman of the board.

However, the proposal was not popular outside the board. The Norwegian press said that Hafslund Nycomed employees had noticed that there were more positions for the Ivax management than for Nycomed managers (Finansavisen, 1995). The general reaction was negative. Why, it was asked, should an extremely profitable and research-based Hafslund Nycomed want to be merged with a US generics company that no one had heard about, that had existed for only eight years, and that had a huge debt? Neither Hafslund Nycomed's top management (outside of Aaser) nor some of the firm's main owners liked the plan.[67] Management protested intensely, fearing for the future of the pre-eminent contrast media business in the world.[68] The CFO was vocally against the merger. His disagreement with Aaser led to his resignation.[69] Before he left, he had led an internal group of executives who had evaluated Ivax and concluded that it was over-valued.[70]

---

[65] RA, Nycomed, 1st part. Ab-L0027: "Fakta om fusjonen," intern meddelelse, October 19, 1995.
[66] Mikalsen to Sogner, March 31, 2020.
[67] Interview with Øyvind Brøymer, October 18, 2019; interview with Jan Fikkan, February 7, 2019; interview with Bjørn Flatgård, November 5, 2019.
[68] Interview with Åse Aulie Michelet, March 4, 2020 and interview with Tore Talseth, March 13, 2020.
[69] Interview with Øyvin Brøymer, October 18, 2019.
[70] Ibid; interview with Helge Lund, November 25, 2019.

Three large owners representing 23 percent of Hafslund Nycomed's A shares opposed the merger: Storebrand, a large insurer (Christensen et al., 2017);[71] Orkla, an industrial company with an investment agenda; and the state pension fund Folketrygdfondet. They analyzed the proposal and even visited Ivax in the United States. Says Tore Lindholt, CEO in Folketrygdfondet:

> [...] the information the administration had, meant that the proposed merger was not a good solution. [...] But the more one got of information and the more in depth the proposed merger was analysed, the clearer it was the Fund could not support a merger with Ivax
>
> (Lindholt, 2005: 61)

As a result, chairman of the board, Mikalsen, had to resign, and he sold his shares.[72] The fate of Svein Aaser was also discussed, but he survived the coming of a new chairman of the board, the independent and experienced Johan Fredrik Odfjell (Lindholt, 2005: 218). The shareholder revolution did not stop the demerging of Hafslund, which was completed in spring 1996. As a pharmaceutical company through and through, Nycomed was still being made ready to be brought into a new constellation.

How could something so unfortunate as the Ivax affair happen? The Merrill Lynch executive Knut Ramel suggests that Aaser was financially motivated:

> The strategic fit was not clear cut and the negotiations went somewhat slow until Philip Frost told Svein what he as president in the American company could expect in salary. "The synergies" increased and one could announce a deal
>
> (Ramel, 2011: 226)

Ramel also pointed out another incident that he characterized as "embarrassing." It regarded options that Aaser had and that Merrill Lynch helped him sell outside the option's time frame; it portrayed Aaser as a leader particularly concerned about his own personal gain (Ramel, 2011: 225).

There is anyway no doubt that the financial approach chosen by chairman Mikalsen and Tharald Brøvig had shifted Nycomed's emphasis as a research-based company to one that also expanded in generics. Going into generics meant that the business could be developed from the top, almost

---

[71] Interview with Hans Henrik Klouman, December 4, 2019.
[72] Interview with Åge Korsvold; Mikalsen to Sogner, March 31, 2020.

without regard for what happened in research. The proposed merger would undoubtedly renew the company's situation but at the price of undermining what from the outside was still seen as a national research flagship with a research and science orientation unprecedented for a Norwegian company. From such a perspective, the merger proposal could be seen as an act of weakness, something that "smelled" of panic. This is why the shareholders took the matter so seriously and investigated so thoroughly and then turned the whole thing down. Aaser and Mikalsen vehemently denied these concerns and argued that this was a calculated act of industrial development.[73] The business was clearly at a crossroads.

Finding a new home

On October 21, 1997, the Norwegian company set off on an entirely new path with a new partner. This followed the organization of a British company called Nycomed Amersham plc. The merger with British Amersham followed two years of intense reorganization seeking a solution to the future of Nycomed. After the demerging of Hafslund in 1996, it had become a pharmaceutical thoroughbred. That Nycomed's future would be through a merger with a smaller British company was, however, a surprising event.

Nycomed's new chairman of the board from early 1996, Johan Fredrik Odfjell had a major role in this outcome. He sought a course the shareholders would trust and support.[74] He observed that in spite of the financial strength of the company, the success within Imaging and the positive development of Pharma, there was no clear and consistent strategy regarding priorities and long-term goals. There was a surprising (perhaps realistic) lack of confidence in the ability to build the future of the company on continued success in research as a standalone firm. Odfjell partly attributed this to the limited number of pharmaceutical companies in Norway and consequently to the lack of experienced Norwegian professionals with relevant industrial backgrounds. Both Odfjell and Bill Castell, who spearheaded Amersham's takeover, suggest that there was room for more confident and imaginative people in top management.[75] In hindsight, one could also see that there would have been room for someone with strong

[73] Interview with Svein Aaser, August 1, 2019 and interview with Terje Mikalsen, August 14, 2019.
[74] Interview with Johan Fredrik Odfjell, January 10, 2020.
[75] Interview with Johan Fredrik Odfjell, January 10, 2020; interview with Bill Castell, December 17, 2019.

218 Norway's Pharmaceutical Revolution

confidence in the commercial position Nycomed had within X-ray contrast media.

The merger decision generated substantial tension within Hafslund Nycomed's management group and people quit. Both the two people who had been most involved in developing the commercial imaging business, Stein Annexstad and Gert W. Munthe, had already left because their roles clashed with that of CEO Aaser.[76] In retrospect, Tore Talseth, who succeeded Gert W. Munthe as head of Nycomed Imaging, suggests that lack of systematic and thorough communication between top management and Nycomed Imaging was a problem.[77] Top management had had unrealistic beliefs about how valuable the research portfolio was and created unrealistic market expectations on the stock exchange. Talseth is self-critical and thinks, for example, that research emphasis within Nycomed Imaging on projects for ultrasound contrast media should have been challenged. These projects carried too much vain hope. On the other hand, Nycomed Imaging's deep knowledge about its X-ray contrast media technology and solid position in the market could have improved Aaser's grasp of the future. Yet, here too, optimism was too high. Åse Aulie Michelet of Nycomed Imaging sees the hope Aaser attached to Visipaque as one important mistake.[78]

Still, CEO Aaser led the process of finding a future for the company that could replace the lack of super profits from research. He did that by following a similar logic to that of the Ivax proposal: Nycomed was not to be built around research outside that of contrast media. Legitimized by perceived tougher conditions ahead and the looming uncertainty of generic competition for non-ionic contrast media in the United States after 1997, he first launched the program "Fokus 98".[79] Research in Austria was shut down, as was Sterling Winthrop's old primary chemical plant in Puerto Rico, and production moved to the main plant in Lindesnes in the south of Norway. Even brand new research facilities in Princeton, New Jersey, based on Sterling Winthrop and Salutar's old projects, closed. In Norway, research at Bioreg—the peptide project and the other therapeutical projects—closed.[80]

Closing Bioreg was particularly noteworthy. Some of the people involved thought that they could have succeeded.[81] Others previously involved saw the closed projects as an undertaking that had been tried out over too

---

[76] Interview with Stein Annexstad, December 16, 2014; interview with Gert W. Munthe, December 5, 2019.
[77] Interview with Tore Talseth, March 13, 2020.
[78] Interview with Åse Aulie Michelet, March 24, 2020.
[79] Annual report for 1996 (Nycomed ASA).
[80] Interview with Geir Gogstad, December 4, 2019.
[81] Ibid.

many years.[82] Ending therapeutic research was perhaps the most surprising development because of the connections to the University of Oslo, the Norwegian Research Council, Norwegian hospitals, and academic and corporate groups internationally. Public money that had been channeled indirectly from state-financed university research and directly from the Norwegian Research Council was shown to have reached a dead end. The ties to the institutions that had created the ecosystem that helped carry Nycomed forward was thereby severed. A less drastic alternative would have been a redirection of research based on key people. Some of the people from Bioreg did start to work for Imaging, but not in their traditional research paths.

The closing of Bioreg was a precursor of the internationalization of research through the formation of multinational pharmaceutical companies in general. The logic of the corporation was no longer grounded in the national, academic–business collaboration model. Some of the nations represented in the multinational corporation became more peripheral than others. Over time, Nycomed Amersham and its successor, GE Healthcare, have scaled down research in Norway even if the Norwegian operation has been highly profitable. And, as just mentioned, prior to the merger with Amersham, Nycomed closed down research in the United States and Austria. The Swedish research communities in Lund and Uppsala, so closely associated with Astra and Pharmacia, have also been badly affected by the new logic introduced by the multinational corporation (Waxell, 2016). Only the Danes, the original Scandinavian outlier that was "present" at the beginning of the pharmaceutical revolution, kept its biggest company (the merged Novo-Nordisk) Danish. This outcome provided great benefits for the Danish medical/pharmaceutical ecosystem (Asheim et al., 2010).[83]

Initially, the Amersham merger "saved" Nycomed's research culture. Research would survive long-term if research results were successful. To some extent, the merger built around Nycomed's imaging research base, which explains why it was preserved. The merger valued Nycomed slightly higher than Amersham, yet Nycomed Amersham became a British company. Amersham International Limited, originally a government enterprise stemming from atomic research, was founded in 1981 on the basis of the Radiochemical Centre Limited. In 1982, the company was privatized under the name *Amersham International plc*. Its talks with Nycomed did not start

[82] Interview with Tore Skotland, March 26, 2020.
[83] Interview with Helge Lund (chairman of Novo-Nordisk board of directors), November 25, 2019.

out as merger talks but, as Amersham's specialty was radiopharmaceuticals, used to detect illnesses, there were obvious commonalities between the two companies.[84]

CEO Bill Castell dominated Amersham. Castell, educated as a chartered accountant, had had a long and varied career beyond finance in the large pharmaceutical company Wellcome when headhunted to lead Amersham in 1989. He swiftly moved Amersham into the medical business through a number of takeovers.[85] Castell prioritized research and went heavily into non-radioactive biotechnology, something that was natural to do for a company coming from the atomic energy sector. Biophysics, a vibrant field in the 1940s that built on nuclear physics, is one of the foundations of the modern gene modification biotechnology that emerged in the 1970s (Rasmussen, 2014). Prior to purchasing Nycomed, Amersham made a huge splurge to secure Swedish Pharmacia Biotech. Nycomed was next in line, with Castell as CEO of the merged company. Nycomed's chairman, Odfjell, became chairman of Nycomed Amersham, while Svein Aaser became number two in the new organization.

Nycomed Amersham soon reflected its British CEO. Svein Aaser quit Nycomed Amersham within a year to become CEO of DNB, Norway's largest bank. Other managers also left. Nycomed Pharma was sold in 1999 to a private equity fund, which reflected Castell's interest in research-based pharmaceutical business. Castell continued extensive imaging research in Norway (in a company with significant Norwegian ownership), but its content was rather heavily adjusted and partly redirected to suit the merged company's requirements. Nycomed Imaging's head of research, Arne Berg, experienced the merger as constructive from a research point of view. Nycomed's people gained access to competence in nuclear science.[86] An important avenue was to develop disease-specific contrast media, something that was very much on Bill Castell's mind.

The merger was one of many in the industry. The two companies fitted together fairly well—at least on paper. Yet, wealthy Nycomed was subsumed by another company rather than continuing the relentless and self-confident expansion of the 1980s. The gap between the investor expectations the company itself had created in the early 1990s and the perceived harsh reality the company faced in the price conscious markets after 1994

---

[84] Interview with Bill Castell, December 17, 2019.
[85] <Amersham plc—Acquisitions from 1980," note given from Bill Castell to Knut Sogner, February 7, 2002.
[86] Interview with Arne Berg, November 21, 2014; interview with Jan Fikkan, February 7, 2019.

just became too wide. Nycomed had not replaced or supplemented Omnipaque as a money machine. Merging Nycomed into another entity was the one way to secure the best shareholder value in the short term. At the time of the merger, there existed no promising long-term plan. Therefore, Nycomed was absorbed by Amersham.

Nycomed entered the merger as a very valuable company. Yet, the value reflected the financial markets' uncertainty about its future. Amersham was less profitable than Nycomed and had a slightly lower turnover, yet its market capitalization was bigger.[87] With an operating income of over 30 percent of sales, Nycomed's profitability was excellent and more than 10 percentage points higher than that of Amersham. Its research effort was nearly 75 percent larger than Amersham's. Amersham was something of an upstart with substantial organizational challenges as Pharmacia Biotech was far from integrated. Yet, its confident agenda and its direction for the future made it a more valuable company. Nycomed did try to be takeover entity in the merger.[88] But Amersham refused and for good reason. Keeping Nycomed Norwegian was not a prerogative for a company without a clear direction, although it was very much what chairman Odfjell and CEO Aaser wanted.

Bill Castell's visionary strategies and articulated and self-confident argumentation made a great difference. His company commanded confidence among investors, and, at that time, Nycomed was unprepared to move ahead alone. That the British firm's most important product, Myoview, a contrast agent for the heart, in 1997 had revenues of $33,4 million, while Omnipaque's sales were more than seven times that amount, did not matter.[89] Nycomed had much the better position within global markets but did not possess the narrative that would point toward a glorious future. Amersham had that narrative and provided—although a foreign company—a research-oriented constructive home for a company whose board and leadership had lost their way.

Conclusion

Nycomed ceased to exist as an independent company in October 1997. Seen from the outside, this was a completely normal occurrence in the

---

[87] "The Proposed Merger of Nycomed and Amersham," Oslo and London, July 1, 1997 (document with the author).

[88] Interview with Johan Fr. Odfjell, January 10, 2014.

[89] Nycomed Amersham's yearly report for 1997.

consolidation of the international pharmaceutical industry. The Nycomed that was absorbed by Amersham in 1997 had become a much more valuable company than the one Hafslund bought in 1985. A lot of value—shareholder value—had been created in those years, and creating shareholder value had become central to Nycomed's owners and to the rest of the international pharmaceutical industry.

Hafslund had changed Nycomed profoundly. In short, business development gradually replaced research as the spirit of the company. Commercial considerations increasingly superseded the research orientation as a core value but not to the extent that research was rooted out or that commercial considerations did not frequently support research positions. Building global marketing organizations for contrast media may indeed have supported imaging research and legitimized it. But through the creation of Nycomed Pharma, commercialization processes became a main organizational task and a goal in itself. Marketing organizations could create new commercial opportunities that did not involve research. By altering the purpose of the company, the core of the company also changed. The short-term success of increasing income within contrast media and the new generics businesses came with a longer-term price, namely the lack of a clear and confident way forward that the national and international financial markets could trust. Catering to the financial markets, as Hafslund Nycomed did, proved to be the downfall for the company's ability to direct its own future in the merger game.

With a top management without a research agenda, the company increasingly became dependent on business solutions once the research departments did not deliver. Nycomed had a large and varied research organization, which, under other and more favorable circumstances, would possibly have succeeded. The comparison with Amersham illustrates that success may come in at least two packages: actual results and the perception of progress. Amersham's CEO Bill Castell could sell the mere idea of biotechnologically clever Amersham to the financial markets and the Nycomed team even if the longer-term development into the 2020s proved the Nycomed team—with its baggage from the 1960s to the 1980s—carried the most valuable package in the form of Omnipaque.

After the merger, however, Nycomed Amersham was a British company, run from the United Kingdom, with research agendas modified to reflect the strategy, that is, the policy logic of the new company. The new imaging research effort was built on a new international company with its main roots in two different countries. This was an ambitious experiment and one that many people believed in. That said, there was a world of difference between the corporate governance logic of the Blix family and the "family company" that put so much emphasis on the success of their small Norwegian entity and the new and sleek stock-market-listed logic of British Nycomed Amersham. This was a corporation with a complex corporate governance logic and many other considerations than the well-being of its Norwegian subsidiary and the Norwegian medical ecosystem.

The board and Hafslund Nycomed's top management had given up control of one of Norway's most exciting, modern companies. They had *sold* control for reaping shareholder value and building a larger international company with a strong British footing. Norway lacked the resources and the strategic orientation that had enabled Denmark to achieve a better balance between its national and commercial objectives. Norway as a promoter of pharmaceutical innovations, after a spurt of ingenuity in the 1970s and 1980s, had thereby regressed several steps down the hierarchical ladder of major pharmaceutical industrial countries.

References

Aaserud, K. 1987. "Nycomed med gullkantet samarbeidsavtale I USA." *Aftenposten*, June 24.

1995. "Overkjøres i Ivax-fusjon." *Finansavisen*, October 25.

Amdam, R. P. and Sogner, K. 1994. *Wealth of Contrasts: Nyegaard & Co.—a Norwegian Pharmaceutical Company 1874–1985*. Oslo: Ad notam Gyldendal.

Asheim, B. T., Coenen, L., and Moodysson, J. 2010. "Two Sides of the Same Coin? Local and Global Knowledge Flows in Medicon Valley." *In*: Belussi, F. and Sammarra, A. (eds) *Business Networks in Clusters and Industrial Districts. The Governance of the Global Value Chain*. London and New York: Routledge, pp. 356–376.

Christensen, S. A., Bergh, T., Ekberg, E., and Myrvang, C. 2017. *Skadeskutt og livskraftig: 1945–2017*. Oslo: Universitetsforl.

Dagens Næringsliv, 1994. "Kurs mot noe større" and "Avviser NHO—press fra Hafslund-styrets side." September 2.

Egenes, G. and Ottesen, G. 1994. "Milliard-thrilleren." *Dagens Næringsliv*, October 15.

Henderson, R. M. and Cockburn, I. 1996. "The Determinants of Research Productivity in Ethical Drug Discovery." *In*: Washington, R. B. H. (ed.) *Competitive Strategies in the Pharmaceutical Industry*. Washington, DC: AEI Press.

Kumar, B. R. 2012. "Mergers and Acquisitions in the Pharmaceutical Industry." *In: Mega Mergers and Acquisitions: Case Studies from Key Industries*. London: Palgrave Macmillan, pp. 1–59.

Lazonick, W. and O'Sullivan, M. 2000. "Maximizing Shareholder Value: A New Ideology for Corporate Governance." *Economy and Society*, 29, 13–35.

Lindholt, T. 2005. *I pengenes rike: beretninger fra den norske kapitalismen*. Oslo: Gyldendal.

Næss, A. 2012. *Fossekraft og lange linjer: Hafslund ASA 1898-1998: en fortelling om kraft, mennesker og kapital gjennom hundre år*. Oslo: Gyldendal.

Ramel, K. 2011. *En finansmans bekännelser*. Stockholm: Ekerlids Förlag.

Rasmussen, N. 2014. *Gene Jockeys: Life Science and the Rise of Biotech Enterprise*. Baltimore, MD: Johns Hopkins University Press.

Waxell, A. 2016. "Writing Up the Region: Anchor Firm Dismantling and the Construction of a Perceived Regional Advantage in Swedish News Media." *European Planning Studies*, 24, 742–761.

10

Conclusion

The Difficult Rise and Rapid Change of an Innovative Culture

The history presented in this study indicates just how difficult it has been for small and middle-sized countries to break into and then maintain a position in high-tech, international industries like pharmaceuticals. Despite the efforts of an array of international organizations to foster modern patterns of economic development for emerging companies and countries to pursue, the burden of promoting and sustaining technical advancement and its associated growth ultimately depends upon national institutions and leaders. Even when they are up to the tasks involved, the long-term outcomes can result—as in the case of Norway—in a shift from national to regional and then to international leadership and control with companies representing collective national efforts. Political resistance to internationalization could potentially slow the process but probably not block it entirely. The cost, at any rate, would be very high.

This pattern of economic development can be seen clearly in the history of the Scandinavian economies in the twentieth century. Coming from behind and catching up with the world leaders in pharmaceutical innovation, the Scandinavia countries did not perform in a uniform way. Denmark was already a promising innovator at the very moment the pharmaceutical revolution began to accelerate in the 1930s; making use of its advanced agricultural sector and its early competence in insulin research, Denmark successfully pushed into international markets in pharmaceuticals. Sweden caught up much later, showing promise in the 1940s and maturity in the 1960s and onward. Sweden adapted a model that had already successfully been applied by the leading countries: establishing strong academic–business links that companies could build upon to create original and internationally marketable new pharmaceuticals. Norway remained the Scandinavian laggard, coming from behind its Scandinavian siblings, with only one real pharmaceutical innovation in the twentieth century.

Norway's Pharmaceutical Revolution. Knut Sogner, Oxford University Press.
© Knut Sogner (2022). DOI: 10.1093/oso/9780192869005.003.0010

The innovation of non-ionic X-ray contrast media—as a basic principle and with specific non-toxic properties—was nevertheless a major achievement on the part of a small Norwegian firm, Nyegaard & Co., subsequently known as Nycomed (and Amersham and GE Healthcare). By 1969, the researchers concluded that they had a breakthrough, and in the next several years they synthesized a number of molecules—some of which became useful products. The first innovation of the new generation was named Amipaque and it was first sold in Norway in 1974. It is, however, its successor, Omnipaque, which, from the early 1980s to the present day (2022), conquered the world market in a profound way. This book explains how all of this was possible and considers to what extent there is something to learn from innovation in the age of the pharmaceutical revolution.

The Norwegian success formula was original to Scandinavia and gives some interesting insights into what it actually entails to "come from behind." The formula is a four-stage model: first came the establishment of a strong scientific research culture; then came insight from specialization of research; then came a shift to a kind of collectivization of the company organization; then, through alliances with doctors and other companies, inventive molecules and subsequent innovative products found significant roles in global markets. There is also a fifth stage, although that is not part of the success formula: once the company in the 1990s achieved independence as a fully fledged innovative multinational corporation, it lost its ability to navigate in a confident and forward-looking manner.

Nyegaard was similar in many regards to other research-oriented startups. But it was also a thoroughly Norwegian company. The story of the success is, at the same time, a story about Norwegian exceptionalism, as this was the only significant Norwegian pharmaceutical invention of the twentieth century, as well as a case study of its industrial context. What had been a remarkable invention turned out to be a remarkable innovation, and the process of getting the initial product on the market, developing new variants, and transforming a 250-employee Norwegian generic producer into the leading global firm in contrast media products was an unusual and noteworthy achievement.

The pursuit of invention

So, the commitment and dedication with which Nyegaard met the opportunities of the pharmaceutical revolution in the 1940s were important elements in the explanation of its later success. Nyegaard turned to science in general and to chemical sciences in particular in the decade of the Anglo–American mastery of penicillin. The early Norwegian state-financed effort in vitamin research had ignited Nyegaard interest in such research, and the plethora of international therapeutic breakthroughs of the 1930s and 1940s built up more and more motivation. With the national economy's strong fishing sector legitimizing vitamin research (similar to how Denmark's agricultural sector benefitted its insulin production), Norway was to some extent better prepared than Sweden to take advantage of the pharmaceutical revolution. Norway, too, had the opportunity to build on the penicillin opportunity with state support, but the society never fully explored the opportunities at that time for Norwegian academic–business collaboration, while Sweden and Denmark did.

The Norwegian industry in general and Nyegaard in particular feared the Norwegian government. Strong forces within the governing Labour Party wanted to nationalize Norwegian pharmaceutical supply. The medical supply sector was already under the control of Director General Karl Evang, a Labour Party member, a man who prioritized cheap medicine for the people within a system that gave him pretty much total control over both Norwegian pharmacies and suppliers of medicine. That double grip—fear of nationalization and low prices in practice—weakened both the motivation and the strength of private enterprise. Nyegaard's research community was adjusted down, some investments were channeled into shipping, and what remained of the research staff was at times directed to development of "free trade" products (i.e. toothpaste, fertilizers etc.) to escape what it regarded as unfair medical regulatory practices.

There were good reasons for skepticism about the Norwegian regulatory regime. Within the regime affecting the pharmacy business, the Norwegian state did not conform to the participatory capitalist model discussed by Rolf Torstendahl as the typical norm in Northern Europe. Rather, a pre-war national system, resembling what Francis Sejersted has called "democratic capitalism," prevailed up to around 1960. The focus was on the pharmacies, prices, and national supply. The state ignored the chance to modernize the Oslo-based pharmaceutical industry in the 1940s, an industry that was geographically close to research communities in the University of Oslo. The industry—for its part—sided with the pharmacies to fight nationalization in the 1950s. This situation helped to confirm the rest of the Norwegian pharmaceutical industry in their generic ways.

Yet the goal of providing important, original research breakthroughs that demanded a deep scientific footing survived for decades in one small Norwegian company. Spurred by how US Merck and British Glaxo had made Nyegaard's own vitamin research useful in their simultaneous discovery of vitamin B_{12}, Nyegaard sent young engineers to doctoral studies in England and commenced work related to the old vitamin research that, at times in the 1950s and 1960s, involved both Merck and Glaxo. But the research effort was limited and spread widely. In pursuit of that elusive research breakthrough, Nyegaard adopted a new strategy in the years around 1960. While struggling to find unpatented ways to make a known contrast medium, the firm stumbled onto a new and patentable substance. That put research on an original development path for several years. The business then explored the new opportunities for academic–business collaboration and for both representing products developed by Norwegian scientists and developing licenses for original products from foreign companies to be sold on the Norwegian market. This path led them forward into a world of broader scientific footing both within the Norwegian market and in export markets. The new leaders of the 1960s were stubbornly committed to the goal of innovation despite the fact that Nyegaard was a small firm without any game-changing product.

Three changes in state policies in the years around the 1960s helped firm up their new strategy: (1) prices in the Norwegian market rose; (2) the threat of nationalization mostly vanished; and (3) the narrow governmental industrial policy that had opened up for nationalization broadened and began to see also the pharmaceutical industry as a research-based national opportunity for growth. Eventually, the state developed new financial tools to help Norwegian companies like Nyegaard.

Now Scandinavian regionalism came into play. Isopaque—the name of the new contrast agent—mattered a great deal. Research learned from the experience, and the rest of the company learned to deal with an original product. The development of Isopaque entailed the building of a Scandinavian network of contacts with doctors. When, in the mid-1960s, Isopaque was well and truly established as a fully developed and fully documented original product, the business had a new and important question to answer: Should the company just move on to new ventures elsewhere or should it take its body of human resources specialized in contrast media as a starting point for something new in that specialty?

The head of research, Hugo Holtermann, argued forcefully and against strong opposition for continuation of contrast media research. His argument is reminiscent of Edith Penrose's theoretical position that businesses develop according to their resource base. Holtermann argued that because of the scientific and commercial knowledge about contrast media, as well as the relevant outside connections, the company was well positioned to succeed. This would establish a three-stage model for research success: First, investment in human resources from the 1940s onward; then, specialization of these resources; and finally, the building of new projects on the basis of that specialization. With this model, Nyegaard succeeded in research. Now they had fruitful research ideas, enough internal capabilities, a productive research environment, and positive political surroundings. The Norwegian industrial policies since the 1940s had what Rolf Torstendahl called a participatory aim, and from the 1960s, Nyegaard and other small enterprises were included in this policy.

The path forward proved to be insights into specialized contrast media, primarily for myelographic purposes. Nyegaard searched for benign molecules with minimal impact on the body. The firm succeeded when teaming up with Swedish radiologist Torsten Almén and his ideas for vascular contrast media with few side effects; this path led to the new group of molecules subsequently known as non-ionic. The invention was based on Nyegaard's insights into the chemistry suitable for new myelographic contrast media and one of Almén's many suggestions. The new products were better than existing ones—for vascular purposes as well— and opened up new uses of contrast media in the upper parts of the spinal canal and the fluid-filled cavities of the brain. They were first used solely for these myelographic purposes, but from the late 1970s their two main advantages—low chemotoxicity and low osmolality (particle density) meant that they conquered the huge global vascular market.

From the mid-1960s, the enterprise that invented this new technology was a flexible, collectivized family business. Research and development of contrast agents became a common purpose shifting the attention from "a hundred generics" to specialized tasks for one product. Organizational integration—constituting a shift from a hierarchical structure—became a feature of the company in the 1960s and 1970s, and this underlines the appropriateness of William Lazonick's concept of collective capitalism. The company succeeded by becoming collectivized; it integrated the results of the conscious building of a scientific culture into a new organizational whole.

The shift in state policy in the 1960s—and increased contact between Nyegaard and university scientists—clearly had a positive effect on the atmosphere within the company. In a general way, Norway was as good a location as any in Scandinavia through the post-war period. It had an up-to-date medical community. Norwegian doctors played crucial roles both in encouraging new products and in furnishing expertise in radiology. The state also provided beneficial financial support from the 1970s. But national locational factors were of little help in the crucial issue—innovation. National environments—innovation systems—are very important in shaping business behavior. They help us understand why the Norwegian innovation system was not very helpful to the development of the nation's pharmaceutical industry.

Nyegaard's three-stage model of research success did not really arise from its national context. Its two main inspirations when it came to formulating scientific ambitions were fulfilling their innovative goals quite differently to Nyegaard. Glaxo and Merck, Sharp and Dohme benefitted greatly from their national research environments. They could easily do that because they could rather quickly build larger staffs than Nyegaard – as could the Swedish industry. They represented different versions of the same story of the rise of the innovative pharmaceutical industry as one firmly rooted in national ecosystems. Merck, more forcefully and earlier than Glaxo, went wholeheartedly along this innovative road and represented one of the earliest and most important examples of pharmaceutical reorientation into the exciting world of science-based innovation. Contrast media research had a different outset, though. It was commercially directed, was in-house as a chemical research project all the time, and its external connections were built from inward in the company and out to collaborators that were not necessarily Norwegians. It was an atypical path as far as the historiography of pharmaceutical innovation goes, although the recent history of Danish Novo-Nordisk tells the Novo story in a similar fashion as very company-driven (Sindbæk, 2019).

Successful international innovation

The collaborative attitude deepened and broadened in the 1970s and early 1980s. On the one hand, getting the new molecules to the market with all that entailed in terms of clinical trials, safety measures in general, and marketing activities, commanded commitment from broad segments of the staff. This meant a many-leveled approach on a global scale, connecting the company to other people and other institutions. It meant the creation of a network for international innovation—Nyegaard, Sterling Drug, Schering AG, and the combined external connections of the companies—which could help a small company get to the world market, while retaining some commercial and technological control.

For a global company to be meeting international regulations—and indeed the strictest national regulations like the US Food and Drug Administration (FDA)—were more important than Norwegian regulations. European regulations were sharpened and followed those of the United States. The partners Nyegaard found to help meet these requirements were not part of Norwegian society; they were other global companies like Schering AG and Sterling Drug. As a result of changes like these, the whole Norwegian pharmaceutical sector lost much of its national character after 1970. Nyegaard grew out of a Norwegian system which resembled Francis Sejersted's term "democratic capitalism." The path, from an initial success with invention through an organizational transformation in the 1960s and beyond, can be seen as a transition from a Norwegian kind of capitalism to a more international one. This applies to its connections with doctors and with other companies—its innovation system. It also applies to its compliance with foreign and international norms rooted in emerging scientific ideals.

Though the firm did not offer formal life-time employment on the Japanese model, its commitment to employees was genuine. The employees' long-term link to the company helped keep scientific success as a stable goal. Shared scientific goals among different levels in the hierarchy transformed the company's organizational structure in the 1960s. The sustained effort of the company's personnel at all levels over 40 years made the business successful; but its growth pattern changed in the 1960s. It is worth asking whether such long-term commitment is more common in the pharmaceutical industry than in Norwegian business generally. The answer is not evident; the issue does not appear to have been studied in either context, and it stands as a worthy subject of future research. The collectivization of Nyegaard owes a lot to the character of its challenges within the pharmaceutical industry, and its collectivization took place as a consequence of innovative ambitions rather than vice versa.

This integrative scientific culture was also important in the network building. The business had well-educated and knowledgeable employees able to build trust relations with employees in foreign companies. A common—collective—culture that forged relations inside and outside shed light on how companies—even small ones—become innovative. Small businesses with a good relationship between owner-managers and their technical department can be more innovative than bigger ones with explicit innovative strategies but without genuine communication between leadership and technical staff.

In the 1970s, Nyegaard benefitted from its Norwegian context. A renewed industrial policy aiming to better the international competitiveness of Norwegian companies included finance that the enterprise could use to build its new chemical plant. The Norwegian ecosystem for medical research provided increased opportunities for scientific collaboration in new fields as well as funding to further some of these new collaborations. The Norwegian state had become a partner, not an adversary. The Norwegian state thereby contributed to lifting Nyegaard out of its position as just a national supplier of pharmaceuticals in a "democratic capitalist" system of regulation.

On a general level, this story clearly supports the innovation-system approach. Nyegaard's innovations came through an interactive, complex process involving numerous firms, institutions, and individuals. The invention of non-ionic contrast media was a collaborative task, and the subsequent process of getting the products Amipaque and Omnipaque to the market involved several doctors and firms. The Swedish radiologist Torsten Almén made an essential contribution in several stages, and because of his role as a research-oriented medical doctor with a stake in the innovation, he could front the push for the non-ionic principle. More specifically, the firm's innovative process was shaped by a purpose, that of the company itself. This is underlined by the fact that the Norwegian environment did not help any other Norwegian company to innovate. What happened was intended, and this reveals much about the character of the network being created, a network that may be likened to "a system." The interplay between the strategies and structures constituting the innovative process reveals that the business was the prime driving force. There was a clear element of "technology push" to this process of innovation. Functionally, it was an interactive process (Elster, 1983). Intentionally, Nyegaard's wants and needs drove the technology push forward. The main lesson that can be drawn from this innovation is that the nature of the company and its leadership were of primary importance.

Its long-term effort to invent and innovate underlines the fact that the changes caused by this firm's innovations were not random matters. This reinforces Alfred Chandler and Louis Galambos's emphasis on the role of the business firm in the long-term, sustained efforts to promote growth in capitalist societies. It does not, however, confirm Chandler's interpretation of the importance of the scale and scope of such companies. It is crucially important to study the individual company in a context and to recognize that the company itself can be the spider that builds different societal webs. The company may be an entrepreneur that more than any other institution influences innovative processes. That interpretation links the two slightly contradictory views of innovation put forward by Schumpeter. On the one hand, it makes the point Schumpeter made in *Capitalism, Socialism and Democracy* that the company drives the innovative process. On the other hand, the reason the company does that is not because it has institutionalized innovation but because it performs the entrepreneurial role Schumpeter emphasized in *The Theory of Economic Development* (Schumpeter, 1934; 1976).

The difficulties of profiting from innovation in the longer term

Nyegaard & Co. changed in the 1980s, once the company name shifted to Nycomed. In the period from the mid-1980s to the 1990s, the business's leaders tried to make the company independent, primarily through the building of a huge international marketing operation. Its crowning moment came in 1994 when old ally Sterling Drug's US contrast media business was purchased. Nycomed also built the generics specialist Nycomed Pharma in the 1990s, a development that marked the replacement of science by business development as the company's main way forward. By 1997, Nycomed—or Hafslund Nycomed as the whole unit was called until 1996—was a successful company in terms of profitability and its position in important markets.

There was, however, an element of duality to the business's development from the 1990s and beyond: On the one hand, the X-ray contrast media were well taken care of and they are ruling the global market in 2022. The Norwegian organization is still an important part of GE Healthcare, and the chemical plant at Lindesnes in Southern Norway is a linchpin in the global value chain. Research, too, still exists in Oslo, within niches. On the other hand, what is left of the Norwegian organization is led from the United States and England, and, of course, there is no strategic headquarters anymore in Norway, no powerful and independent research and development organization, no expanded role in the Norwegian innovation system. Indeed, Nycomed failed to innovate at the very moment it could be said to have become a big company.

In 1997, Nycomed was merged with British Amersham, one of many acquisitions of the international pharmaceutical industry. By then, Hafslund had changed the collective culture and introduced a financial orientation. Research—or, perhaps more precisely put, science—had been replaced as the company's main goal by business development activities. The 1997 merger met requirements for a sensible business solution at the same time as it took care of shareholder value considerations. At the time, there was a looming threat of expiration of patents for the most important products, uncertainty about future price-cutting efforts of new and strong purchasing organizations, and the disrupting possibilities of new modalities like magnetic resonance imaging (MRI) and ultrasound. The logic of the shareholder value dimension of the financial culture seemingly kicked in, and shareholders cashed out through the merger with Amersham. The huge research-and-development organization built on the basis of contrast media income had failed to deliver the new products that could excite markets.

The Nyegaard story also has a bearing on the theory of the transition from participatory capitalism to corporative capitalism. In Torstendahl's view, an economic crisis in the 1970s rendered the old order unsustainable. The state could not maintain its leading role in partnerships. It lost power to private firms because it could no longer redistribute wealth, which was no longer created in the same quantity as before. When Hafslund Nycomed closed down the research company Bioreg, it cut itself off from important networks in the Norwegian medical ecosystem.

There is no necessary contradiction between building a shareholder-value-oriented company and pursuing innovation through science. But the prioritization is important to keep in mind, not least when the alluring world of new commercial avenues outside of research are opening up. Avenues like mergers with other companies looking for synergies and rationalization may follow. Such developments characterized the situation in Hafslund Nycomed in the 1990s. The fate of science-based innovation—being submerged by commercial operations eventually ending in a merger—sheds some light on the general failure of pharmaceutical innovation in the period. Too much commercial orientation, too many mergers, too little faith in the possibilities to invent and innovate became the norm. Nycomed going into the 1997 merger had become a typical international pharmaceutical company of its time. Indeed, it had become the equal of the large Swedish companies Astra and Pharmacia that also were (sub)merged into larger international units, with deep consequences for the Swedish medical ecosystem (Waxell, 2016). Only the Danes, the original outliers "present" at the beginning of the pharmaceutical revolution, kept their biggest company—as the merged Novo-Nordisk—Danish, and with huge benefit for the continued national ecosystem (Asheim et al., 2010).[1]

The early Danish start in innovative pharmaceuticals gives an insight into why Denmark kept its control of its research-based large pharmaceutical business. August Krogh, the Nobel-prize-winning scientist who started the Danish insulin snowball rolling, created the company Nordisk in the 1920s as owned by a foundation with the purpose for further scientific research in insulin and to be active in insulin-related activities (Sindbæk, 2019). In 1951, the owners of Novo followed along this path because they wanted to preserve the company progress and created a foundation "to secure the company's future through an independent institution" (Richter-Friis, 1991: 127f). The foundation, so to speak, for the continued Danish ownership of Novo-Nordisk is *the new and merged foundation* that owns a controlling interest in the company. The creation of the foundation obviously reflects a collective attitude that also characterized the Blix family in Nyegaard, yet when the Norwegian family looked for succession possibilities for a wealthy and vulnerable company, they did it on the doorstep of the new shareholder climate of the 1980s. The Danes came prepared for the 1980s having taken precautions about the volatility of international capitalism, while the Norwegians delivered their fast-growing and long-time-coming entity to the destiny of the stock market.

The Norwegian story mirrors the story of the international pharmaceutical industry's two distinct phases. From the 1940s onward, the one Norwegian innovative enterprise was not only driven by the goal of achieving scientific breakthroughs but it also delivered. And Nyegaard delivered in its own distinctive way, coming from behind the leading companies from the two leading Scandinavian nations. From the 1980s onward, they all still put forward ambitious goals involving scientific breakthroughs, but that was also the start of a major consolidation into new and huge stock-listed international enterprises. These new enterprises did not deliver new products to the same extent as in the prior period. Of course, that may be related to scientific opportunities being exploited and eroded.

[1] Interview with Helge Lund (chairman of Novo-Nordisk board of directors), November 25, 2019.

Yet, this book points to another explanation, which is that the scientific cultures that brought forward the new and research-based pharmaceutical industry were squeezed and hindered in these new, financially motivated enterprises.

They were transformed—as was their role in their respective national innovation systems—when they became units in great financially oriented enterprises. Financial goals turned the logic upside down. Financial logic asked for specific products that were wanted immediately in the market. In some cases, financial goals were achieved by saving on research. Science does not work that way, and there is reason to lament the loss of firms like Nyegaard that changed a vital medical process by pushing the science of imaging in a new direction. At the same time, we can learn from what Novo-Nordisk did to strive for corporate governance solutions that value the longer term and includes enough idealistic purpose to motivate path-breaking innovations of the kind Nyegaard delivered.

References

Asheim, B. T., Coenen, L., and Moodysson, J. 2010. "Two Sides of the Same Coin? Local and Global Knowledge Flows in Medicon Valley." *In*: Belussi, F. and Sammarra, A. (eds) *Business Networks in Clusters and Industrial Districts. The Governance of the Global Value Chain*. London and New York: Routledge.

Elster, J. 1983. *Explaining Technical Change: A Case Study in the Philosophy of Science*. Cambridge: Cambridge University Press; Oslo: Universitetsforlaget.

Richter-Friis, H. 1991. *Livet på Novo*. Copenhagen: Gyldendal.

Schumpeter, J. A. 1934. *The Theory of Economic Development: An Inquiry into Profits, Capital, Credit, Interest, and the Business Cycle*. Cambridge, MA: Harvard University Press.

Schumpeter, J. A. 1976. *Capitalism, Socialism and Democracy*. London: Allen & Unwin.

Sindbæk, H. 2019. *De renfærdige. Fortellingen om Novo-Nordisk*. Copenhagen: Politikens forlag.

Waxell, A. 2016. "Writing Up the Region: Anchor Firm Dismantling and the Construction of a Perceived Regional Advantage in Swedish News Media." *European Planning Studies*, 24, 742–761.

11
Epilogue

The new and merged company formed in 1997 in some ways developed steadily along the historical lines created by Nyegaard & Co., Actinor, and Hafslund. In other ways, it diverged a great deal. Two main long-term developments are visible up until the present (2022). One is that Omnipaque and Visipaque are still the main products of the Norwegian imaging company, formerly called Nycomed Imaging and now known as GE Healthcare AS. In particular, Omnipaque is a hugely successful product globally. The other development is that the generics business formerly called Nycomed Pharma is a prominent part of the huge Japanese pharmaceutical house Takeda.

The fortunes of these two parts of old Nycomed have much to do with how Nycomed Amersham's Bill Castell shaped the new enterprise. His main aim was to build a research-oriented company to use molecular science to develop personalized medicine. This pushed the renewed research organization into new and—for some—exciting avenues. Castell was a visionary leader. During his seven years at the top, the Norwegian Nycomed Imaging part of the (Nycomed) Amersham organization prospered as a rewarding science-infused venture. Huge investments in the Lindesnes plant for chemical substances in these years proved to have very beneficial long-term effects. By contrast, Castell was not enthused by the generics parts of the organization and was quite critical of some of the products in its portfolio. In 1999, Nycomed Pharma was sold to a private equity firm. In the following years, the organization merged with a couple of other generics companies to form one of the world's largest generics companies. In 2011, this was purchased by Takeda for $13.7 billion (€9.6 billion).

In 2003, General Electric purchased Amersham plc, which since 2001 had been the name of Nycomed Amersham. The $9.5 billion deal was formally completed in 2004. General Electric was a supplier of various types of medical equipment used in the imaging procedures and had expressed an interest in such a deal over several years. Bill Castell named the main contributing factors in the sale: the expiration of patent protection of some key products and a desire to reap "shareholder value." In some respects, Amersham plc in 2003 mirrored Nycomed in 1997 in that its research portfolio lacked clear and exciting new products. In the longer term, although some research lines started under Castell are still alive, little has come out of the huge research effort that took place after 1997.

Under the leadership of General Electric, GE Healthcare AS (Norway) developed in a rather different direction. General Electric emphasized earnings in an era characterized by falling margins. In 2008, it initiated a rationalization program that gradually streamlined and downsized research. Over five years, a couple of hundred employees were made redundant. Later, the relatively new (1990) and imposing Blix research center in central Oslo was torn down and rebuilt as a residential complex. Increased international competition and pressure on prices were contributing factors; in the mid-2010s, the Norwegian organization felt pressurized and vulnerable.

GE Healthcare AS returned to great profitability in the late 2010s. This was due to increased sales volume and sunk investments in four plants (Lindesnes, Norway, for primary and Oslo, Cork, and Shanghai for secondary production) and the reorganization of production. Production costs were greatly reduced. The changes were particularly significant and impactful at the primary production plant in Lindesnes. Here, technical progress was combined with reorganization and the deep involvement of workers in finding new and improved methods that reduced production time. Omnipaque is still the number one product, as a significant product worldwide. It is sold at a significantly lower price than in the 1990s but is made in much larger quantities (see Figure 1.1) at much lower cost. GE Healthcare AS's sales volume and income compare well with what was achieved in the 1990s. There is no doubt that the foundation with which Nyegaard & Co. entered the 1980s could have been used to build a significant Norwegian-owned pharmaceutical enterprise.

In the early 2020s, GE Healthcare AS is a very profitable company and is still conducting research, although on a much smaller scale. It reports to GE Healthcare's British organization.

Sources

Nyegaard & Co./Nycomed

The main source for this study is the company archive, which is located in the National archives of Norway (private archive 1229, named as Nycomed). This archive consists of several parts that have been delivered in two stages. The author has used the archive in two periods, 1991–1995 and 2019–2021. This division of work has impacted the references.

By far the larger part of the archive was created from scratch in the period around 1990 by a team comprising retired employees of the company and experienced archivists working for the Business history unit of BI Norwegian Business School. This book generally uses this archive's original key (cited below). When the original historical archive was dispatched to the National archives, and supplemented by additional material, the National archive applied a new key (private archive 1229). This did not involve a complete reorganization of the material. The old archive information is therefore a good approximation to the new archive key. For the material that was consulted in the period from 1991 to 1995, I have used the original key.

The main body of the original historical archive consists of material collected from the company's various departments and was initially done by pharmacist Fridtjov Rakli, who therefore is named as the creator of the main body of this archive. Nycomed employees have also donated personal archives to this archive. Archive references in the notes refer to the background of this original historical archive:

NAA = Nycomed, A. Arntsen's papers
NADM = Nycomed, administration
NAFI = Nycomed, AFI's archive
NBA = Nycomed, Biochemical department's archive
NFR = Nycomed, Fridtjov Rakli's archive
NKT = Nycomed, Knut Tjønneland's archive
NOS = Nycomed, Odd Kåre Strandli's papers
NRBP = Nycomed, Rolf Bjerke Paulssen's papers
NSL = Nycomed, Søren Laland's papers
NTA = Nycomed, Thor Andersen's papers
NUB = Nycomed, Ulf Blix's papers.

Archival references in the text to minute books and general assembly books prior to 1986 have been omitted to save space. They are easily found through the company archive (private archive 1229, Nycomed) in the National archives.

Some material not included in the historical archive was also used when the main body of this work was researched in 1991–1995:

Hafslund Nycomed's archives

H-N.Actinor = Actinor archives

Nycomed Imaging's archives

N.Pers.avd = Department of personnel's archives at Nycomed Imaging.
This material is also expected to be transferred to the national archives.

References to material consulted from 2019 to 2021 follow the archive key created by the National archives (private archive 1229).

In this later period, I also used material belonging to Hafslund (demerged in 1996 but possessor of minutes of board meetings of Hafslund Nycomed prior to the demerger). This was consulted in two locations: a power plant in Sarpsborg that may become a permanent home and an attic in an office building in Oslo that was to be vacated.

Interviews have also been an important part of this project. The details are given in the notes.

The Directorate of Health

This study also draws on the archive of the Directorate of Health, to which I have had free access for the period from 1940 until 1985. The older records (up to 1960) were located at the National Archives (RA.HD.H7 = Health Directorate, Office H7, Pharmacy office). More recent records were consulted within the institution itself. These are periodically transferred to the National archives, but here I use the keys from when the actual research was conducted at the Directorate.

The industrial committee in New York

I have used some material from The Industrial Committee in New York. This archive is located in the National archives (RA, IKNY)

SNI's archive

I have used some material from Studieselskapet for norsk industry (SNI, the Norwegian Industries Development Association). This is located in the National Library's archives (UBO.SNI).

List of Abbreviations

AFI = A/S Farmaceutisk Industri
AL = Apotekernes Laboratorium
CEO = chief executive officer
CERN = European Council for Nuclear Research
CoU = Cofactor of Urgocyton
CPI = The Consumer Price Index of Statistics Norway
DVM = Doctor of veterinary medicine
EEC = European Economic Community
EFTA = The European Free Trade Association
FDA = (US) Food and Drug Administration
GATT = General Agreement on Tariffs and Trade (1947)
GMP = good manufacturing practices
IBT = income before taxes
IRAS = The Norwegian Office for Industrial Rationalization
MRI = magnetic resonance imaging
NAF = Norwegian Association of Proprietor Pharmacists
NMD = The Norwegian Medicinal Depot
No-Fa-Ki = Norway's Pharmaceutical–Chemical Industry Association
NOMI = No-Fa-Ki's successor, Norges Medisinindustriforening
NOP = net operating profit
No-Re-Farm = The Association of Foreign Pharmaceutical Companies of Norway
NTH = Norwegian Institute of Technology
NTNF = Royal Norwegian Council for Scientific and Industrial Research
OECD = Organisation for Economic Co-operation and Development
PIA = Pharmaceutical Industries Association of EFTA
PMB = pharmacy benefit managers
PROFO = The Production Engineering Research Institute
R & D = research and development
RIA = radioimmunoassay
SNI = The Norwegian Industries Development Association
SOL = solidity
SOP = standard operating procedures
SSB = Statistics Norway

Index